THE FABRIC OF HOPE

THE FABRIC OF HOPE

An Essay

Glenn Tinder

WILLIAM B. EERDMANS PUBLISHING COMPANY
GRAND RAPIDS, MICHIGAN / CAMBRIDGE, U.K.

First published 1999 by Scholars Press for Emory University

This edition published 2001 by Wm. B. Eerdmans Publishing Co.
255 Jefferson Ave. S.E., Grand Rapids, Michigan 49503 /
P.O. Box 163, Cambridge CB3 9PU U.K.

Printed in the United States of America

07 06 05 04 03 02 01   7 6 5 4 3 2 1

Library of Congress Cataloging-in-Publication Data

Tinder, Glenn E.
The fabric of hope: an essay / by Glenn Tinder.
p.   cm.
Includes bibliographical references.
ISBN 0-8028-4857-5 (pbk. : alk. paper)
1. Hope — Religious aspects — Christianity.   I. Title.
BV4638.T56 1999
234′.25 — dc21
99-047191

CONTENTS

PREFACE TO THE EERDMANS EDITION

More than two years have passed since I finished writing *The Fabric of Hope*. Now, a new printing, under a new publisher, is being done, and this is the occasion of the present preface. Hope has been on my mind a great deal since the completion of the manuscript. This is due partly, no doubt, simply to habit — habit formed during the eight or nine years spent working on the book. It is due also, I believe, to the importance of hope in our lives; anyone trying to think seriously about human matters is bound to think a good deal about hope. At any rate, whatever my motives, I've had the inclination, as well as the time, to reconsider the ideas embodied in the original book.

What has come of this is not a change of mind nor even anything I could conscientiously call a "deeper understanding." It is rather a simplified perception. I am able now, I think, to characterize the source of hope, and the role of hope in human life, more simply, and in that sense more effectively, than I could two years ago. To do this briefly, thus perhaps helping readers peruse the following pages, is the aim of the present preface.

As a Christian, I believe that Christ is the one source of human hope. That, one might almost say, is what it means to be a Christian. The simplified version of hope I have arrived at stems from my realization that Christianity is a simple creed. With its numerous and seemingly abstruse doctrines, such as the Trinity, the dual nature of Christ, original sin, atonement, and so forth, it does not look simple from the outside. But at the center there is a single fact, tiny when seen from the perspective of the vast universe and its long history, yet all-encompassing when seen from the perspective of faith. This is the crucified Christ. If this center is fully understood, even the most abstruse doctrines also are understood. The crucified Christ is a microcosmos, where everything human and divine is brought to a radiant focus. This, of course, is not a bold new generalization. It is a mere restatement of Paul, who wrote to the Corinthians that he had decided "to know nothing among you except Jesus Christ and him crucified" (I Corinthians 2:2).

Anyone who understands Christ crucified understands hope. The Son of Man on the Cross created and set before us the possibility of becoming new men and new women. This is the source of our hope. Christ offers us both wisdom and righteousness. He offers us wisdom, not primarily by words, but by bowing before the will of his crucifiers. In his suffering and death he summarizes and sets forth the infinite yet concentrated understanding Christians call God's Word. The human state is understood, and the manner of God's presence among us is also understood.

Christ offers righteousness by expiating our crimes and misdeeds, thereby releasing us from the past and opening the way to sanctity — the sanctity that lies in reproducing in our own lives the self-sacrificial love Christ displayed in accepting the Cross. Christ was not only God incarnate; he was also incarnate humanity. Hence, in the Crucifixion, that universal self, confined by ignorance and error, and deformed by unconditional love for merely conditional realities — the fallen self evident in every particular self — died on the Cross. Following on this death, a transfigured self came to life.

Creating us anew was tantamount to placing us in a new universe — under new heavens, on a new earth. Possessing greater powers of understanding, we could see realities long obscured by the tenacious self-imprisonment inherent in accepting the conclusions of sense and intellect as ultimate truth. And with heightened powers of love we were liberated from the stultifying illusion that the most lovable things are things we can see and touch. We could thus live in a universe far wider and more glorious than the universe we had long inhabited.

The self-confinement humans so obstinately practice has been described by great philosophers — by Plato, for example, in the Myth of the Cave, and by Kant, in his analysis of our inability, given our limited sensory and intellectual faculties, to know things-in-themselves. And more than one great writer, Dostoevsky among them, has imagined that somehow, if we could only awaken, we would find ourselves in Paradise. There is a word often used for designating the prison in which we confine ourselves, that is, "world." A derivative word, "worldliness," designates our determination to be thus confined. Fallen man, in his proud insistence on living amid realities that reason can comprehend and will can manipulate, construes the world as the totality of being. In doing this, he surrounds himself with illusions, mistaking worldly reality for lasting substance. More specifically, he blinds himself to God and makes objects of his neighbors. This recoils on his own selfhood, with ironic results. Having proudly set out to achieve comprehension and command, he falls into error and weakness. He dilutes his own being and diminishes his own stature. It is this diluted and diminished creature that perishes on the Cross.

A signal characteristic of this shrunken creature is that it necessarily dies. It might be said, therefore, that when it perished on the Cross, death itself perished. In re-creating humankind, by informing it with wisdom and charity, and in placing human beings in this way in a new universe, reflecting the glory of primeval creation, Christ conquered sin. He necessarily conquered death at the same time, as is manifest in the Resurrection. Sin is worldliness, stubborn self-confinement within the objectified realities that make up the world. Death is the fate of anyone who is a mere worldly being. But the crucifixion of Christ is the crucifixion, or end, of the world. Those who learn the wisdom and righteousness of the Cross are set free of the world, and with no one left to sustain it through objectification, the world dissolves. There is a sense in which every person's death has already occurred — on the Cross. This is why the author of Colossians can write, "You have died, and your life is hid with Christ in God" (3:3). The effect on hope is plainly revolutionary. Hope no longer is hemmed in by death. Its horizon is eternal life.

The simplicity of Christianity is reflected in Jesus' simple characterization of the transformed situation inherent in his life and death: "The kingdom of God is at hand." One way this kingdom is at hand is in being composed of realities that are familiar, or could be familiar, if we but opened our eyes. It is composed of your neighbors and of the things around you in their original splendor; of you yourself in your authentic being; and, of course, of the being who is closer to you than any other and evident in a far greater number of everyday signs than we ever notice, that is, God. It is also at hand in a way that bears importantly on our understanding of hope. It can break in at any time. Hope does not have to resign itself to the passage of millennia. Every beloved face, every flicker of beauty and glint of truth, every hint of meaning in seemingly meaningless events is a foreshadowing of the kingdom of God. Hope must, to be sure, be patient and enduring. It can also, however, take the form of momentary expectancy.

Jesus' affirmation of the kingdom of God as being *at hand,* however, tells us something else vital to the idea of hope. While Jesus' death on the Cross has opened the gates to glorious realms, we still must pass through those gates. In principle, this is not difficult ("For my yoke is easy, and my burden is light" [Matthew 11:30]). In our worldliness, however, we are very reluctant to do it. Hence the threatening tone in which Jesus sometimes addresses his listeners. Seriousness is essential.

There is a suitable word for characterizing our situation. The kingdom of God lies before us, not as a present possession, but as a *destiny.* It is the destiny of the human race as a whole and of each one of us. A destiny is not a fate. It is not forced upon us, and someone who is intensely fearful and stubborn may even be able to evade it. But neither is a destiny merely a desired or ideal end. It is that for which we were born, and evading it would entail, not deprivation of this or that particular good, but loss of self, or soul. Living our destiny is therefore not merely one way among others of living. It is the life given us to live. This is true even though, in order to fulfill a destiny, one must be crucified. (Thus Dietrich Bonhoeffer's well-known dictum on human destiny: "When Christ calls a man, he bids him come and die.") The Crucifixion, in rectifying the disorientation of our intellect and will, thus re-creating and resituating us, authoritatively defined human destiny. At the same time, it defined hope, which from then on had to be understood as fidelity to the destiny given us on the Cross.

To use an overused, but useful, word, destiny is "dialectical." The Resurrection is preceded by the Crucifixion. The wisdom bestowed by the Cross is received by foolish men and women; the righteousness achieved on the Cross comes to us as forgiveness of our unrighteousness. We enter into the splendor of God's kingdom from out of the desolation of the world. The emphasis some Christians place on being "born again" is questionable, for rarely is it said forcefully enough that before we can be born again we must die. There can be moments of ecstasy in our lives. These depend, however, on our following the pattern of the life of Jesus: suffering death, perhaps in various ways, and only then living in the plenitude of the being God has given us. The joy that accompanies hope, therefore, is not always unalloyed. It is sometimes the kind of joy Paul had in mind when he spoke of rejoicing in his suffering. At these times, hope is the strength to endure suffering, knowing that suffering is not our proper and final — not our destined — end.

I scarcely need to say that these are not original themes. They run throughout the letters of Paul. This is particularly true of the theme of suffering. For Paul, we should not recoil from suffering. In a certain way, we should welcome it. We can do this because we know that suffering, patiently endured, brings hope, and that the hope it brings will not be disappointed. Hope is fulfilled when God's love is "poured into our hearts," signaling the coming of the kingdom of God (Romans 5:3-5). In the same vein, Paul declared that he would "boast" of his weaknesses, and that he was "content with weaknesses, insults, hardships, persecutions, and calamities." This was because of a paradox inscribed in all faithful suffering by the suffering of Jesus: when he was weak, then he was strong (II Corinthians 12:9-10).

The prospect of death did not imperil Paul's fundamental tranquillity any more than did the prospect of suffering, for even when our outer nature is perishing, "our inner nature is being renewed every day" (II Corinthians 4:16). The destiny bestowed by the Crucifixion recasts human agony so that in every instance it can be incorporated in a life of hope. In the dying of the God-man — the incarnate God who is also incarnate humanity — everything we have to fear is deprived of its horror. Our unrighteousness is broken and pardoned, our mortality is set aside. We can live. Hope is not merely possible; it is required of us.

Hope clearly is at the center of a Christian life. Without hope, it is tempting to say, there can be no relationship with God. This could be illustrated in several ways. Prayer, for example, cannot be genuine without hope. To end a prayer in despair would be, in effect, to cancel the prayer. As another example, divine forgiveness cannot be accepted without hope. Forgiveness is a grant of further life; to submit to a feeling of being doomed by past misdeeds would be to scorn God's mercy. But perhaps the best vantage point for perceiving the centrality of hope in Christian life is provided by the so-called theological virtues.

That faith and charity are in principle more basic than hope is obvious. Someone entirely lacking in faith could not have hope, at least not Christian hope. And someone without charity, without love for God and neighbor as encountered in the present time, could not aspire to eternity in the company of God and neighbor. Hope, then, is secondary. This very fact, however, accords it a kind of primacy. Depending on faith and charity, hope is impelled to summon them, for otherwise it is groundless. Moreover, if it fails to summon them, faith and charity die. They are nothing unless they enter into life, and they enter into life only through hope. It is hope that implants them in temporal existence. They would wither and die in the soul of a despairing person.

Hope plays its part through a companion virtue, trust (meaning by this trust in God). Trust is discussed in the following pages, but I am not sure that I realized, when I wrote those pages, how uniquely indispensable trust is in the life of hope. Only when faith and charity issue in trust do they issue also in hope. Christian hope does not depend on knowledge of the things impinging on us in the world. Worldly knowledge provides only calculable probabilities, and these offer only the setting, not the basis, of true hope. Nor does Christian hope depend on knowledge of God, for we have little such knowledge. We cannot comprehend the intellect and will of God. We can, however, trust in God. Indeed, we must, as people of faith, and only so far as we do can we entertain hope.

Enabling us to live hopefully in time is not the only role of trust. It also enables us to contemplate hopefully the end of time. Trust gives us assurance of eternal salvation. Christians often assert that while they *hope* to be saved, they are not *sure* of being saved. Can such assertions be entirely serious? People who feel that their future holds a real possibility of eternal damnation, even though the chances seem to be against it, can hardly live except in a state akin to terror. They cannot live with the joy and expectancy characteristic of true hope. Yet to claim absolute assurance of salvation, it is said, is to claim knowledge we cannot possess and is thus to offend against God's majesty. The validity of the objection may be granted. But knowledge does not necessarily enter into the question. Surely we do not offend against God's majesty by *trusting in his love,* that is, in the love demonstrated in the crucified Son of God. Indeed, one may think we offend against God's majesty if we allow our trust to falter. Paul calls on us to rejoice in the Lord always. He warns explicitly against anxiety and asserts that, through prayer and supplication with thanksgiving, we will unfailingly experience "the peace of God which passes all understanding" (Philippians 4:4-7). How could we heed Paul's counsel without some assurance concerning our eternal destiny? To say that we *hope* for salvation continues to be appropriate, for we have no objective knowledge in the matter. We have no demonstrable certainty. Through trust, however, we do have certainty, and in that way joy and peace.

Not every hope, of course, is bent on salvation. Our days and years are carried along by hopes for things of far less moment. We live much of the time toward merely temporal goods, some of them sweeping, many of them trivial. In every hope we harbor there is uncertainty, hence potential anxiety. Yet assurance of salvation can erase the anxiety inherent in every lesser hope. If the ultimate issue of one's earthly existence is not in doubt, then doubt in every other case is readily supportable. Even death loses its terror. Thus the words T. S. Eliot attributes to Thomas à Becket in *Murder in the Cathedral*. Pursued by the king's assassins, Becket seeks to reassure his frightened aides. "I am not in danger," he says to them, "only near to death."

Hope is a universal human need. To live is to relinquish present circumstances and to move in the direction of circumstances that are more or less unknown. It is impossible to do that without hope. People without hope falter and eventually die. This is true not only of individuals but of societies as well. When the future becomes very ominous, civic life breaks down, as it did in Germany between the two World Wars. For believers and unbelievers alike, whether in solitude or in the public square, hope is the breath of life. This is a matter of utmost concern to Christians.

For Christians to think only of themselves when reflecting on hope is to betray their faith. Christ is the ultimate ground of all human hope; his purpose was the salvation, through Israel, of the entire human race. This means that Christians, as custodians of hope, bear responsibilities in relation not just to other Christians but to all human beings. What sort of responsibilities? Above all, of course, for making known all over the earth the name of Christ; and doing this, moreover, not only through their words but also through their lives. These, however, are commonplaces, in little need of comment here. Far less commonplace is awareness of a great danger that arises whenever Christians address the vast human multitudes who are not Christian: that of failing to accord full respect to those they address. This happens if they are condescending. And they are condescending when they assume that there is no deep truth outside of explicitly Christian truth. In doing this they falsify their relations with the human race as a whole. And they falsify hope, which for Christians is hope for all humanity.

The assumption that serious truth is a Christian monopoly is an easy one for Christians to make. The idea that Christ is the sole and unique savior of the world is intrinsic to Christian faith. Someone who believes in Christ but believes that there are other saviors equal in status and significance is not a Christian. Hence Christians readily infer that all who are not committed explicitly to Christ dwell entirely in darkness. Such an inference, however, is unnecessary. From the earliest times Christ has been looked on by his followers as the Logos, the ultimate principle in accordance with which the world was created and is guided. But unbelievers surely know something about the created universe and something about the history God providentially guides. Doesn't it follow that they know something about Christ even though they are ignorant of his name?

If so, there must be intimations of Christian truth in many places outside the bounds of Christendom. And plainly there are. Didn't Socrates manifest a keen appreciation of righteousness and speak eloquently of human immortality? Didn't Plato demonstrate an awareness of the fallenness of the human race and of a truth in which men and women can find salvation? Didn't the later Stoics, with their sense of our moral equality, seemingly see something of the dignity of every individual? Granted, these were only glimpses, not the fullness of truth which Christians believe is implicit in the Cross. Still, many Christians have drawn from pagan thinkers in order to give structure and clarity to their faith. That so great a Christian as Thomas Aquinas could be an Aristotelian (as well as, in some ways, a Platonist and a Stoic) testifies strikingly to the universality of truth. (I have tried in *The Fabric of Hope* not only to adhere closely to the truths of biblical revelation but also to discern adumbrations of such truth in the secular mind. Usually I could, and I endeavored to bring these out in the essay.)

Christians have learned from Paul — and recently from Karl Barth — the dangers of such universalism. It can lure us into forgetting the singularity of Christian truth: a truth that comprises in one integral and comprehensive revelation all that is only glimpsed in other places, a truth that is unattainable by human efforts alone, and, finally, a truth that lays on those who receive it unique responsibilities in relation to the human race. However, the illegitimate inference that this singular truth is an exclusive possession can be very damaging to the Christian spirit. Encouraging an attitude of disdain toward all who are not Christians, it weakens the standard of love. Only Christians are viewed as neighbors (in contravention of the fact that the wounded man by the side of the road, in Jesus' parable, was a Samaritan). The most devastating consequence of this disdain has been anti-Semitism, but anyone can easily think of other examples. And not only does Christian exclusivism tend to weaken the standard of love; it tends also to undermine awareness of the universality of God's mercy. A god who consigns much of the human race to total darkness seems cruel or negligent rather than merciful. These consequences might be characterized summarily as loss of charity — toward neighbors and toward God. With that loss, the gospel is distorted. The glad tidings so movingly announced in the opening chapters of Matthew and Luke take on the aspect, for most of the human race, of a decree of damnation.

True hope, as I understand it, encompasses all human beings. Only thus does it conform with the charity that underlies it. This is why Christians must take care not to let their faith, and their sense of that faith as a singular gift, separate them altogether from those innumerable persons all over the world who do not share it.

My universalist concept of hope may help to explain the strong political cast of the following pages. To harbor hope is to situate oneself in the midst of the human race. This in turn — universal humanity being an empty abstraction for anyone who spurns the particularities involved in the life of a people or a nation — is to take on the obligations of membership in a particular society. Hope in this way implies politics. Conversely, since the patience needed for resolving conflicts through persuasion rather than force is not likely to inhabit the hearts of desperate peoples, politics presupposes hope. All of this is to say that hope is not a private dream. It unites us with the concrete human beings inhabiting our own historical time and place, and with their concrete tribulations and perplexities. It connects us with the multitudinous crucifixions and resurrections that make up the destiny of the human race. To live with hope is, if my reflections are valid, to live in one's full humanity.

GLENN TINDER
Lincoln, Massachusetts
January 2001

PROLOGUE

This essay is addressed to everyone interested in hope, regardless of their religious or philosophical beliefs. By intent, it is universal. At the same time, however, it is based on an assumption which ordinarily reduces drastically the range of willing readers. The assumption is that our main source of hope today, and indeed in all times, is Jesus Christ. Because Christ lived and lives, hope is not only reasonable but is morally imperative. A second assumption follows necessarily: that reflecting on Christ, and on the tenets of Christianity, is the only way of coming fully to understand what hope is and how it is attained. A great many people today find such assumptions, in works addressed to the general reader, offensive.

Isn't this essay, then, a self-contradictory undertaking? No more so, I think, than any work written by someone who occupies a particular intellectual position yet invites attention from people who do not occupy that position. Marxists, for example, believe that the essential truths of human nature and history are contained in the major doctrines of Karl Marx. When they write on a subject such as hope, however, they do not necessarily assume that only fellow Marxists will read what they have written. They commonly address themselves to people of varying views. Nor do most readers assume that Marxist writings are appropriately read only by Marxists. They take it for granted not only that they should know what Marxists are saying but also—more significantly—that they might learn from reading them. In short, Marxists and non-Marxists are related by the ordinary courtesies which form an intellectual community. They pay attention to one another. Why shouldn't Christians and non-Christians be related by like courtesies?

I grant at the outset that the obligation of mutual attention bears on Christians just as definitely as it does on non-Christians. This is so in spite of the strain of exclusivism that can be heard in the words of some of the greatest Christians. One of these, the Apostle Paul, expresses disdain for secular doctrines and enjoins his fellow-Christians "not to be mismated with unbelievers," and asks "what fellowship has light with darkness?" (II Corinthians 6:14 Revised Standard Version) In some ways, Christians should no doubt follow Paul's counsel. For example, they should be ready—far readier than they usually are today—to shun fashionable secular opinions and to enunciate opinions which are not merely distinctively Christian but, in the eyes of the world, absurd. Yet Christians should not seek complete separation from the world. On the contrary, through universal attentiveness and speech they should position themselves in the very center of the world, sustaining spiritual relations so far as they can with all human beings. Such a stance is required both by the example of Christ, who immersed himself in crowds where anyone who wished to might touch the fringe of his garment, and by the will of God, who "will have all men to be saved." (I Timothy 2:4 King James Version) In short, Christians are bound into unity with the world by their own highest moral standard, that of love.

For Christians, the idea that there is a potential community in the truth, binding together all human beings, whatever their religious views, has strong grounds in the ancient doctrine that Christ is the Logos, the incarnate meaning and order of all reality. Logos means reason, or word, and is what is reasonable in all valid reasoning and true in all true words. Although this doctrine was advanced by a particular school of theology in the early years of Christianity, all genuine Christians, in all times, are bound to accept the doctrine in one form or another. It is implicit in the Christian conviction that the ultimate truth is expressed in the life, death, and resurrection of Jesus of Nazareth. On this premise, Christians and non-Christians inhabit common ground. The truth they seek is one truth. Christian thinkers and writers, therefore, cannot rightfully ignore secular thinkers and writers. The latter may reach truth to which Christians cannot be indifferent. A great thinker such as Friedrich Nietzsche, who styled himself the Antichrist, may paradoxically attain insights into the Logos which Christians cannot ignore or reject.

Christians should be mindful of the fact that secularism still maintains a vital existence. Believing as they do in a providential God, Christians must be open to the possibility that the endurance of secularism accords with God's will. The God of Christ may intend for Christians to share the world, and the truth of the world, with people who reject Christ and God and every other form of religious belief. Perhaps Christians are not wise or righteous enough to have exclusive custody of the truth. Granted, a genuine Christian must believe that in Christ there is truth that surpasses in scope and depth and certainty all other truth—truth that is all-inclusive and inexhaustible. Still, this is not truth of the sort that can be acquired, possessed, and passed on as if it were a piece of material property. It is a human version of an incomprehensible mystery. It is given by God, not attained by research. And it is not unchristian to think that there may be in God resources of magnanimity and kindness by virtue of which this mystery is made accessible even to those who, like Nietzsche, declare themselves to be God's enemies.

It is a surprising fact, however, that in our time it is not so much Christians, as their irreligious opponents, who refuse the obligations of mutual attention. Non-Christians are more likely to withhold the courtesies of common discourse from Christians than are Christians from non-Christians. Christian intellectuals typically read extensively in non-Christian writings, and it is not only in the present time that this is the case. Augustine knew thoroughly, and was deeply appreciative of, pagan writers such as Cicero and Plotinus, just as Karl Barth, in our own day, was well-versed in secular philosophers such as Jean-Paul Sartre and Karl Jaspers. But the converse is not true. Non-Christian intellectuals, at least in the twentieth century, do not as a matter of course try to stay abreast of theology. The average university professor is unashamedly ignorant of Christian literature. Christian writers must, accordingly, assume that their writings will be of interest mainly to other Christians and not to many others.

It is difficult to conceive of any adequate justification for this state of affairs. Secular minds are very likely, even in their understanding of worldly realities, to be impoverished by a doctrinaire inattention to Christian voices. Reality is not entirely simple and one-dimensional. It is not merely a collection of facts open in its entirety to casual inspection and easy understanding. Thus we speak of the "depths" of reality, and we distinguish between wisdom and mere knowledge, and between insight and ordinary apprehension. Even those who reject Christianity's central claim, that Christ is God's definitive address to humankind, may find wisdom and insight in Christian ideas; this is exemplified in the appreciative attention given by numerous non-Christians to Reinhold Niebuhr's use in political analysis of the doctrine of original sin (an exception to the indifference usually characterizing secular attitudes toward theologians). Although secularism does not bar wisdom and insights, it may nonetheless encourage efforts to reduce understanding to rational principles and scientific laws. As a result, it may have an inherent tendency toward the kind of systematic superficiality which might be called objectivism. Nothing is real, according to objectivist assumptions, except realities that can be empirically investigated and rationally explained. Not only do such assumptions involve a constricted view of the things that are; they may also block off insight into the things that ought to be, that is, into moral principles. If so, then secularism contains an inherent tendency toward amorality as well as toward objectivism. Here Christian discourse may help. It may take cognizance of realities which in their depth and in their moral character escape the notice of the secular mind yet are not invisible to that mind. In this way it may help secular knowledge take on a weight and penetration it would lack if framed altogether within the bounds of an exclusively secular community.

I propose as a principle underlying my argument—that people of a secular persuasion should at least listen to Christians—what might be called "openness toward transcendence." This principle arises from the fact that the realm of objective knowledge is situated within an encompassing mystery. Every object known is abstracted from a background that, objectively speaking, is not known. As is demonstrated in the writings of Immanuel Kant, the utmost extension of objective knowledge will not alter this state of affairs. The light of intellect will always shine in the darkness. We cannot know what the darkness conceals. We cannot know whether, beyond our knowledge of the finite and temporal, there is anything infinite and eternal. It follows, to speak simply, that, in spite of all secular doubts, God may exist. To many, such an assertion is annoying and even offensive. Nonetheless, rejecting it out-of-hand amounts to an arbitrary closure of mind. It is a closure, moreover, in relation to what is by far the most significant question concerning the human condition. No other issue has so decisive a bearing on how we conduct and understand our lives as that of the existence of God.

Such openness is incumbent on us, however, not just because the word "transcendence" may stand for something supremely important to us, but also, as my remarks above indicate, because it may shed light on the realities affirmed by secularism, those that make up the world around us. These realities are more or less hidden. We all know they are there. But what they are and how we should deal with them we do not know. Anyone familiar with the history of philosophy realizes that it has taken centuries to bring some of them to light. Ostensible disclosures of transcendence concern worldly realities in their relations to transcendence as well as transcendence itself. Hence, even if such disclosures told us nothing of transcendence, they might enable us to see hitherto unknown worldly realities.

An example is offered by what seems to us now a plain fact, although for many centuries it was more or less unseen, that is, freedom of the will. The full reality of such freedom was brought out by Christians absorbed in what was for them the dreadful fact that human beings could rebel against God. In time, such theological concerns faded in many minds. But the stark reality of freedom remained; and it became of great concern to secular thinkers such as Marx and Sartre. The concept of natural law may serve as another example. The idea that moral guidance can be gained by observing the order of nature—specifically, the order of human powers and faculties making for fulfillment and happiness—was developed by religious philosophers, pagan as well as Christian. The idea was implicit in Plato and Aristotle, and became explicit in Cicero and Augustine. Yet it has been detached from its religious sources, an event occurring early in the modern era, particularly in the writings of the great seventeenth-century jurist Hugo Grotius, and has played a role of immense importance in secular thought. In short, "transcendence," even if unreal, may bring to light realities which otherwise would remain unseen. This too is a reason why secular minds should not be closed toward transcendence.

Finally, in addition to the possible existence of God, and the partial hiddenness of worldly reality, the trials and uncertainties of moral life also require openness as we approach the borders of knowledge. One of the most incontrovertible facts of our existence is that we are conscious, practically all of the time, of various obligations. To seek and to tell the truth; to be considerate of those who are close to us; to be careful of things that are beautiful—such imperatives as these have great authority. Why? Are they divine commands? Are they inscribed somehow in human nature? Do they derive merely from custom and tradition? Would they lose their authority if we could know certainly that they have no transcendental ground and (human sanctions aside) may be violated with impunity? If the very idea of an infinite and eternal ground of morality vanished from our minds, would morality disappear? Could we then say, as Dostoevsky so feared we someday would, that "everything is permitted"? Questions such as these, arising from an elementary sense of responsibility toward the social order, bar indifference toward transcendence.

On the basis of the principle of openness toward transcendence, a distinction can be drawn between two different kinds of secularism, one legitimate and one not. These are alike in eschewing any claim to transcendental knowledge and in being disposed, in consequence, to attend to worldly realities as the only realities we can assuredly know. It is this worldly orientation that constitutes their secularism. They are divided, however, by their attitude toward transcendence; one is closed, the other open. The former assumes that there is no transcendental reality to be revealed; it can accordingly be called *radical secularism*. It is typified by Marx, Nietzsche, and a multitude of less distinguished minds. It is illegitimate, in spite of the unquestionable greatness of its foremost protagonists, because it is arbitrary. The other kind of secularism, it might be said, acknowledges that we do not know what lies beyond the bounds of objective knowledge (we do not know what we do not know). It can thus appropriately be called *agnostic secularism*; it is legitimate because it faithfully reflects our epistemological condition.

Agnostic secularists do not inhabit a completely different universe from that of Christians, for Christians too must be open toward transcendence. By writing a meditation on hope which seeks light in Christian principles but tries continually to appeal to reason and common experience, I resist a conviction strenuously upheld both by radical secularists and by many serious Christians: that a vast chasm divides Christian faith from all non-Christian attitudes. Both seem to say, of their antithetical commitments, "It's all or nothing." But life is not so simple, nor is Christianity. The history of the human intellect since the time of Jesus is replete with examples which should constrain secularists to admit that the life of reason depends on minds sensitive to the mystery of being; and the same examples should constrain Christians to acknowledge that God does not teach the human race only by making them professed Christians nor does he confine the wisdom that radiates from Christ to those who publicly declare their allegiance to Christ.

My belief in universal communication does not imply what is usually called, in a theological sense, liberalism. Christianity is not simply a dramatic set of symbols representing truths which unbelievers may readily gain through reason and ordinary human experience. As Paul emphasized, Christianity rests on principles which are foolishness to "Greeks"—to those who rely wholly on natural human faculties. Christianity which fits harmoniously into a context of secular convictions certainly has something wrong with it; one might even say that tension with secularism is a test of authentic Christianity. But tension is one thing, incompatibility another. Christian and secular principles, so far as they are supported on the Christian side by revelation and on the secular side by empirical evidence and reason, cannot be incompatible if Christ is the Logos.

Thus while the premises of this essay are not theologically liberal, neither are they radically dualistic in the manner of thinkers such as Blaise Pascal and Søren Kierkegaard. Christians need to be wary not only of allowing Christian truth to be comfortably merged with secular truth but also of envisioning Christian truth as flatly contradicting secular truth and thus as attainable only through a "leap of faith." Christians sometimes dramatize the miracle of Christ's appearance in the world by speaking of the "absurdity" or the "offense" inherent in Christian faith. While they express in this way a certain truth, they also practice a perilous strategy. They risk dividing God's universe, in Gnostic fashion, and limiting the significance of Christ. Christians therefore cannot be indifferent to the task of speaking comprehensibly to the secular world and even, from time to time, hearing expressions of understanding and assent from secular minds. I address this essay to everyone interested in hope, rather than only to those who accept my Christian premises, because I would like to be understandable to all people who sensitively consult human experience and who reason carefully about it, whatever conclusions they reach.

Someone might object that if Christians wish to share the public realm with non-Christians they must practice a terminological and even theological self-restraint. They must not speak explicitly of Christ or of matters of faith such as the Incarnation. Otherwise, they violate the canons of objectivity which define the public realm. Knowledge of scientifically-ascertained population trends, and of other such social conditions, is true for Christians and non-Christians alike; it is objective and thus constitutes public knowledge. Knowledge of Christ, however, *even if it be true,* is not in the same sense objective and therefore does not belong in the public realm; properly speaking, it is *personal* knowledge.

My response to this argument is that it draws an unreal line of demarcation across the public realm. The line is unreal because most of our knowledge is either personal altogether or is blended with personal knowledge; it is not for the most part publicly demonstrable. In public discourse, the personal and the objective are inextricably fused. If all personal knowledge were excluded from the public realm, public discourse would become a desert of abstractions, lacking reference to the human purposes, premises, intuitions, and undefined and undefinable understandings which render communication vital. What would be left of Abraham Lincoln's "Second Inaugural" if all personal knowledge were cut out of it? This response is closely linked with another. While Christians can sometimes put their understanding of things in secular terms (as I hope often to do in this essay), they cannot do so invariably. They cannot leave out distinctive Christian terms entirely and still speak as Christians. Hence to forbid Christians to use Christian terms in the public realm is tantamount to excluding them from the public realm.

Finally, it ought to be said that there is no good reason why the boundaries of the public realm should be drawn so narrowly. Public life would be enriched, rather than threatened, by the presence of Christian words and voices. For Christians to speak publicly in Christian terms is rather a different matter, in modern liberal polities, from their burning their opponents at the stake. And secular minds would gain from hearing Christian claims, even if they were led thereby only to a reasoned repudiation of them. They would become familiar with possibilities of thought never before considered; they would enter into relations with multitudes of human beings heretofore barred from their intellectual universe; and they would be compelled to clarify their own convictions. On grounds such as these it may be suggested that one of the main standards for gauging the quality of a society is the degree of its openness to all manner of serious and responsible speech.

If Christianity is compatible with a communal disposition toward people who reject religion, what is the Christian attitude toward people who follow a religion other than Christianity? Again we find Christian faith intrinsically capable of greater openness than either Christians themselves, or their opponents, have often realized. Construing hope in Christian terms does not necessarily mean saying things entirely unacceptable to Buddhists or to Muslims. One who believes seriously that God is love—that is, a Christian—cannot hold with very clear logic that the great world religions, aside from Christianity, all are utterly false. That would require the paradoxical assumption that the God of love had consigned most of the human race, century after century, to the darkness of erroneous beliefs. Here too the doctrine that Christ is the Logos has significance. If Christ is the meaning and order inherent in reality, the truth he incarnates cannot be entirely unknown to anyone, nor can the revelation that occurred through Christ be in the nature of a private communication, relevant and comprehensible to only a portion of the human race. All truth must partake in some way and measure of Christ, and no one who apprehends a fragment of the truth in any form can be entirely ignorant of Christ. Hence Christians must grant not only that there is truth of some sort in all of the great religions but also that this truth, as genuine truth, is tacitly Christian. Precisely how the Christian truth in Hinduism, or Confucianism, or Islam, is related to the truth in Christianity, is a question with diverse possible answers and cannot be considered here. What is important in the present context is simply that a Christian understanding of hope can be universal—of potential interest to people of various faiths, as well as to people without faith.

If Christians have bonds with adherents of all the great religions, they are, or at least they ought to be, particularly close to Jews. It is true, as often charged, that Christianity has been a major source of anti-Semitism. It has been shocking to Christians that Jesus has been largely rejected by his own people, by the nation Christians regard as chosen by God to carry ultimate truth in human history. Many Christians have no doubt felt, however unconsciously, that such an incongruity cast doubt on their faith. In response, they have cursed the Jews. There are signs of Christian animosity toward Jews even in the New Testament. Spiritually, however, such animosity is scandalous and intolerable. Not only were Jesus, the apostles, and Paul all Jews. Religious Jews worship the God who speaks in the Psalms, in the books of the Prophets, in the Mosaic law, and everywhere else in the Hebrew Bible which Christians treasure as the Old Testament. Jews worship, even though they interpret differently, the same God Christians worship. And Jesus was not only ethnically Jewish; he was religiously Jewish as well. Although he offended Jewish leaders by the authority he claimed, his spiritual matrix was Judaism, and his attitudes toward human beings and human history were fundamentally Judaic. It is easy to see why many Christian writers have felt that turning against the Jews was for a Christian not simply wrong but an act of apostasy. All of this has a bearing on the present inquiry. To base a concept of hope on Christianity does not imply that the concept is not at all Jewish. If it is authentically Christian, it is bound to be in significant ways Jewish as well.

In view of these comments, one might ask why I base the present inquiry on Christianity rather than on religion in general. One answer to this question concerns methodology. To try to abstract from the various religions a single outlook, made up of elements found in all faiths, would result inevitably in the equation of religion with a partially-subjective construct; there is no objectively-adequate definition of religion. But even if there were such a definition, it would be a ghostly abstraction; it would lack the particular symbols and the concrete texts and traditions which are essential for a religion to be vital. For this reason the present discussion must be based on a particular religion and not on religion in general.

But why on the Christian religion? Partly because of the simple but compelling consideration that the author is a Christian and knows Christianity far better than any other religion. An additional consideration is that Christianity is the principal religious possibility for most people in Western societies. Even one who believed that all religions are substantially equivalent, and that whether God is found in one religion or another is immaterial, would have to admit that for most people in Western societies God will be found either in Christianity or not at all.

Further, Christianity is decidedly a religion of hope. It might be said that Jesus' preaching did not concern a God above so much as a God ahead. The kingdom of heaven, Jesus declared, was at hand, and the whole of a person's life and being should be placed in readiness for its coming—however this event might be envisioned in relation to the other events of history and personal life. Nothing else mattered. It might be said, accordingly, that Jesus sought above all to call forth hope. The faith and love he so dramatically demanded took their character from hope. The God in whom we have faith is known to us primarily as the God who has taken in hand the human rebelliousness called sin and is leading the human race toward a state in which God in his glory will be everything to everyone. And the human beings whom we love can be fully known to us only as destined sharers in that glory. Faith and love in this way were anticipatory attitudes. It was logical for Paul to declare that "we are saved by hope," (Romans 9:24 KJV) and to tie faith, hope, and love together as a triad of primary Christian virtues.

Finally, in asking why the reflections making up the present inquiry are based on Christianity, something has to be said which earlier passages may have obscured and which may to some be offensive. As a Christian, the author believes that the truth in Christianity is all-inclusive and unsurpassable and that this cannot be said of any other religion. The revelation that came about through Christ was unique and final. The truth in non-Christian religions is of great splendor and can be saving truth; yet such truth is a portion of the truth of Christ the Logos. Many people today see such statements as intolerably condescending. Yet they are absolutely inseparable from what Christianity has been from the beginning. Anyone who argues that there are various pathways to God, all equally legitimate, is simply not a Christian—not, at least, in the traditional sense; and it is doubtful that the traditional construal of Christianity can be set aside while all the rest of Christianity remains intact. For Christians, Christ is a singular representation of God's mind: his Word, his Son. The pathway Christ marked out between God and man was God's pathway, not a pathway human beings might use if they happened not to find another one they preferred. Things I have already said should make it apparent that in such statements I am not expressing contempt for other faiths. Rather, I am trying to make clear the meaning of Christianity and to show that it is at once—however paradoxical this may seem—in favor of universal speaking and listening, and sure of its own truth. And I am expressing my confidence that to base an inquiry into hope on Christianity is to have access (whether or not such access is used to full advantage) to every significant truth concerning hope.

In sum, this essay is a Christian meditation on hope. It seeks light in the human being who stands at the center of Christian faith and thought, Jesus of Nazareth, called Christ as an expression of the belief that he was not only a human being but also God incarnate and that his words and life consequently illuminate every corner of human existence. My essay addresses everyone, however, asking only that readers, within their own frameworks of thought, reflect on the nature and conditions of hope. All who are human entertain hope at times, and all are tempted at times by despair. Thus we have common concerns. And in human life and experience we have common grounds for addressing these concerns.

Two comments on other matters, both very brief, may help to prepare readers for the essay that follows. The first concerns the nature of this essay. It is a work of philosophy, not scholarship. This means that I have tried to understand hope by thinking about it rather than by carrying on any sort of scientific research. I have tried to do this in a sustained and logical fashion. By thinking, however, one reaches what are, in the final analysis, mere opinions, although these will be worth considering if the thinking has been well done. There are few footnotes, and the nature of the essay is such that footnotes could not contribute much to supporting the main claims I make. Readers who find what seem to them gross misjudgments may be right. It is in the nature of thinking, as contrasted with scholarship and science, that basic disagreements cannot usually be definitively resolved. So I can only hope that I will be read sympathetically.

There is another implication involved in characterizing my efforts as philosophical. At its best, philosophy is not a specialty; it looks at life as a whole. In this essay, accordingly, I try to see a great deal all at once. Not that I feel my own ability to do this is uncommonly great. Rather, I am convinced that looking at life as a whole is a task some people must undertake. Some must expose themselves to the charge of "trying to do too much," for otherwise all serious study will be left to specialists, and our vision of life as a whole will disintegrate. But broad statements are bound to be annoying to some readers; they will seem presumptuous and arbitrary. I can only say in response to such readers that what I am trying to do is not to foist mere personal opinions on others but to help people think. Here again I need indulgent readers.

My other comment concerns my title—*The Fabric of Hope*. I chose this title, after literally years of indecision, for the simple reason that hope is woven of many threads and colors. One of the main conclusions I reached is that hope is not simple. Even though it has a single key, that is, Christ, it contains many elements. This is not surprising, for having hope is having the spirit that enables one to live, and living is a many-faceted enterprise. Hope is as wide and richly-textured as life itself. To characterize the richness and complexity of hope I thought of using the word "tapestry," instead of "fabric," in my title. But a tapestry is something to look at, whereas hope is something to be worn, like Joseph's coat of many colors. I think of hope as a fabric each one of us must weave, and then fashion into a garment, good for wearing, like Joseph's coat.

────────── ❧ chapter one ❦ ──────────

THE FAILURE OF MODERN HOPE

The Need for Hope

Hope is as necessary to life as light and air. Fear weakens and paralyzes us. These are matters of common experience. Hopelessness is a kind of death; one is immobilized by the dark and threatening visage of the future. But hope enlivens us. When viewed with hope, the way ahead is open and inviting. Hope draws us into the future and in this way it engages us in life.

Hope is no less essential in our lives together than in our lives individually. Politically, it is indispensable that our common future, the future of our city or country, be inviting. If it is not, each one will be tempted to seek refuge from the grimness of common life in a private life hermetically sealed against the outside world. And withdrawal into the private realm is not the only possible consequence of hopelessness. Another is a fanatical and despairing effort to break down whatever seems to block the road into the future. This necessarily means, where a reasoning hope is lacking, raising up fictional—and destructible—obstacles. By promising their destruction, demagogues can arouse hope that is exhilarating and politically potent even though it is thoroughly false. The Jewish people have many times served as a tragically convenient fiction of this kind; capitalists were such a fiction for many Communists (and Communists for not a few capitalists). Without a common hope, in short, people flee from common life, either into an alienated private life or into the meretricious public life that arises from fanaticism.

In other words, hope lies at the source of civic conscience and behavior. Civic life depends on a widespread willingness to delay action, even on cherished projects, in order to listen and speak to opponents. Forbearance of this sort is possible only where there is hope, which tells us that everything will work out finally and that therefore we need not fear taking our time. When people in power are patient with those who threaten their plans, they demonstrate their hope. They show by their bearing that they enjoy the light and air on which all good human life depends.

If our need for hope is a common experience, then, it may seem, we must know what hope is. It is doubtful, however, that we do, or that very many do. Even though we recognize hope when it arises in us, and miss it acutely when it dies out, most of us would have difficulty defining it. Partly at least this is because hope concerns time, and time is a notoriously difficult subject to reason about. To have hope is presumably to inhabit time in a particular fashion. But to think about inhabiting time is to face certain well-known and extremely puzzling paradoxes. What is past, for example, is presumably non-existent, since it is past, and yet for the past to weigh upon the present and the future is a common human experience, as instanced when there are acute feelings of guilt; the present we think of as unquestionably real, yet attempting to grasp the present is like trying to seize a handful of water from a flowing stream; the future, being not yet present and having never been present, may seem less real even than the past, yet countless people (Vladimir Lenin, for example) have carried on lives shaped in every detail by the future, or at least by interpretations of the future. The Czech novelist Milan Kundera plays on such paradoxes when he writes, "People are always shouting that they want to create a better future. It's not true. The future is an apathetic void of no interest to anyone. The past is full of life, eager to irritate us, provoke and insult us, tempt us to destroy or repaint it."[1] To entertain hope is to relate oneself in a certain manner to the past, present, and future. How? Not, as we shall see, precisely as one might expect.

Another difficulty in defining hope is that our ultimate earthly future invites despair, seems even to render despair inevitable. Eventually, each one of us will die and finally the earth itself will die, in the sense of becoming uninhabitable. For a clear-sighted person, mortality blankets our existence. One is tempted to feel that hope requires willful short-sightedness; one must not look too far ahead. Religion of course adopts a very different expedient—that of looking beyond all rational expectations, beyond earthly time itself. For many this is no less desperate an expedient than willful short-sightedness. It will be obvious to the reader that the present essay in some way argues the "religious expedient." The point I am making,

---

[1] Milan Kundera, *The Book of Laughter and Forgetting,* trans. Michael Henry Heim (New York: Penguin Books, 1981), p. 22.

however, is that hope is not an easy and natural attitude for creatures who must, with the capacity for looking far ahead, inhabit mortal time.

I am not suggesting that hope is more mysterious than other inner states, such as faith and love. But it is not less so. Hence in reflecting on hope one must be prepared for anomalies and surprises. Hope may turn out to be something quite different from what common sense had taken it to be. And if the nature of hope is other than is often supposed, its attainment may be harder—or, of course, easier—than is often supposed, and its strength and stability may depend, both for individuals and societies, on conditions rarely linked with hope in our minds. In short, although hope is a familiar experience and a familiar concern, thinking about it may lead us to the realization that it is not a familiar concept.

We can hardly avoid the task of working out this concept. Perhaps we could if our lives were filled with hope. We could let ourselves be carried along in time, rejoicing in the future before us. If hope is contradicted by our mortality, however, living in this way would be an illusory enterprise, destined sooner or later to be rudely interrupted. And there is not only the natural difficulty of hope; there is also the spirit of our times. We live in an era of unusual despondency. In some periods of history, as during the Renaissance or the Enlightenment, human morale is generally high and people look ahead with anticipation. The twentieth century is not such a period. Nor is America, in spite of its traditional optimism and its roots in the Enlightenment, different from other societies in this regard. Although Americans today are expected to display high spirits and a cheerful demeanor, their hearts are often burdened with uneasiness and foreboding.

Modern Despondency

Even people with little historical knowledge cannot avoid an undercurrent of awareness that our century has suffered devastating disappointments and tragedies. The century before ours was apparently one of the hopeful centuries. Nineteenth-century optimism, however, disarmed us. When the twentieth century began, we were unprepared for the misfortunes and crimes of our age, and our disillusionment was more profound than it might otherwise have been. The hope we inherited was laid waste by trench warfare, by totalitarianism in major civilized nations, and by the death camps. These were unprecedented evils, and in most quarters unexpected. Henry James, during World War I, found nearly unbearable the thought that the long centuries past had been leading up to, and in that way were given their meaning by, the horrors transpiring in the trenches. By now we have seen evils more numerous and shocking than James had seen. How can a realistic person at the end of the twentieth century avoid James's dismay? How can one entertain anything but frivolous or delusory hopes in the century of the Somme and Verdun, of the Gestapo and KGB, of Buchenwald and Auschwitz, of Iwo Jima and Hiroshima?

Further, and at the risk of misunderstanding, it must be said that the failure of communism must also be counted among the severe disappointments of our times. Granted, this failure came as the climax of a long series of crimes and culpable miscalculations. Witnesses of the Soviet disaster cannot altogether avoid feeling the grim satisfaction inherent in seeing despotic and arrogant men brought to grief. Nonetheless, the delight with which many have greeted the Soviet collapse has been too simple to be appropriate. It is oblivious of the fact that the Soviet Union, even though born of proud illusions and sustained with terror, represented an ideal of justice and cooperation which arises spontaneously in human imagination and which capitalism cannot match even in theory, much less in practice. Capitalism is far more realistic, and on the whole immeasurably more beneficial, than communism; still, it is inseparable from the love of money, from the competitive pursuit of profits, from great material and social inequalities, and from various other conditions which, although far preferrable to conditions of the kind communism creates, can hardly be regarded as better than necessary evils. Hence it is that the collapse of communism means lost hopes and, even though those hopes were from the beginning presumptuous and illusory, will weigh on the mood of generations to come.

It is not only the recent past, however, which encourages despondency. So does the impending future. No one today can escape the realization that we face problems that, appraised realistically, are probably insoluble. There is, for example, the destitution endured by countless millions all over the world: Can one, without entertaining science-fiction fantasies, think that economic sufficiency for all human beings is apt to be achieved even within centuries? And there is the problem of nuclear proliferation; it seems virtually certain that sometime in coming centuries nuclear weapons will fall into the hands of an irrational leader and be used. Finally, there is the terrible tenacity of racial hatred. Can we envision a time, even within a thousand years, in which such hatred will have vanished from the earth?

In whichever direction we look, then, and however far, we see things telling us that hope is irrational. The sources of our despondency, moreover, are not known just to specialists. They are components of modern consciousness. Scarcely anyone is so ignorant of the past as to be entirely unaware of the evils that have marked the history of our century, or so uninterested in current conditions and events as to think that the future is promising. Hence modern despondency is neither a momentary mood, caused perhaps by a passing circumstance, nor is it the mood merely of those professionally engaged in reading and writing books. It is deeply rooted in our historical situation and is felt in some measure by everyone. Surely the preoccupation of industrialized peoples with entertainment and pleasure represents in some part a widespread desire to think as little as possible about the past and the future and rather to be absorbed entirely in the present moment.

In addition to the disappointments and fears I have mentioned, there is a condition less fearful than trench warfare or death camps, and less ominous than world poverty or racial hatred, but nevertheless evil enough, and in addition difficult enough to manage and even to define, as to encumber seriously our efforts to live into the future. This is "mass society." The term is used to designate one of the strangest and most unsettling conditions affecting Western societies in the nineteenth and twentieth centuries. Numerous nations today are in some ways ideal societies; most people within them enjoy reasonable economic security, stable freedom, and multiple opportunities to participate in public affairs. What more can we ask? Many of the major aspirations of the modern age have been in fair measure fulfilled. In this sense, as Francis Fukuyama has argued, we have reached the end of history.[2] Yet many perceptive people contemplate life within these societies and find it repellent. Economic plenty seems to impose materialistic limits on imagination and people devote themselves to recreation, entertainment, and physical pleasure. Freedom consequently becomes trivial; the most dramatic alternatives before an individual may be in the nature of those faced in a supermarket. Freedom may be subtly nullified in another way as well. Even though legally one can live in any of a great variety of ways, in fact everyone lives in about the same way, and it may be difficult even to think of a different way; and this is to say nothing of of the problem of carrying on a distinctive life under the surprised or censorious regard of one's neighbors. And not only is personal freedom thus palsied. Public freedom likewise, in a mass society, suffers from unforeseen illnesses. Election campaigns may come to consist largely in expensive and professionally organized marketing campaigns for candidates for office. And politicians may be so disabled by the pressures put on them by monied interests and unreasoning voters as to lose the dignity essential to a legitimate government.

Alexis de Tocqueville, as a visitor to Jacksonian America, was one of the first to perceive the strange ambiguity of liberal democracy—the ambiguity introduced by mass society. He strongly approved of the general principles of the American polity, principles such as liberty, equality, and popular rule. Yet he found many of the actualities of American life to be quietly subversive of the principles ostensibly underlying them. Americans on the whole were a constrained and uneasy people. Like ambiguities are apparent today. On one side, patriots who idealize America do not wholly misrepresent the realities. America is a highly prosperous nation, with the vast majority enjoying material benefits and vital opportunities unmatched in

---

2 Francis Fukuyama, *The End of History and the Last Man* (New York: Avon Books, 1992).

any past society; it probably provides more durable and diverse liberties than any other nation in the world; and it still practices, over two centuries after its founding, the politics of representative democracy. Yet critics who see America as a degraded society do not wholly misrepresent the realities either. They are justified by such well-known conditions as the squalor of many inner city neighborhoods, the shallowness of popular culture, the irresponsibility of the schools, the omnipresence of advertising, and the commercialization of politics.

Mass society is discouraging not just because the conditions defining it are undesirable. Perhaps more important is the fact that it is hard to know how to deal with those conditions. Humans can sometimes act rationally and effectively in order to create just economic and political forms. But there seems to be little they can do when the life that fills those forms turns out to be spiritually worthless. We know how to resist poverty and enslavement; but a spiritual decline leaves us bemused. Hence, although modern constitutional government and social democracy marks the end of a long journey, the event of arrival has been surprisingly unhappy, and no one knows quite what we can do about it. There is little doubt that this situation reinforces modern despondency. Mass society seems at once to fulfill and to foreclose hope.

It may seem that the term "despondency" oversimplifies the emotional coloring of our age. I have chosen the term, however, to cover a variety of emotions—resignation, apathy, fear, despair, apprehension. All of these are conspicuous, in different degrees and among different groups, in the happiest of twentiety-century societies.

Notably lacking in the modern world is the quiet confidence that signalizes hope. This is the occasion for the present essay. Thinking about hope would be unnecessary if we possessed it. We could simply rejoice in the serenity it bestows. But not possessing it, and needing it, we are forced to seek it. To do that, however, we must try to understand what it is and what it rests on. How can we best approach these problems? The despondency of our times gives us a lead. The failure of modern hope is not due entirely to modern events and conditions. It is due also to defects inherent in that hope.

Modern Hope and Its Weaknesses

Present despondency represents a fading of the hope that had with growing power sustained and inspired the modern era. This hope lends itself to examination, because it was given clear conceptual formulation. It was expressed in the doctrine of progress. The main features of this doctrine are well-known. Progress was typically seen as natural and, in the long run at least, inevitable. It was thought to consist in increasing knowledge, increasing command of the physical world, and increasing material abundance. It was also envisioned as a steady, if gradual, approach to justice and peace. And, finally, it meant liberty, ever more widespread and secure. This advance in understanding and efficiency, in fairness and well-being—in a word, in amplitude of life—resulted from a spontaneous unfolding of human powers. The greatest of these powers was reason. Human beings were held to be reasonable, which is to say, capable of learning and of acting on what they learned. Mistakes are not endlessly repeated. Given the premise of human rationality, the idea of progress made a great deal of sense.

The idea had deeper roots, however. The Hebrew prophets, and later on the Church fathers, planted deeply in the Western mind the faith that there is a single history, a unified and meaningful unfoldment of events, embracing the entire human race. Human beings were envisioned as participants in a single great pilgrimage, the goal of which was life with God. Such was not, of course, the goal envisioned in the doctrine of progress. Nevertheless, the ancient Jews and the early Christians instilled deeply in Western minds the notion that human life on earth is not scattered and pointless. It is a common life, and it has a direction and an end. The argument that the doctrine of progress was a secularization of this faith is old and familiar. But it is nearly irresistible. The vision of human history as unified and directional is not natural to the human mind; this is demonstrated by its absence from the philosophical and historical writings of antiquity. It almost certainly depends on the conception which the ancient Hebrews brought into Western thinking: that one God created and governs the universe. In the age of the city-states the doctrine of progress was virtually impossible.

The religious version of this doctrine faded, not because it was disproven; rather, it ceased to hold people's interest. This was due, presumably, to rising confidence in human powers and in earthly possibilities. But why, in our own time, did the secular version fade? People did not lose interest in it—at least not in its goals, such as prosperity and justice. Something more decisive happened. It suffered the fate which the religious version was spared. It was disproven. The doctrine of progress was demolished by the terrible events of the twentieth century. This is why modern despondency is so serious; it is not merely a matter of shifting moods. It comes out of a collision with reality. This means that confidence in historical progress is probably gone forever. We cannot respond to its disappearance simply by trying to revive our spirits. We have to deepen our understanding, and this requires, first of all, that we understand why the very idea of progress, as formulated by the modern mind, was false. To learn this is to see why modern hope was ill-founded and to lay the groundwork for true hope.

From the vantage point of the late twentieth century, several grave weaknesses in the doctrine of progress can be readily seen. The most obvious of these is simply its excessive optimism. It left human beings entirely unprepared for the tragic events of our time, for it implied that such events were precluded by the logic of history. The use of violence would steadily diminish; cruelty would be replaced with kindness; hence war and despotism would vanish into the past. True, there were relatively pessimistic interpretations of progress. These, archetypically in Marx and his great philosophic predecessor, G. W. F. Hegel, construed progress as dialectical; history advanced by way of tensions and catastrophes. The dialectic, while preserving high long-run expectations, allowed for conflict and violence in the short run. But modern catastrophes have surpassed the dimensions of the Hegelian dialectic. To think of the global devastation wrought by twentieth-century wars, and the desolation of the death camps, as simply an antithesis to the thesis posed by the Enlightenment, and destined to be subsumed in a higher harmony lying before us, would be to indulge in offensive fantasies. In none of its forms did the doctrine of progress prepare people for life in the twentieth century.

How extreme and uncritical the optimism underlying the doctrine of progress was can be seen in one of its main premises: that there would be a corporate human advance toward perfect wisdom and righteousness. We still are so habituated to progressive modes of thought that the idea may not strike us as particularly problematic. But how could such an advance possibly occur? Can wisdom be passed from one generation to succeeding generations and steadily deepened in its passage? Surely not. Objective knowledge can be thus transmitted, but wisdom (without which objective knowledge is of doubtful value) cannot. A wise father cannot at will call into being a wise son; ordinary human experience makes this abundantly plain. Neither can a righteous father call forth a righteous son. One generation cannot achieve righteousness and then bestow it on the next generation. Perhaps laws and customs can be gradually elevated, just as objective knowledge can be extended. But righteousness is a more vital and creative state than mere conformity with law and custom; this being so, perfecting the existing order is not the same as perfecting righteousness. Wisdom and righteousness alike have to do with personal qualities which we cannot even assuredly define, much less hand over to others. It is likely that the doctrine of progress, and with it modern hope, could survive as long as it did because of the growing self-satisfaction of Western peoples; they were able to assume unthinkingly that they were steadily becoming better and better human beings. Progress seemed natural, and hope mere common sense.

Someone may object that were this argument valid the human race would spiritually still be where it started. In their moral standards and actions, for example, men and women would be no better now than they were thousands of years ago. Is it clear, however, that they are? True, there are practices such as the Roman games and slavery which are no longer tolerated. But practices as terrible, or worse, such as the Nazi death camps or Cambodian and Rwandan genocide, have been carried on very recently. Granted, social norms have in some ways been refined, for example in efforts to make the public world accessible to the handicapped, and there must be moral meaning of some sort in this fact. But the most we can say is that something of moral significance appears to have occurred during the history of civilized societies. We cannot even crudely express this significance in terms of the steady and natural advance affirmed in the doctrine of progress. Indeed, one of the most striking phenomena of the twentieth century is that of demonic evil. The unqualified proposition that human beings are better than they were in the distant past has been refuted.

Nor are human beings clearly wiser than they were in the distant past. The television culture of Western nations today certainly marks a decline compared with the state of the populace in medieval Europe (nourished spiritually by the Church) or in ancient Athens (nourished by the tragedians and philosophers). Granted, in earlier times most people experienced a state of intellectual deprivation which relatively few today experience. But the process of equalization has come to rest on a very low level. It is not obvious even that Christian revelation has made us wiser. Thomas Aquinas had access to a far greater treasure of wisdom than did Plato, but would anyone say flatly that Thomas Aquinas was wiser than Plato? He stood on higher ground, but whether he was taller is debatable.

At any rate, whatever their causes and whatever their nature, the optimism written into the doctrine of progress is gone. We know now that a nation in history has no more security than explorers floating on a raft down an unknown river. Anything can happen. We can easily share the emotions of Hegel when he contemplated the pervasive passions and violence in history, and the "Unreason" that he found in the company not only of evil designs but of "good designs and righteous aims" as well. "When we see the evil, the vice, the ruin that has befallen the most flourishing kingdoms which the mind of man ever created," Hegel wrote, "we can scarce avoid being filled with sorrow at this universal taint of corruption." And in the same passage he speaks of history as presenting "a picture of most fearful aspect" and as exciting "emotions of the profoundest and most hopeless sadness."[3] No one living in the closing years of the twentieth century, and looking back on the series of world tragedies that began to unfold in 1914, can think Hegel's comments exaggerated. Indeed, today we can realize the justice of those comments more fully than Hegel could himself. We have seen far worse than Hegel had seen, and by now we are doubtful that there is, or even could be, any dialectic at work—at least within the bounds of earthly history—that will finally redeem the enormities of our age.

---

[3] Georg Wilhelm Friedrich Hegel, *The Philosophy of History,* revised edition, trans. J. Sibree (New York: Willey Book Co., 1900), pp. 20–1.

How, then, as persons and as peoples, can we learn again to hope? This is to ask, since hope is the state of mind which enables us to enter with assurance into the mystery of life, how can we live? From the standpoint of modern hope, as embodied in the doctrine of progress, no realistic answer, no answer divested of sentimental dreams and fancies, is apparent. No wonder many people take refuge from history in the distractions of buying and consuming.

Optimism, however, is not the only weakness in modern hope. The doctrine of progress depended on a grossly exaggerated account of human powers. It raised man to historical sovereignty, sometimes tacitly, as in the minds of American industrialists, sometimes explicitly, as in the projects and ideals of Russian Marxists. This view, too, has also been refuted by events in the twentieth century. Our times would not have been so inhuman if humans had been in control of history. Modern disasters have not been due only to evil men, although evil men obviously have had a hand in them. They have been due also to good men, or at least to men who were decent as judged by prevailing standards. World War I was brought about by blundering but ordinary, not demonic, leaders; the Russian Revolution, which prepared the way for decades of despotism and terror, was effected by people who were no doubt arrogant but also were idealistic and heroic; the Great Depression— a matrix of tyranny and war—was precipitated by businessmen and government officials who were selfish and short-sighted but far from diabolical. Needless to say, diabolical men have played a role in our times. Human beings are potential tyrants and terrorists, and that is one reason they are incapable of reliably steering nations on progressive courses. But often they are merely unwise or morally mediocre. And even leaders with exceptional abilities and strong consciences, like Woodrow Wilson and Lyndon Johnson, may unwittingly bring great historical misfortunes.

Historical examples are not strictly necessary, however, for showing that we cannot comprehend and control history. Nor, if we come to speak of human nature, are references to our deep and persistent sinfulness strictly necessary. It suffices simply to take into account that we are finite. Being finite, we are immanent in history, incapable of the unqualified transcendence which the idea of human historical sovereignty presupposes. Like explorers on a raft, we can see only a little way ahead, and there is inevitably a great deal of guesswork in our navigational strategies. In more familiar terms, we cannot foresee all the consequences of our actions. Among those who pressed for universal suffrage and the other rights that make possible participatory democracy, how many foresaw the rise of mass society? And among those who fought for the seemingly impeccable cause of economic and social justice, how many realized that even an approach to that goal would give rise to vast bureaucracies—elites that are at once highly privileged and startlingly inefficient?

It becomes ever more apparent, as one reflects on the doctrine of progress, that regaining hope through mere psychological maneuvers, such as refusing to worry about evils that are only possible but not yet actual, or "learning to look on the bright side" of every situation, is out of the question. We face conditions—our mortality, our finitude, our bent toward evil—which seemingly render hope unreasonable. These are conditions our century compels us to face, and they point in the direction of an enduringly tragic course of human affairs. This is why modern hope has waned; the principles underlying it have become incredible. Manifestly, to recover the hope that is the light and air of human life we shall have to search for wisdom lacking from the doctrine of progress. Before undertaking this search, however, two further flaws in modern hope need to be noted.

One of these is its confinement to worldly possibilities. Many today, reflecting the secularism of our age, are reluctant to admit that any other possibilities exist. Nietzsche enjoined his readers to "be true to the earth," and if this means being defiantly resistant to the idea of there being anything more real than the realities we see and touch or anything more conclusive than events of the kind reported in the press, Nietzsche's advice has been widely followed in our time, particularly by academicians and intellectuals. As sensible and solidly-founded as this attitude may seem to be, however, it is in fundamental conflict with human nature. It takes no account of the boundlessness of human imagination and is, in this sense, unnatural. Humans have the capacity—a source of ceaseless anxiety, yet integral to the human spirit—to inquire of every existing state of affairs, however blissful, "Is this all?" and of every plan and prospect, "Then what?" This capacity draws their attention irresistibly toward eternity. Followers of Nietzsche—and of Marx, Freud, and other secular writers—can pour as much scorn as they like on the inclination to look beyond the earth and history. This inclination arises from the essence of our humanity. Although we are immanent in nature and history, we are also, whether we like it or not, transcendent—unable to contemplate any existing or imagined reality without being aware that there is something unknown beyond it. And confining our gaze and understanding to a particular state of affairs, present or anticipated, is not only impossible. Were it possible, it would be idolatrous; it would be treating as ultimate and infinite something which is ephemeral and finite.

Human transcendence has a decisive impact on hope. Hope confined to worldly possibilities is scarcely hope at all; it is so limited as to warrant the label "resignation" rather than "hope." Marx is often thought of as having delineated a sweeping and inspiring prospect, thus arousing a magnificent hope. But that is not true. For Marx, death was final, and earthly history had no eternal sequel. The most one could hope for was some years of essentially animal satisfaction, culminating in foreknown and inevitable nothingness. Marx of course presented a version of the doctrine of progress; he was, indeed, the most powerful exponent of modern hope. If the hope he expounded was in truth resignation, then we must say that modern hope is delusory. It tries to persuade us to dismiss from our minds that which concerns us more than anything else, our ultimate destiny. In this sense modern hope is not optimistic at all. It is common today for defenders of worldly progress to argue that we would not care about eternity, and would die contentedly, were we to experience true joy and fulfillment on this earth. But this argument begs the question, which is whether there can be true joy and fulfillment on earth for creatures able to ask, "Is this all?" and "Then what?" The answer surely is negative; boundless imagination cannot be satisfied with bounded and mortal realities. And even if it could, it is far from clear that such satisfaction would be any more fitting a goal than the "satisfaction" found in drugs, alcohol, or any other device for obscuring the realities of our situation. What would our humanity amount to if we lost all consciousness of the mystery that encompasses us in space and time?

Note must be taken finally of a problem inherent in modern hope and closely related to the characteristic secularism of such hope. The confinement of hope to the world, and to worldly history, involved the doctrine of progress in an insoluble moral problem. The era of perfect peace and justice to which history was supposedly leading could, in view of human mortality, be enjoyed by only a portion of the human race. Only those still living when history reaches its climax will reap fully the benefits of progress. Even if progress is conceived of as endless, and therefore lacking any precisely identifiable climax, the principle remains the same. Measured by the standard of historical possibility, multitudes of human beings will suffer at least a degree of deprivation and many from very severe deprivation. In effect, these multitudes will have been sacrificed in the cause of historical development.

Modern hope has no way of avoiding an implication disastrous to its moral spirit: many members of the human race are destined to be merely means to the great ends toward which history is moving. The notion that every individual is an end and not merely a means fades from human consciousness. This is far from being a mere theoretical consideration. The fact that Soviet leaders reconciled themselves so quickly after the October Revolution to murderous measures, and descended in little over a decade into an abyss of genocide, reflects this logic. The idea that historical progress requires the expenditure of many lives found ready lodgment in Soviet minds.

Thus it cannot be said that modern hope was benevolent but shallow. It was not, in the final analysis, benevolent. It could not envision a transcendental community in which every human being would have a part. Human beings were looked on as participants, not in the City of God, but merely in the process of history. Their reduction to the status of means became inevitable.

These, then, are the weaknesses of modern hope: obliviousness of the insecurities and tragedies inherent in history; neglect of the finitude and moral imperfection affecting all human understanding and action; failure to realize that man, although finite, has an imagination without determinate limits and therefore cannot rejoice in ephemeral satisfactions; and finally, implicit in its denial of eternity, an incapacity for according unqualified respect to every person.

In focusing on the doctrine of progress we have, of course, been discussing modern hope in its collective form. But individual forms of hope cannot, in the nature of things, differ very much from collective forms. It is difficult and often impossible for an individual to hope for things in personal life which the surrounding society, normally with the collaboration of that very individual, declares illusory. We are justified in saying, therefore, that both in their common and in their personal lives humans have in recent centuries inhabited time on the basis of presuppositions at odds with human nature and the human condition.

This is why we have fallen into despondency. Our hope was built on spiritual sand and swiftly collapsed when struck by the floods of war, tyranny, and revolution. And that is not the only unhappy consequence of modern errors. A concept of hope presupposes a comprehensive view of the world and history. Thus Augustine's philosophy of history was grounded in his Christian theology as a whole, and modern hope arose from the secularism of the modern world. What particularly concerns us here, however, is that not only does any particular concept of hope presuppose a particular world view; things also work the other way around. A concept of hope, particularly one that is widely and enthusiastically adhered to over a period of centuries, has an impact on the world view underlying it. Thus the doctrine of progress, as long as it flourished, encouraged the secularism on which it rested. We may draw the conclusion that a false concept of hope tends to reinforce, and in some circumstances to produce, a false view of life, and people who inhabit time and history with unwise hope will tend to be unwise in general.

The Subversion of Wisdom

To speak plainly, modern hope has in many ways made us superficial (as well as confirming a superficiality already present). It has made it hard for us to see certain things and therefore hard for us to learn from experience. There is no better example of this than the modern attitude toward suffering.

For a society to understand suffering adequately is not a small matter; it concerns the equilibrium not only of individuals but of entire peoples. The Greeks and Romans were taught by tragic drama, ancient Jews by the afflictions undergone by the Israelites and by the Prophets, and Christians by the vision of the Cross. In all of these cases, suffering was instilled with meaning and reconciled with the dignity of the sufferer. The doctrine of progress, however, implied that the great evils heretofore experienced in history are passing phenomena, not enduring characteristics of human existence. Suffering, therefore, might be largely eliminated from our lives, and if it might be then surely it should be. But if a society in which there is little or no suffering is possible and desirable, it follows that suffering is avoidable and useless. The logic of such a thought is remorseless. When people suffer there must be some human failure involved, perhaps on the part of the sufferer; moreover, the suffering itself is sheer waste, an incursion of absurdity into what ought to be under rational control. Thus the wisdom of tragic drama, of the forty years in the wilderness, and of the Cross was lost. Suffering, however, was not thus lightened; it was made worse, for now it was shameful and senseless.

Another example of the subversion of wisdom by modern hope concerns values. The belief that humans can control reality, and that their vocation in the world is consequently one of action, led logically to concentration on those values which humans could readily create and enhance. These were material values. Human agencies cannot with any assurance provide people with spiritual insight or righteous inclinations; this is true even of schools and churches, and more so of governments and private corporations. They can, however, provide them with wealth, comfort, and physical pleasure. Even though business cycles, class conflicts, and other conditions can mar such achievements, the fact remains that, when it comes to dealing with material realities, humans enjoy something that at least feels like mastery and looks like spectacular success. In dealing with spiritual realities, however, they are on entirely different ground. Here they will fail entirely unless they admit, right at the outset, their weakness. That, however, is an unpleasant necessity, and there is a way of avoiding it: simply to ignore spiritual realities and spiritual values. The doctrine of progress, with its emphasis on human powers, invited such a maneuver. In this way it contributed naturally to a preoccupation with such values as money, material security, and physical gratification.

This preoccupation has lowered the level of American political life. It has done this by giving rise to a material acquisitiveness which has in turn called forth an unnatural concern with gaining and preserving material privileges. True, there are "culture wars," arising from such issues as abortion rights and sex education in the schools. These issues, however, are spiritual. They do not degrade American political life nearly so much as does the love of money, which calls into being a tangle of pressure groups, many of them armed with a great deal of money and fighting for conditions which will enable their members to acquire yet more money. Hatred of taxes, which supposedly rob people of their money and eventuate in no commensurate benefits, has taken on an entirely unrealistic intensity. The virulence of the "culture wars" may derive partly from the desire of some to devote themselves to more dignified causes than making money. It is understandable that Hannah Arendt, seeking to ennoble politics, wished to exclude distributive questions from the realm of public debate. As it is, the Greek conception of a life that is harmonious and whole, and the Christian conception of a life turning on the axis running from God to man, have been replaced by the simple idea of a life that is materially secure and physically pleasurable. Ironically, by affirming human powers, modern hope has constricted human imagination.

A final example of the deleterious spiritual consequences of superficial hope concerns religion, the arts, and literature. As for religion, the assumption that earthly existence has no transcendental dimension and earthly history no eternal sequel, has made religious creeds appear entirely arbitrary. There is no reason for anyone lacking religious inclinations to give them a moment's serious consideration; hence the casual neglect with which modern academicians treat theology. As a commitment and a way of life, correspondingly, religion is thought of as simply an indulgence in personal proclivities, suitable for people moved by them, but not as an orientation which might possibly be connected with the essence of our humanity. Indeed, religion comes to be thought of in somewhat the same way as sex—as a purely private matter. As a public matter, however, it is regarded as threatening to freedom, since its practitioners are inclined to take it with disproportionate seriousness. Religion, then, although intrinsically insignificant, can be dangerous. From this perception follows the readiness of American courts to confine religious groups to the periphery of life, sometimes even depriving them of privileges and rights accorded as a matter of course to other groups.

Not only religion, but also art is trivialized where there is no openness toward the transcendent and eternal. Most, if not all, works of art which we think of as masterpieces are either tacitly or explicitly transcendental. Sometimes this is simply because they are beautiful. They set before us splendors and dramas that are not visible to the eyes of realism and practicality, and in doing this they tell us that existence in its depths is not absurd but has meaning. But even nihilistic works, such as novels displaying human life as cruel, disorderly, and pointless, may, by relativizing everything in the world, paradoxically invoke a consciousness of transcendence. And something of the same sort can happen through comic works; in laughing we discover, as Kierkegaard insisted, that the comical is very near to the religious.

It is undeniable that even in these secular times many works of art that are beautiful, or in some other way powerful and moving, have appeared. It is noteworthy, however, that many works that are unsightly, or merely strange and unsettling, also have appeared. And these works are taken seriously—displayed in museums, played in concert halls, staged in theatres, published and widely distributed. And the most unconditional and unyielding form of secularism in modern times, that of Communism, produced visual art that was relentlessly sentimental and in large part void of artistic value. It is noteworthy, too, that even works of unchallengeable beauty and power are on all hands challenged in their significance. They provide, we are told by the gentler critics, a fictional world where we can enjoy harmonies not available in the actual world. According to the more astringent critics they express only the sentiments of a dominant class, race, and gender. Thus at best they offer relief and diversion, at worst misrepresentations and lies. The idea that they provide access to the depths of reality is contemptuously cast aside.

In sum, the way we hope is the way we live. Modern hope has embodied serious misunderstandings and has inevitably, therefore, been spiritually stultifying. It has rendered suffering incomprehensible, encouraged materialism, and trivialized religion and art.

It has also been politically stultifying. This is best exemplified, perhaps, by its repercussions upon our attitudes toward historical change. By teaching us to trust in the spontaneous course of affairs (which must be distinguished from the deep necessities constituting human destiny), modern hope has instilled a kind of historical recklessness. This is manifest, in different ways, both in the liberal, capitalist West and in the Communist nations.

In the West, confidence in the beneficence of history has led above all to willing acquiescence in every form of technological change. As a spontaneous unfolding of historical forces, technological development is assumed to be benign—not even needing to be very closely observed, much less to be deliberately checked. In recent years, the rise of environmental concerns has marked a decline in such confidence, and for decades nuclear weapons have been a reminder that technological inventiveness is not always salutary. For the most part, however, it has been taken for granted throughout the industrial revolution that whatever was technologically feasible was historically inevitable and bound in the long run to be humanly beneficial. This frame of mind has been particularly evident among proponents of laissez-faire economics. However, we are not speaking of a particular ideological position but of a reigning temper of mind. Technological moderation was scarcely thinkable. In no ideological camp could leaders have contemplated the regulation, or even careful monitoring, of the transformations technology was bringing about. Thus, in America, changes like the disappearance of family farms due to the mechanization of agriculture, and the breakdown of cities into clusters of suburbs because of the proliferation of automobiles, have been as astonishing and disruptive as natural calamities. My point is not so much that developments as profound as the industrial revolution can or should be entirely under human control. It is rather that the cult of progress inculcated a mood of historical irresponsibility, an attitude of idolatry toward all historical possibilities.

In the Communist nations historical recklessness took a different form, that of faith in revolution. Human beings, or at least certain groups of human beings, were thought—mainly by themselves—to have the capacity to transform society. They set out to perform the miracle of revolution. Of course, revolution can be defined in a way which justifies such a faith. If throwing off imperial domination constitutes a revolution, then Americans in the late eighteenth century proved that revolution is within human powers. But if such an act as that is a revolution, then we need a different word for what was done in Russia in 1917. Lenin and his comrades attempted to transform abruptly and comprehensively the whole economic, social, and political order. An effort of that sort requires that the whole structure of institutions and habits constituting society, that is, the social forms which have shaped the expectations, daily lives, and emotional attachments of a people, be suddenly dismantled, or at least placed in question. This unleashes such a deluge of confusion, fear, and ambition that government by negotiation and consent becomes impossible. Despotism arises inevitably. Moreover, since a sweeping transformation of long-established habits of behavior and thought is impossible, the old ways return. The new order replicates in many ways the old order, while being more violent and unconstrained.

The truth is that revolution can be justified only as a tragic necessity, not as an effective way of improving society. This surely would be obvious to people not blinded by the illusion of inexorable worldly progress. Only those who assume that revolutionary efforts will be sustained and furthered by the very logic of history can confidently launch a revolution. But this, of course, is precisely what was assumed by the Russian revolutionaries in October of 1917. Bolshevik leaders never undertook a sober analysis of Russian realities in order to determine whether their designs were feasible. They felt no need to. They were carried forward, exuberantly, by the faith that these designs were underwritten by the dialectic of historical progress.

The deficiencies of modern hope point toward the characteristics of authentic hope. We are thus in a position, now, to begin the task of rethinking the concept of hope.

──────── ❦ chapter two ❧ ────────

THE NATURE OF HOPE

Hope and God

Seeing the errors of modern hope enables us to see also, at least dimly, the way out of our present despondency. Hope must be defined in terms of transcendence. For hope to be regained—not only better understood but also made alive within us—our minds must cease to be confined altogether to the realm of things we can rationally comprehend and control; and the scope of our lives must no longer be identified with the realm of human faculties and powers.

Laying hold of a hope defined in terms of transcendence, however, requires something more than the openness toward transcendence discussed in the Prologue. And it requires more than the kind of striving to understand transcendence which might arise from this openness. Transcendence cannot be reached through human powers alone. The finite intellect by its very nature objectifies reality and in that way builds the world which shuts us off from transcendence. Sin exacerbates this disability; the pride which for Christians is the core of sin renders the intellect blindly imperious and the world it builds more confining than it has to be. And even the simple openness which underlies the struggle of the mind to reach transcendence is contrary to some powerful inclinations. We would like to think that reality can be wholly understood and mastered; we are thus led to close our minds to transcendence. Hence, for transcendence to be known, transcendence itself must act. Transcendence must disclose itself, and call forth the openness in which its disclosures can be freely accepted. There must, in traditional Christian terms, be revelation and faith.

Human attitudes toward revelation are decidedly ambiguous. On the one hand, we are put off by the very idea of revelation. Some people in marked degree, and all us in some degree, are hostile toward transcendence; hence the phenomenon of radical secularism. One source of such hostility is always the desire to maintain our independence—to live according our own judgments, and not to be humbled or thrown into doubt by a reality supposedly beyond human criticism and comprehension. We want to live our own proud lives. But sometimes the motive is hedonistic: the desire, without censorial oversight, to discover and enjoy our own pleasures. Another factor in our hostility toward transcendence may be fear, however vague and ill-defined. The Christian concept of God as merciful and kind, after all, is not the only possible version of divine character. God has been thought of as cruel, or capricious. The gods supposedly revealed to various men have not infrequently inspired uneasiness or even dread.

It is scarcely necessary to say that Christianity condemns our tendency to repudiate and close ourselves off from transcendence. Ostensibly trying merely to guard our human independence, in fact we are trying to seize a sovereignty for which finite and erring creatures are ill-suited; and in pursuing what we think of as harmless satisfactions we are usually trying to lose ourselves in worldly pleasures. When proud or pleasure-seeking men affirm their own lives in defiance of transcendence they embark on a project that is bound to end badly. They place their trust in an entity—the worldly self—that is passing away into dust and oblivion. Nor is the fear of God (except for the fear felt by believers, which partakes more of awe and reverence than of mere human fright) any more defensible. It comes from ignoring the paramount principle disclosed in the life of Christ—that God is love. Whatever our motives, Christianity tells us that we cannot live in our full humanity apart from God, and that God is present to us mainly on his terms, not ours. All hope based on a denial of transcendence—on radical secularism—is false. This applies to Marxism, to the "liberal hope" discussed in Chapter One, and to every other radically secular version of progress.

On the other hand, denial of transcendence is by no means a universal human impulse. Many are strongly drawn toward transcendence. The most striking evidence of this is the prevalence of religion, in all periods of history and in all parts of the globe. Of course religion always expresses a measure of fear, and religious ceremonies are always in part efforts at propitiation. But the great scriptures of the world, such as the Upanishads and the Bhagavad-Gita, show incontestably that fear is not the predominant motive. The motive rather is love of transcendence. It is hard not to think that human beings in most times and places have had an intuition of transcendence as merciful, glorious, life-sustaining, or in other ways deeply consonant with human taste and need.

In Western philosophy, the human love of transcendence is manifest from the beginning. Again and again the great thinkers envision, and mark out avenues leading toward, the infinite and the eternal. Thus for Plato the ultimate object of human striving was the supreme source of all being and all knowledge which Plato likened to the sun and called "the idea of the Good." For Aristotle, the highest human felicity lay in contemplation of a similarly quintessential and primal reality, a cause of all other beings, itself uncaused—"the unmoved mover." The Stoics argued that serenity amid life's mischances and troubles could be found only by living in conformity with the Logos, the divine order underlying all the things and happenings around us. Plotinus set forth the concept, and reportedly more than once attained a mystical vision of, a being beyond being—in that sense a nonbeing—which he termed "the One." Modern philosophical literature resounds with words like "the Absolute," "being itself," and "transcendence."

The love of transcendence grows spontaneously in the soil of human nature. As we saw in the last chapter, a human being is distinguished among all creatures by the ability and tendency to ask such questions as, "Then what?" To put it simply, we are able and inclined to look beyond whatever we have before us, even if what we have before us is an image of the whole universe. In this sense, we are at home and at rest only when we have reached the unsurpassable and the ultimate. This is the truth embodied in Plato's vision of man as moved by an erotic passion which was only diverted and threatened with extinction if it sought satisfaction in carnal relations. It is also the truth expressed with such poignancy in Augustine's avowals of love for God in his *Confessions*.

Only against this background can the role of Christian revelation, in defining the nature and grounds of hope, be understood. For Christians, Christ is the axis of history, which is to say that he enters into history both as climax, in relation to all that has gone before, and as origin, in relation to all that follows. It is the former, the climactic, role that concerns us particularly here. Aside from consummating the revelatory history of the Jewish people, Christ answered to diverse human impulses in relation to transcendence. He rebuked the efforts of some to live in proud defiance, or in hedonistic negligence, of transcendence. But also, by disclosing the nature, and the relationship to the world, of transcendence, he fulfilled the efforts of others to reach transcendence through human intellect and imagination. Christ was God's response to Socrates.

Not all of the questions to which Christ responded were known in advance of the answers, however. This is a vital point. Humans are not so clear-sighted or conscientious that they are able always to ask the right questions or to anticipate the answers they will receive. It is not inappropriate that the word "revelation" should be somewhat jarring. Given the distance between humans, in their pride and love of pleasure, and God in his infinite holiness, revelation is bound in some measure to be surprising and unforeseen. Karl Barth goes so far, in his *Epistle to the Romans,* as to claim that Christianity is not basically a religion, which is a human institution. It is a divine act, different in kind from every religion. Illustrative of the degree to which revelation can be strange and even offensive is that fundamental tenet of Christian faith—that God died on a cross. This belief does answer human questions, such as whether God can be found here among us or is unreachably beyond us. Still, there is something unsettling and offensive in the notion that God was executed as a criminal. And—such are the limits owing to human finitude and perversity—the questions such a notion might be found to resolve could not be clearly asked until the answers began to be known.

At the same time, revelation does not explode among us like a terrorist's bomb. It corresponds with our profoundest desires, and these are partially seen and haltingly voiced before revelation ever occurs. Above all else, revelation enables us to know that transcendence is a divine and ultimate reality, not a mere abyss at the borders of human knowledge. Without revelation, openness toward transcendence is at best a courageous confession of ignorance. Such is by no means a negligible achievement; but it is an uncomfortable, if not impossible, resting place. Philosophy, in principle spurning revelation, provides powerful intimations of the reality of transcendence; but any particular philosophy depends on particular premises and can therefore do little more than undergird an attitude of openness. Only revelation provides unconditional assurance. To be sure, those who only hear and assent to reports of revelation, and are not direct recipients of revelation, can entertain doubt. But all to whom God is revealed, whether by an immediate ecstatic experience or merely by reports of such experience, are either relieved of doubt altogether or are given powers which enable them to deal with doubt in a way that deepens their faith. In brief, through revelation alone are we able to become securely rooted in the primal ground of our being—the fathomless and infinite freedom Thomas Aquinas called the divine *act* of being.

Aside from the ultimate, indefeasible reality of transcendence, the most significant disclosure that comes to us from the side of transcendence concerns the character of transcendence: that it is deeply and entirely personal. It is not the kind of reality we can observe, comprehend and master; rather, we must hear, listen, and respond. It is arguable that only when envisioned as a person—as a "Thou"—does transcendence wholly correspond with our needs. Once personality has come to light it is seen, under the authority of an irresistible intuition, as morally prior to everything impersonal. Having become cognizant of the personal, the only realities we can think of as valuable beyond measure and therefore as intrinsically ends in themselves, are those we can love and trust, listen to and address. Impersonal realities are properly at our disposal; we can use them as we please, or ignore them.

Hence transcendence cannot fully quench our dissatisfaction with the finite and temporal if it is nothing more than a very large and splendid object, like a cathedral. It must come to us as the kind of reality that might be a friend and companion, that might speak and listen. It seems likely that the impersonal transcendence which concepts like "the idea of the Good" and "the unmoved mover" invoke, could be completely satisfying only in a civilization which, like ancient Greece, had not fully awakened to the personal dimension of reality. And one can think that efforts in our time to return to pagan impersonality, as in philosophies centered on "the Absolute" and "being-in-itself," put human personality at risk by according prior value and reality to the impersonal dimensions of the universe.

The personal character of the Christian God becomes plain when we note that not only is Christ, as God incarnate, a bodily person who might be seen, heard, and spoken to—as well as ignored, hated, and crucified. Christ, as the Logos, is the speech (or "Word") of God. Revelation is not a dictate reducing us to abject silence but rather the opening of a divine-human dialogue. God is a potential conversation-partner, even though a conversation with God cannot be the kind of tranquil interchange of opinions that a human conversation is at its best. If the notion of God as a conversation-partner seems too casual, that is perhaps because the conversation of human beings is usually frivolous and debased, not because God is too august to enter into so personal a relationship as a conversation. The Old Testament states that God talked with Moses "face to face, as a man speaketh unto his friend." (Exodus 33:11 KJV) God is personal not only for Christians and Jews, of course, but also for Muslims, whose faith is based partly on Jewish scripture. However, for the great Greek philosophers, relying on human powers, God was impersonal, even though possessed of far greater value than any human person. In the Far Eastern religions, too, divine reality in its ultimate depths is impersonal. The concept of a divine personality is far from a universal intuition, and indeed it might never occur to human minds apart from revelation.

In any case, having noted that revelation establishes the reality of transcendence, and the personal character of that reality, we can begin to grasp the nature of hope. Very simply, hope is for God. It is written into our nature as rational, thus critical and questioning, beings that we can come to rest only in the presence of the infinite and eternal; and it is inscribed in our nature as personal beings that we can fully respect another being, even one that is infinite and eternal, only if it too is personal. In this way, we are oriented naturally toward God. This, of course, does not imply that God exists. Our transcendental orientation would be a preface to tragedy were it no more than a query spoken into the darkness surrounding us. But out of the darkness there comes a response. We hear the Word of God. Christ is the light shining in the darkness, and this light reveals a universe which renders realistic the only hope that can quiet our natural restlessness—hope for a life with God.

What does it mean to say that hope is for God? What kind of relations can there be between a person who is human and the person who is God? Both metaphors used in the paragraph above—word and light—suggest an answer to this question. If hope is for God, then it is manifest in listening for the Word in which the depths of divine reality are expressed. It is manifest also in attempting to respond. Very simply, hope is for a conversation with and in eternity. Hope envisions God as an interlocutor. However, we do not ordinarily feel that we know someone we have conversed with (perhaps by letter or telephone) but have never seen. Hence in theology, visual metaphors are at least as prominent as auditory metaphors. We must say, then, that we look toward a conversation that is, like Moses's, face-to-face. Not only do we listen for the Word of God; we also look for the light in which we can see God. The most definitive formulation of the object of hope is perhaps the Thomist concept of the beatific vision: seeing the face of God—not in transfixed solitude, however, but rather in the kind of devout and dialogical search through which there is gained an ever-clearer vision. The prayers and rituals of the Christian Church are clearly illustrative of hope.

It will be obvious at this point in the essay, I think, that I am not suggesting that only Christians can be hopeful. Such a suggestion would sharply restrict the range of Christian wisdom, which, if Christ is the Logos, must be secreted in all human wisdom. And it would clash with a major premise of this essay: that *Christian* hope can provide us with an understanding of *human* hope. Hope has various forms and fulfillments. Wherever there is a vision of transcendence, as in Plato and Aristotle, there must be hope. Wherever there is a consciousness of true values (which are always reflections of transcendence) there are grounds for hope.

Not that one can be casual about such matters. The Christian God is "jealous"—intolerant of the worship of other gods. Hence agnostic secularists are called—when Christians address them—to a resolute and demanding recognition of the finitude and temporality of all those things that are finite and temporal. In pursuing truth, they are warned to beware of scholarly arrogance, in enjoying beauty to be cognizant of the imperfection and ephemerality of all beautiful things, in loving other persons to remember that every earthly grouping of persons, the most intimate as well as the most august, is earthly and not divine. And radical secularists, those who deny transcendence, are challenged—by Christians—to live with the resignation their principles imply. Idolatry is a potent temptation, and, as an enthronement of false gods, it may come near to being irresistible among those unaware of the true God.

Nonetheless, openness toward transcendence is possible for all, and in that openness there is hope. The glory and goodness of God spill plentifully over the edges of the Christian vessels which, Christians believe, are their primary receptacles. They pervade the created universe. Thus, for example, the love of poetry and literature can determine the atmosphere of a hopeful life, even in the absence of explicit Christian faith. A life set on courses dictated by a sensitive conscience can be hopeful apart from all theological convictions. And someone capable of behaving with courage, perhaps in military, perhaps in civil, settings, is capable also of true hope. It should be noted, moreover, that in all such forms, just as God is known primarily through revelation, transcendence comes unbidden. Poetry and conscience may be silent, and courage may fail. In the final analysis, for Christians and secularists alike, human beings must abide a mystery they can never fully illuminate and can never master.

For Christians, revelation is not simply a matter of epistemology, having to do with *how* we know and not with *what* we know The very fact of revelation, apart from its content, tells us something of its author. Revelation is a compassionate overture on the part of God toward the human race; it is a manifestation of what the prophet Isaiah refers to as God's "everlasting kindness." (Isaiah 54:8 KJV) This kindness, as Christians understand it, is particularly accentuated by the symbol of the Fall. The rebellion against God, mythically attributed to Adam, but psychologically evident in the universal, natal selfishness of every human being, does not merely spell alienation from the good, with human nature left intact. Since human nature is defined by its orientation toward God, in rebelling against God humans have disfigured their nature. They have, so to speak, rendered themselves unsightly. Hence revelation testifies not to the attractiveness of men, but rather to the indefeasible fidelity of God to his human creatures, soiled and unlovely as they are.

The content of revelation confirms these inferences. This is apparent in the central proposition of Christian faith, the Trinity. This great doctrine is sometimes seen, even by Christians, as a piece of theological legerdemain which ordinary Christians neither can, nor need to, understand. But the general idea embodied in the concept of the Trinity is easily stated: God is communicative, and this implies not only that he is disposed to speak but also that he has the power to do so perfectly. Hence the Word of God does not, like human words, merely reveal aspects of the author; it is substantially identical with the author. This is why the Word of God is called, alternatively, the Son of God; the Son, begotten and not made, is the same in being as the Father. But the Word is not launched on the seas of human history, perhaps only to capsize and sink. God's Word does not return to him void. Through the third person of the Trinity, the Holy Spirit, God assures that his Word is understood in the ways and in the measure that he intends for it to be understood. In the Word is God's truth, in the Holy Spirit his compassion.

All of this has important implications for hope. It suggests that God is not only the *object* of hope but is also the *basis* of hope. Not only do we hope *for* God, we hope *in* God. Hope is a human possibility, not mainly because of anything in human nature or in human historical circumstances—in themselves profoundly discouraging—but because the visible world is not the compass of being and human energies and faculties are not the only powers working in history. Seen in the context of God's universe, the plight of the human race is far less desperate than it appears to be. Hope arises not from objective appraisal but from transcendental trust.

This trust explains the mysterious disproportion between hope and fear in the mind of a hopeful person. Hope and fear do not vary inversely, as reason would lead us to expect. Christian hope dramatically witnesses to this fact. Christians hope to live eternally in the presence of God; the alternative is the unthinkable horror called damnation. But hope is not the same as objective certainty; hence, to hope for salvation is to entertain the possibility of damnation. Reason tells us that so great a hope, matched by so great an uncertainty, must be accompanied by terror. But this is not ordinarily so. Hope seems not merely to reduce fear but rather, like the "perfect love" John speaks of, to *cast out* fear. It cannot be claimed, of course, that in those who hope to be saved there is no fear at all. But fear does not, so to speak, occupy all of the territory which hope, in its objective uncertainty, leaves it. Rather than terror, there is a mysterious fusion of suspense and serenity. This fusion cannot be understood in terms of specifiable conditions but only in terms of something beyond all such conditions, that is, the transcendence we hope for, or God. When those who hope for salvation confess their objective uncertainty they are not confessing their cosmic peril but rather their entire dependence on God. Conscious of such dependence, they realize that there are no rationally-comprehensible circumstances to sustain them. They are not objectively sure of salvation. Nevertheless, relying on God, they are sure in a way that surpasses all calculations. Fear, held at bay by transcendental trust, cannot contest the sway of hope.

In sum, hope is directed toward God and rests in God. In the Christian vision, we are privileged, through revelation, to harbor hope. It is essential to note, however, that this is a privilege we cannot with impunity refuse. Hope is an indispensable link with God. Lacking in hope, we must be lacking in faith as well, since a faith without hope must be dead and meaningless. We must also be lacking in love, for we cannot love—if love is more than a despairing and ephemeral affection—those we cannot see as fitted and destined for life in the presence of God. To repudiate hope would be to fall into an abyss of finitude and mortality.

The role of deliberate choice in the harboring of hope is a difficult matter, analysis of which must be postponed to the following chapter. Suffice it here to say that despair is not a sinless state but rather, we must think, is reprehensible to God. It is disbelief and mistrust, whereas hope is a state of receptivity, of reliance on God's kindness. When Christ, walking on the sea, calls on Peter to approach him and Peter, on starting out, falls into a panic and begins to sink, Christ scornfully refers to him as a man of little faith. It is reasonable to think that God expects of us the receptivity that is hope, just as he expects the prayerfulness that underlies hope. There is a sense in which those who hope for nothing deserve nothing, even though God again and again gives us things we were too faithless to hope for. Allied with the receptivity of hope are several attitudes intrinsic to the life of hope: waiting, watching, standing fast. These will be examined in the course of our discussion. Here, however, in closing, we need only take into account certain ways in which the concept of hope for God is easily misconstrued.

Non-Christians sometimes speak as though what Christians hope for mainly is life after death, with the life hoped for being principally one's own. Hope expresses only an instinctual recoil from death. But mere personal survival, in all of the loneliness, confusion, and imperfection of worldly life, is not what anyone who has reflected on the matter hopes for. To find oneself after death condemned to carry on forever the same kind of life one has lived on earth—a life in which, at best, one's achievements are ambiguous, one's relationships tenuous, and one's understanding of creation and history clouded—would be frightful rather than fulfilling. The idea of personal immortality, truly understood, is an idea of life undistorted by moral failure and unbounded by time, finitude, and mortality. It envisions an amplitude of being infinitely transcending the being of any mortal and erring creature. That is, it envisions God. Hope is for a share in the primal and limitless life we attribute to the creator and sovereign of the universe. It is not surprising that atheists, denying God, find it easy to affirm the finality of death. If there were no hope of seeing God, we would shrink from from the prospect of living—who knows how or where?—eternally.

Closely allied with the misconception that Christian hope is mainly for personal survival after death—but less easily refuted—is the notion that, whatever you hope for, you are always looking for something for yourself. In other words, the supreme object of love is not God but the self. To hope for God is to hope for some benefit you can derive from God. Precisely understood, God is in the nature of an absolutely efficient means rather than a final end. This is a plausible charge since it seems impossible to hope except for things which you yourself can possess and enjoy. Is it, then, a valid charge? When we hope for God are we always hoping in the final analysis for something we can get from God? Probably so—but not in a sense which conflicts with the proposition that hope is for God.

Jesus himself tacitly recognizes the legitimacy of self-love. This happens, as often noted, when he commands you to love your neighbor as yourself. In thus phrasing his command, Jesus was surely realistic. It is hard to see how love for God can be divorced from a certain kind of love for yourself, for in loving God you very much want something for yourself, namely, to dwell eternally in the presence of God. Isn't this, however, the kind of self-love Jesus sanctioned? It is love for a self defined by its relationship with God. Who you are, it may be said, depends on what you love, and you become the one you authentically are only when you come to love, above all else, that which *deserves* to be loved above all else. Authentic selfhood, then, belongs to those who love God. This is presumably why, before implying the legitimacy of self-love, Jesus commanded the love of God—with all one's heart and mind and soul. Self-love is wrong when it is love for a self that cares nothing for God. But such a self is an imposter, pretending to an authenticity it does not possess. Such misidentification of the self is the very essence of sin, whereas accurate identification of the self, which can derive only from love for God, is at the heart of righteousness. In sum, when you identify yourself accurately, you render self-love compatible with hope.

Hope fixed on God is—to use a somewhat forbidding yet irreplaceable word—eschatological. It anticipates an advance through time to the end of time. If hope is for God, for eternal life, then it looks beyond the temporal and spatial framework of natural reason. And since all events, both those confined mainly to the lives of individuals and those occurring in the large social world, take place within this framework, hope is for something beyond the whole course of worldly happenings. In a word, a hopeful person anticipates the end of history. The word "eschatology," as recondite as it may seem, is simply a name for the sober fact that human beings are not at home, and cannot be content, within the cluster of realities which make up our commonsense world. They naturally, even if unconsciously, wish for the end of that world.

It is vital to the practice of hope, however, to recognize that even though hope is for God, and is in that sense eternal, it is necessarily temporal too. It is for things experienced in time. This is clearly implied by the principle that all true values, such as truth and beauty, participate in the infinite value that is God; indeed, values strike us and make themselves known to us as values precisely by virtue of the absolute which shines through them. Values are experienced in time, and to be without hope of encountering them in time—to be confined, that is, to a purely eschatological hope—would be to cut hope in half, as it were, and to render it scarcely viable. More basically, it would be tacitly to deny the sovereignty, and hence the grandeur, of God. If God is not found within time and in the values that help give meaning to time, he is a diminished and disappointing being. He is not the natural consummation of hope. And he is not the basis of hope, since, not being the sovereign of time, he is not infinite and not fully reliable.

There is, to be sure, a sense in which everything transpiring in time is intrinsically insignificant. Temporal events are significant, not in themselves, but only in relation to eternity. It matters very little what happens to us during our brief days on earth and in time except as earthly and temporal happenings influence our eternal destiny. But of course these happenings do not merely influence our eternal destiny, they decide it. More precisely, the happenings which we bring about decide our eternal destiny. What matters is how we conduct our temporal lives. At least that is the Christian claim. Living irresponsibly or despairingly in time means forsaking the eternal and almighty God. Being loyal to God, means bearing responsibility in time for truth and for the fellow creatures with whom we share the truth, and doing this means entertaining temporal hopes. These hopes, however, are never for mere temporal goods. They are for God, who guides time and can be glimpsed in time.

Hope proves itself, therefore, by staying alive and strong, *as a temporal orientation,* in spite of temporal disappointments and fears, and in spite of the eternal goal which overshadows all temporal goals. True hope is indefeasible. It is anchored in eternity. The eternal goal does not, when properly envisioned, threaten temporal goals but rather is present within them. The only legitimate temporal goals are those which are emblematic of eternity, and in this sense hope is always eschatological, whether related to temporal goals or not. Hence temporal disappointments are never final. There can be no happening so grievous that we cannot, with God's help, look beyond it and begin again to live with hope.

Of course hope is never so strong that it provides immunity from every threat of despair. The flesh is almost always, when first faced with great earthly dangers, weak. Paul unhesitatingly confesses his fears. But he is never mastered by them. When he is weak then he is strong. And his strength enabled him to live in time. Paul's temporal hopes are plainly stated: for harmony and for perseverence in faith among members of the churches he has founded, for the health and well-being of his friends in the Christian mission. The God in whom Paul had faith was clearly like the God of Jesus. A sovereign and merciful creator, who noted even the fall of a sparrow and numbered the hairs on the heads of his beloved human creatures, he was a God interested in time and history. The new creation, repairing the ravages of sin in the first creation, was historical work. It follows that while temporal affairs have only relative importance, it is God who establishes their relativity; hence anyone who neglects them and fails to bring them into the circle of hope, neglects God. This is why eschatology must not be allowed to swallow up temporality.

But the opposite—becoming preoccupied with temporal hopes and forgetting eternity—may be the greater danger. Our need for hope is so urgent, and our concern with transcendence so weak and erring, that hope readily becomes concentrated upon visible, worldly objects. When that happens, what is good becomes evil by being put in the place of God. A finite value is treated as though it were infinite, which is idolatry. In other words, we take things good in themselves, as elements in God's universe, and try to incorporate them in a universe we ourselves have made and can control. This is what is meant by worldliness. We are all of us spontaneously idolatrous and worldly. We strive unceasingly to suppress the eschatological component in hope.

The key to true hope, plainly, is balance—between eternity and time, eschatology and history, the ultimate and the penultimate. Ways of cultivating a balanced hope will be discussed in the following chapter, on the spirituality of hope. Our present concern, however, is with the nature of hope. To probe further into this matter we must now take note of the fact that although hope is for God, it is not for God alone.

God, Community, and Self

That God is immeasurably distant from us—unlike any other reality, and, although omnipresent, unapproachable—is an elementary tenet of Christian faith. In both the Old and New Testaments an encounter with God is always on God's initiative and often elicits, instead of joy, dread and fear. Although God is eminently in accord with the desires of our created nature, he must seem dissonant and threatening to someone who, fallen from the glory of primal creation, simply wants to enjoy sensual and worldly life and be left alone. The sense of God's absolute singularity is expressed dramatically, even if too unconditionally, by Karl Barth when he speaks of God as "wholly other."[1] God cannot be a comfortable, everyday friend, always available, always conforming with our expectations. Needless to say, Christians have often neglected or denied the disquieting incongruity between the human and the divine. In doing this, however, they have allowed themselves to worship a man-made image of God—an idol of some sort, not God.

In striving to set God apart from every worldly category and affirm his utter uniqueness, however, it is easy to think of him as alone, dwelling in sovereign and heavenly solitude. In doing this, we again are thinking of something other than the Biblical God: a god of our own making and thus an idol. For God is love. And if the omnipotent God, creator of the heavens and the earth, is love, presumably he always has companions. Indeed, this does not put the matter strongly enough. In Christian doctrine, the very essence of God is companionate; he is Father, Son, and Holy Spirit—three persons, distinct, yet perfectly at one. Moreover, God lives, in the words of the Anglican Book of Common Prayer, in the midst of "angels, archangels, and all the company of heaven." (Angels, according to Thomas Aquinas, are multitudinous, far more numerous than human beings; we may imagine clouds of angels.) And finally, we must think of God as destined, in accordance with his own providential intent, to dwell in eternal and perfect communion with the saintly, with the unsaintly but forgiven and transfigured, and perhaps even with the least of his earthly creatures—with immortal fish and birds, plants and trees.

---

[1] See Karl Barth, *The Epistle to the Romans,* trans. Edwyn C. Hoskyns (London: Oxford University Press, 1933).

It follows that true hope is never for God alone but is rather for an all-encompassing and never-ending community, centered in God. By "community" I mean perfect unity among personal beings. (The word "communion" may sometimes be used, for the sake of convenience, to designate, not something essentially different from community, but rather community in its essence, purified of all the imperfections adhering to it in its earthly embodiments.) The statement that hope is for a perfect community, for communion, is not mere speculation. It is grounded in Scripture. Jesus proclaimed the coming, not of God alone, but of the *kingdom* of God. And the core of the Christian ethic, as we all know, is the radical love called *agape*—a love transcending justice and fully expressed in the absolute affirmation of the other which occurs in self-sacrifice. Accordingly, if hope is for God, it is for a triumphant community—for a final and eternal reunion of God and his human creatures.

The notion of God's communality, and man's consequent communal destiny, enables us to apprehend more fully than before the eschatology by which hope is defined. As the doctrine of "the last things," eschatology is concerned not simply with God but with God's final arrangements for all creation. If God is love, these arrangements presumably involve the ordering of all life and reality under the standard of love. The end of the ages must bring a community as deep and immutable as God himself in the perfect life and vitality of the Holy Trinity. Contrasting with this ultimate harmony is history, a tale of conflict and estrangement. Indeed, it is conflict and estrangment that give rise to history by impelling human beings continually to move beyond every existing state of affairs. If love governed all things on earth, there would be no history. Yet history is not sheer disorder and senseless movement. It transpires under the sovereignty of God and hence has meaning. It leads toward the tranquillity of communion, that is, toward the end of history.

Hope clearly depends on love—both for others and for God. Without love for others, you cannot care about or hope for community. Nor can you hope to see God without loving God. Understanding hope clearly depends on understanding love. This is not entirely easy, for the Christian concept of love is strange by worldly standards. Its basic principle, however, can be readily stated. Love for your fellow human beings depends on love for God.[2] Of Jesus' two great commandments, love for God precedes love for your neighbor, the reason being that only by obeying the first commandment can you obey the second. What does this tell us about love?

The answer lies in the concept of the neighbor, the one you are commanded to love. Love is not for someone you have selected on the basis of special qualities of personality or mind. Rather, it is for anyone you find in your pathway or your immediate vicinity; your neighbor is the one who happens to be near you. Your

---

2 I John 4 contains a concise statement of these principles.

neighbor, therefore, might be anyone in the world. It might be someone who is not particularly admirable or attractive in your eyes; it might be someone who is malicious or psychologically disordered or physically repellent. Neighborly love is utterly indiscriminate. This is the quality connoted by the word "*agape.*" Such love embraces everyone, yet not by embracing humankind, an abstraction. It is a concrete love and embraces *everyone* by embracing *anyone* who happens to be encountered. But how is *agape* possible? How can I love someone whom I do not, perhaps, altogether respect or even like?

The Christian answer is simple. A person is worthy of love, not mainly because of intrinsic merits, which are always finite, unstable, and affected by sin, but because that person reflects, in the eyes of faith, the perfections of God. In the acts of creation and redemption, God impresses on each one the divine image. Love for a human being is in the last analysis love for God. Hence it is limitless and uncritical. (Be it noted, however, that since the divine image cannot be totally effaced in one's neighbor—who could not live were this to happen—love is never exclusively for God, with the neighbor merely a neutral medium. One who sees in the neighbor nothing whatever worthy of love is not seeing the neighbor.) From none of this does it follow that love for someone admirable or attractive is necessarily wrong; the qualities you prize may be truly good. Love that is exclusive, however, separating those loved from numberless multitudes who are regarded with indifference or disdain, is wrong. Nor is love for a blood-relative, whom you may be attached to by a strong if irrational bond, necessarily wrong. Love is wrong when it is possessive and partial, flowing out of your own preferences rather than out of God's mercy.

It follows that the hope of dwelling eternally in the presence of God, *with a noble elite,* would be a sinful and illusory hope. The hope of dwelling for all eternity in the company of wife or husband, daughter or son, or special friends—in the company of people prized as somehow mine rather than God's—would also be a sinful and illusory hope. Authentic hope is for eternal life in the company of one's neighbors, although it is perfectly fitting that those admired or found attractive for special qualities be among one's neighbors; and it is fitting that wife, daughter, and so forth, be among one's neighbors. One of the most difficult, yet indispensable, disciplines of hope is that of loving *as neighbors* those you find particularly admirable or attractive or those to whom you are attached by a blood-relationship. Insofar as love discriminates, on the basis of visible qualities and worldly ties, it turns away from God and leads toward despair.

The principle of neighborly love encapsulates the balance between time and eternity which is so vital to the practice of true hope. Since love is not for an ideal human being, living in a state of abstract perfection, but rather for someone in particular, someone encountered in your daily life, love places you inescapably in time. It is an unavoidable temporal entanglement. But it also lifts you above time, for your neighbor as such is not confined to the here and now. Your neighbor stands before you as a representative of every human being and of the God who has created and dignified every human being. In short, your neighbor is an eschatological presence. Neighborly love is at once an involvement in time and an orientation toward eternity.

The universality implicit in neighborly love is one of the primary characteristics of hope. To live with hope is to live with the thought and image in mind of all generations and all peoples. There are few for whom this thought and image can take on very many of the features of actual human beings. The universal community envisioned by hope will be an extreme abstraction. Such universality, however, is not inconsequential. It means that true hope can never be tribal or exclusive or hateful. It will tend always toward tolerance and wider understandings. It will situate itself in the most ecumenical institutions. Nothing human can be alien to those who have hope. In the following pages these things—the "final things" for which we hope—will be explored and explained.

It may seem that so strange a love can have little meaning for a secularized world. It is a noteworthy fact, however, that the concept of "the dignity of the individual," a quality presumably invalidating the invidious distinctions we make among individuals, holds an important place in the secular mind. It has survived the fading of faith, in spite of increasingly bold defenses of practices like abortion and euthanasia. Moreover, this concept grounds the ideal of a universal and enduring human community, realizing perfect equality and justice—which also continues to hold an important place in the secular mind. In logic, these survivals make little sense. It is inconceivable how a fallible, finite individual, in a strictly secular universe, can possess "dignity" or "infinite worth." Nevertheless, life does not work with perfect logic, in either the secular or the Christian spheres, and it would be hard to deny that just as Christians have many times offended against the law of love, so atheists and agnostics have, to the advantage of the world, sometimes acted in accordance with that law. This suggests that *agape,* and the all-inclusive communality based thereon, do not fly so flagrantly in the face of common intuitions as one might expect.

It should not be supposed that the secular vision of community can serve equally well in place of the Christian vision. One of the major flaws in a secular vision is the assumption—nearly inevitable among those lacking any conception of divine agency—that community can be a human creation. Thus Marxists have entertained the illusion that the nature and requirements of community can be fully known through dialectical materialism and that community can therefore be brought into being purely through human design and purpose. The truth is, of course, that while we can deliberately unify material objects, such as bricks and boards, we cannot deliberately unify human beings. Community consists in communication. It is an act, not a settled state of being, and for this reason it is in essence free and uncoerced. Ignoring these rudimentary facts leads naturally in the direction of forceful tactics. And since such tactics are self-defeating, they tend to inspire frustration and fury. In this way, the pursuit of community leads to violence, and it lures men into something at the opposite extreme from community, that is, totalitarianism. Such are the fruits of distorted hope. One of the main contributions Christians can make to the world's understanding of hope is that of an uncompromising eschatology. By this means Christians can help to shield secular minds from the perilous illusion that community can be reached through human energy and resolution alone.

Secular communality can, however, help to keep the transcendental communality underlying authentic hope in balance. A serious weakness to which transcendental communality, and thus Christian hope, is susceptible lies in the tendency of Christians, under the spell of otherworldly expectations, to avert their gaze from historical injustice and suffering. This manifests, in the collective realm, the imbalance between eternal and temporal hope discussed in the preceding section. Saint Augustine typifies, with magisterial authority, the occasional willingness of Christians to think of the City of God as coming only with the end of time, and of the earthly city as so largely under the governance of sin, and so intrinsically insignificant, that its improvement is scarcely worth considering. This willingness works against not only historical responsibility but eschatological faith as well. The rule of neighborly love is that those who do not love the human beings encountered here and now, in their immediate world, do not really love anyone; love for imagined inhabitants of heaven, without love for inhabitants of the earth, is spurious. Hence an eschatology which induces forgetfulness of worldly suffering and injustice cannot be genuine. It is based on a meretricious love. Christians would clearly do well not to ignore entirely their secular opponents who, in their denial of any life beyond time, may sometimes take their temporal obligations more seriously than Christians do. In our time, liberation theology, in spite of its multitudinous shortcomings, indicates that Christians can learn even from so decided a secularism as Marx's.

The striving for community manifests our need for a certain kind of clarification—not the kind that comes from a theoretical explanation but the kind that is found in intuitive insight. The other person is in some degree always an enigma. This is true even of those we most love and admire, even of those we are most intimate with. We cannot have the same experience as another person, except in a rare sympathetic glimpse or shared emotion. We cannot confidently judge the motives of anyone—not of those we love, far less of the billions of human beings making up the human race. The part played in anyone by upbringing, by biogenetic inheritance, and by choice is unknown to all of us, even to psychotherapists. The enigma of the other person is manifest in the unpredictability of human actions, and we acknowledge this unpredictability in the simple act of establishing laws and governments. By these devices we try to render in some measure predictable what would otherwise be so unpredictable as to render civilized life impossible. This mutual ignorance, on which love invariably runs aground, is one of the most disturbing signs of our fallenness.

Yet love remains. Almost everyone loves some of these enigmatic companions. Even when others have been rendered harmless by laws and governments, we cannot acquiesce contentedly in the ignorance which sets them apart from us. Philosophers sometimes refer to the enigmatic character of the other person as "incommunicability," and they speak of human persons as essentially, although in varying degrees, "incommunicable." We might say, accordingly, that striving toward community involves a struggle against the incommunicable. The eschatological concept of communion is a concept of full discovery—of those we love but know imperfectly.

From this standpoint, we can see one of the most vital—yet hitherto, in this essay, unnoted—characteristics of our longing for community. It is a longing for light, not just on others, but on the self as well. Hope for communion envisions self-discovery. The self is in some ways as enigmatic as the other. At first glance, this may seem not to be so. Since you have access to your own intimate experiences in a way no one else does, it is easy to fall under the illusion that you know yourself even though others are strange to you. And it is true that you know your inner world as no one else possibly can. That you do not know yourself, however, is shown not only by the common preoccupation with "finding out who you are," but also by our frequent inability to comprehend our own motives. When a wrong has been done, it is as difficult to estimate the role of extenuating circumstances in your own case as in the case of someone else. Is it not intolerable, however, that you should be incommunicable even to yourself? Surely it is. Hence the urgency of dissolving the enigma not only of others but of the self as well.

That these two tasks are inseparable—that the search for community is also a search for self—arises from the fact that apart from community selfhood is impossible. This is a principle as old as Aristotle. Human communality cannot be adequately defined by saying that community is pleasurable or satisfying; rather, what needs saying is that community is the source of a human being's very identity. Something of this sort can be said even of many animals; a dog in the wilds is a greatly diminished being in comparison with a dog in a human household. But a human being without human relationships simply would not be human. Hence we identify someone by specifying his parents, brothers and sisters, friends, vocational associates, and so forth—his relationships. There is no exaggeration in saying, as Aristotle did, that the quest for community is a quest for self-realization.

Such a quest can be fulfilled, however, only in a community centered on God. In Christian faith, the only companion who can bring about a complete unfoldment of one's being is God. Implicit always in the enjoyment of a finite value is a desire for its infinite completion. As Plato said so unforgettably, in enjoying a beautiful work of art, we wish, even if unconsciously, for beauty itself. In apprehending a single truth, we inevitably look beyond it, toward all truth. But a human being is a finite value; hence in all human companionship there is an urge toward divine companionship. In loving someone who is an image of God, we inevitably love— in the sense of seeking—God himself. To the extent that we allow ourselves to rest in finite values, we limit our own selfhood. We fail in self-realization. To use earlier terms, the being who can ask continually "Then what?" is fulfilled, and *thus achieves identity,* only when this question is no longer possible—that is, only in God.

Seeking selfhood apart from God is inescapably a tragic quest. This is shown in the life of Friedrich Nietzsche, who pursued the search for godless selfhood to depths which few have had the intellect or courage to plumb. The result was a profound and highly dramatic philosophy, but one which hardly anyone has had the strength to adopt, except with qualifications which have changed it essentially. The strain of working out and living that philosophy had a part, one may surmise, in Nietzsche's final breakdown and insanity. We owe an incalculable debt to Nietzsche for demonstrating the impossibility of the path which he followed to self-destruction. Dostoevsky, who shared many insights with Nietzsche (although apparently unacquainted with his writings), yet chose a path leading in the opposite direction—toward Christian faith. He saw the truth so eloquently denied by Nietzsche in his writings but tragically demonstrated in his life: that a human being apart from God cannot remain fully human. Dostoevsky dramatized this truth through fictional characters such as Raskolnikov and Stavrogin, one a murderer, the other a nihilist who committed suicide. The twentieth century has dramatized the same truth through characters terrifyingly real—atheistic tyrants of the right and left whom we spontaneously characterize as "inhuman."

The conclusion we are brought to is that hope is not only for a knowledge of God but for a knowledge also of one's fellow creatures and of oneself. Hope delineates an eschatology of light. It envisions a culmination of history in which all things are clarified. Such an end would be an untanglement and illumination of all the bewildering and shocking occurrences in personal lives and in history. And in this process the God who designed and governed history through his Word, and the human beings—self and others—shaped by their historical deeds and sufferings, would come vividly before us. Let us remember, however, that we are speaking of a mystery. God, others, and self are not three objects added on to one another. As infinite and eternal being, God is not an entity to which any addition can be made; and even with human beings, as Dostoevsky declared, two and two do not make four. We might better think of three concentric circles. The self is found in the encompassing presence of others, and others are found in the encompassing presence of God. But all such metaphors are awkward attempts to grasp realities beyond the reach of discursive reason. What is essential here is to perceive the fullness of hope and to see this fullness as implicit in the hope for God.

The idea that hope is essentially an aspiration toward a community centered in God establishes continuity between Christian history and all human history. This needs to be emphasized because the opposite might seem to be the case. If community is centered in God, and God is revealed fully in Christ, it might seem that any true community must be a Christian community. As I said in the Prologue, however, the concept of Christ as the Logos implies that Christian truth is implicit in all truth. Christ fills out, corrects, and confirms the truths held in common wherever there are humans, and Christian history draws together the threads running through all of human history. Thus, for example, Christians can hear, and learn from, the philosophers of classical antiquity, such as Socrates and Plato. Indeed, a Christian may feel almost as close a bond with Socrates as with Abraham and with Plato as with Isaiah; Kierkegaard exemplifies this fact. Not that the pagan philosophers can stand independently of Christ. Even so great a mind as Plato made egregious errors, as in his acceptance of slavery; the pagan philosophers had scarcely an inkling of the *agape* that transcends justice; and non-Christian philosophies all need confirmation from revelation, for otherwise they are defenseless against deconstruction. Nonetheless, Christians can listen to them and in listening can include them in a community that encompasses two-and-a-half millenia of history.

This can be put in terms of dialogue. Revelation is of course prior to reason, in the Christian understanding, and this suggests that the Word of God, as known by Christians, must be ascendant over the word of man, as known by secular and non-Christian minds. But the divine and human words are not mutually exclusive. The very idea of Christ as the Word implies that the truth revealed in Christ is reasonable. It is therefore congruent with all that is reasonable in non-Christian thought. And it is consequently constrained to approach non-Christian minds, not with commands, but with rational arguments. Christian faith leads logically in the direction of dialogue, and the ultimate community of the human race imagined by Christian hope must be dialogical. To say this, admittedly, is to abstract from the limitations inherent in the state of fallen humanity. It indicates, nevertheless, the encompassing vision inherent in authentic hope.

Here, however, we face the possibility of an immensely serious challenge— one that we can neither meet, altogether satisfactorily, nor ignore. Christian hope is not for community, it might be charged, but for a system of terror based on an eternal bifurcation of the human race. With this charge we come up against one of the most disturbing tenets of Christian faith and thought. Alongside the paradise of eternal communion there will be the horror of God's Inferno. How can we give the name of "hope" to expectations which include the frightful concept of Hell?

As disquieting as the concept of Hell may be, Christians have never felt free to shrug it off. It has been said that perhaps no one will actually be sent to Hell. But Christians have been decidedly reluctant, throughout their history, to assert flatly the principle of universal salvation. One motive for this reluctance certainly has been the pain of seeing evildoers flourish in the world, with the consequent conviction that they must be punished in eternity. Biblical faith, particularly in the Old Testament, is closely linked with the cry for justice, so poignant amid the gross injustices of history, and God has been seen as one who will finally right the scales. It is questionable, however, whether this motive is decisive. For one thing, Hell is not conspicuously just: Can anything done in the short span of an earthly life merit eternal suffering? Further, Christianity is centered on the principle of divine forgiveness, and we are bound to ask whether this principle can be reconciled with the affirmation of eternal torment. No doubt the desire to see people, especially hated people, receive what they deserve, has played a part in preserving the idea of Hell in the minds of Christians. But a better motive, if not a stronger one, has been quite a different idea, namely, that of freedom.

In creating the human race God brought forth creatures fitted for eternal companionship with God. Such companionship is not imposed on us, however. It is not fated. It is merely something we are free to choose, and in being free to choose it we are free also to reject it. If we do reject it, we reject our own happiness. God is the ultimate object of every human desire; we would always choose divine companionship if we fully understood and consistently pursued our own good. Hence to live eternally without God is to suffer radical and irreparable deprivation. It is to live in unsurpassable and endless agony. Yet that is a fate God allows us to choose. In creating us with freedom, God opened the doors of Hell. In doing this, God did not withdraw his love but he limited his power; he refrained from determining that at the end of the ages we would all, as it were, be herded into a single great heavenly corral. Such a determination as that would have drained freedom of all significance. It would, indeed, have sanctioned the notorious maxim that all is permitted. I could engage in torture as an experiment and in murder for the excitement of it, sustained throughout by the confidence that nothing could keep me finally from entering into God's heavenly dwelling place and taking my place alongside the saints. Without Hell, freedom would be without lasting consequences. Rather than raising us to a position of unique dignity among creatures, it would be merely an invitation to frivolity.

Still, we are left with a disquieting picture of the state of God's universe once the whole human adventure has ended. To be sure, we see a perfect and joyous community, the kingdom of heaven. But alongside it we see something sickeningly different—a cosmic concentration camp (Augustine and other leading Christians, of course, believed that most of the human race would be sent to Hell) in which inmates are tortured unremittingly and forever. It is understandable that some Christians, such as the brilliant Russian philosopher Nicolas Berdyaev, have recoiled from such an image and denounced it as placing Christianity under the sign of terror. Even if we think of everyone inhabiting this ultimate scene of torment as fully deserving to be where they are; and even if we think of them as having freely chosen the appalling destination to which their lives have brought them; and even if we think of them as, through some demonic perversion of their natures, preferring Hell to Heaven—even with all of these suppositions granted, it is impossible to avoid the sense that evil has gained a victory. In spite of God's limitless power and mercy, the divine act of creation has turned out to be a venture that did not entirely succeed.

These, no doubt, are matters beyond our comprehension. We can hardly avoid reflecting on them, however, in the course of inquiring into the nature of hope. The question we face can be simply stated: If at the end of mortal time and history the universe will contain the horror of Hell, how is hope possible? How is hope based on neighborly love possible if most of our neighbors—or even some of them, *or even one of them*—is destined for Hell? There is presumably no definitive rational answer to this question, no answer of the sort we could demonstrate to any doubter, or to ourselves in moments of doubt. We can, however, formulate the question in a way that directs our attention to the mystery in the depths of which Christians believe the answer will ultimately be found.

First of all, let us note that those who suffer complete and final separation from God cannot experience a reality different from and apart from God's good creation, for there is no such reality. Rather, they experience the utter absence of reality. Hell is a void. It is like the void, one may surmise, which existed before God's act of creation, when "darkness was upon the face of the deep." (Genesis 1:2 RSV) Near the end of his life Augustine discussed Hell in terms which, to say the least, sit uneasily with the notion of Hell as Nothingness. He applied himself energetically to the task of proving that bodily human beings might burn eternally without being consumed and thus relieved of their sufferings. Not only does he thus reveal with embarrassing candor the vengefulness which has so doubtful a place in the worship of the God of love. He seems also to lay bare an assumption that there is reality apart from God and God's creation—a reality one would have expected Augustine, in view both of his attack on Manichean dualism and his doctrine of evil as absence of being, to reject. The concept of Hell one might have looked for in Augustine is powerfully presented in a work of modern literature, Thomas Mann's *Doctor Faustus*. True, Hell is somehow sensually and terrifyingly present in human life, for otherwise Faust's bargain would be a sham; yet Hell is nothingness, unreality. To speak in this manner may be self-contradictory. But it may also be the only way we have of approaching eschatological truth.

Something else must be borne in mind concerning those whom God rejects. No one who is loved by another human being can be destined for Hell. At least the argument pointing to this hypothesis is compelling. Presumably God does not love those whom he damns (although it may be that none are damned and none unloved by God). To think that someone who is loved by another human being is damned is to assume that some human beings—those who love the damned person—have a profounder and more capacious love than God's. I am speaking, it must be said, not of deluded attachments, pathological dependencies, and the like, but of the authentic love which is a gift of grace and an intuition of the eternal glory of a human being. Hell cannot be the destination of people who, although worthy in some ways of love and accordingly loved by at least a few other people, have fallen afoul of a tyrannical or capricious God; it can be the destination only of those who have fallen outside all circles, divine or human, of genuine love. One must conceive of Hell as occupied—if occupied at all—exclusively by those who are of no concern whatever to anyone.

All this having been said, Hell remains a disquieting thought, one we live with—in hope—only by remembering that it pertains to a universe governed infallibly by love. How can this be? Perhaps, after all, none will actually be damned, even though this cannot be guaranteed in advance without undermining freedom. Otherwise, we must look on the reconciliation of God's sovereign love and the same God's eternal reprobation of some persons as a mystery—beyond our present comprehension but certain to be entirely acceptable, even glorious, when finally comprehended. In any case, in the eyes of faith, the concept of Hell does not destroy or weaken or disfigure hope. To fear damnation, one's own or another's, is a transgression against the indefeasible mercy shown forth in the life, death, and resurrection of Christ.

Summarizing, insofar as the nature of hope is determined by its ends, hope can be defined as life consciously oriented toward the discovery of God, and toward the discovery—in God—of one's fellow human beings and of oneself. To live with hope is to anticipate the dissipation of the darkness which not only hides God so completely that it is easy for intelligent people to deny that God exists, but that hides in some degree even our friends and ourselves. Hope cannot be defined, however, only by its ends. It is defined also by its presuppositions. Hope would not be meaningful in any sort of universe whatever. It would not make sense in a universe in which nothing of significance ever changed. Nor would it make sense if everything were ruled by chance or caprice, or if all events were blindly determined by mechanical causality. To understand hope, therefore, we must explore the nature of the universe it presupposes.

The Universe of Hope

Day-to-day life is carried on in the world, the complex of visible, comprehensible, and controllable things that surround us, organized in some measure by nature and in some measure by human artifice as a rationally-coherent totality. The world is an assemblage of objects, with the human beings that inhabit it standing as objects of a peculiar kind: objects because they are bodies, in principle no different from any of the other organic entities among the objects of the world; peculiar because there seems to be something about them which is disturbingly non-objective, sometimes called their freedom (which places them beyond causal explanation), sometimes called their dignity (which requires that they be treated as ends, never merely means). Some worldly entities seem to be fully accessible to empirical observation and rational analysis. Rocks are entities of this kind—objects and nothing more. But other worldly entities have an aura of inscrutibility about them. This is true not only of human beings, in view of their "freedom" and their "dignity," but also of natural realities like light and sky, trees and tigers, sun and stars. If we treat realities of this kind as purely and simply objects, we ignore their inscrutability and in that way falsify them. Further, if we conceive of all objects as making up a self-enclosed totality—a single vast and intricate object, called perhaps the universe—we falsify reality again, for there can be no envisioned assemblage of objects so vast that there is nothing more beyond. To perceive and understand is essentially to objectify; that, in turn, except with entities like rocks, is to falsify; and even with rocks and other such realities, it is to engage in an act of abstraction from an encompassing mystery. Hence the world is not the same as the universe or divine creation. It is in some measure a human construct, an imposition on reality of forms utilized by our sensuous and rational faculties. The philosophical grounds for looking at things in this fashion can be found not only in Kant's *Critique of Pure Reason* but also in the writings of Thomas Aquinas, particularly in his analysis of the agent intellect.

In our unexamined daily lives we are inclined to take that which is structured by human faculties, and is therefore more or less unreal as entirely real, and to regard as unreal, or even to forget or deny, that which is real. We do this in shaping and maintaining the world. We assume that the highest degree of reality belongs to something we can see and rationally understand—an object—and that the real universe is a hypothetically-total complex of objects—an all-encompassing world. Thus something like an apple or a shovel is entirely real, whereas an angel or God is a figment of imagination. Radical secularism is affirmation of this point of view as a metaphysical premise, sometimes on the basis of critical thought, as with a philosophical materialist like Thomas Hobbes, but often uncritically and casually. Human beings, at least in their fallen state, seem to tend instinctively toward radical secularism.

Light is cast on the nature of the world by noting that the terms "world" and "society" are sometimes used synonymously. To live in the world is to live in society, in the established order. The connection between the world and society is easily seen. We objectify in order to understand and control the realities around us. That is also, in part, why we set up and maintain societies. It goes without saying that we are naturally sociable and therefore societies are intended, as Aristotle asserted, to serve a full and human life. But they are also intended to serve certain particular ends which are forced upon us by our bodily nature—ends like economic sufficiency and military security—and to serve these ends they must be devoted to understanding and control. Thus societies classify people, necessarily and always in terms of function and ability, less necessarily and often quite gratuitously in terms of race and gender; they uphold laws, customs, and rules which render people predictable and enhance the orderliness of reality. An efficient society greatly magnifies our powers of objectification, as exemplified in organized technology, and it inculcates habits and skills of objectification. In short, a society tends always to become a world.

Some kinds of objectification are necessary and relatively innocuous. These occur when realities are construed and organized without greatly distorting their true nature, as when people are classified with some regard for their actual desires and capacities and with a view to social functions which are legitimate, hence potentially fulfilling. But other kinds of objectification are unnecessary or even vicious, violating the nature of those who are objectified. They are carried out perhaps carelessly, or perhaps for the sake of the thrills and satisfactions of domination; these are exemplified by classifications according to race. Sin might be briefly defined as unnecessary and untrue objectification. The world, in the degree to which it becomes an all-inclusive and all-pervasive totality, obscuring and crushing all that is non-objective, is a product of sin.

Sin is worldliness, the will that all realities be objectively comprehensible and readily controllable. The primary motive of sin is always pride. One who reduces everything to worldly objectivity stands above all reality, like a god (although pride is not always in one's own particular self, but may be vested in one's nation, profession, race, or some other collective entity). A secondary motive—secondary in the sense of coming to the fore as a supplement or replacement when pride is weakened or defeated—is despair, issuing in the desire to abandon selfhood. Here even the self is treated as an object, as when someone sinks uprotestingly into an organizational function which consumes all energy and life. The height of pride, it might be said, is found in the tyrant, the depths of despair in one who gladly submits to the tyrant. Both pride and despair are ways of fleeing from reality—from concrete selfhood and the burdens of finitude and responsibility which selfhood imposes. Society, as a reinforcement of the world and of worldliness, is in a sense more sinful than an individual, a truth Reinhold Niebuhr brought out in the title, as well as in the contents, of his book *Moral Man and Immoral Society.* Thus it is particularly difficult for rulers and high administrators, in official relationships, to overcome pride and to subordinate objectification to love. And in relations among societies, virtues such as humility and self-sacrifice are almost unheard of and are even, in view of the candid concentration of nations on their own self-interest, largely inapplicable.

In our fallenness, then, we aspire to create and inhabit a world. We have not fallen so far, however, that our minds are entirely insensible to the values that lie behind and often shine through the natural and human realities around us. Hence we experience life in the world as exile, even though it is self-imposed. We are aware of not being at home in the world. There are numerous ways in which our exile is made plain to us in the course of daily life. Whenever one person loves another person, for example, and realizes that the two of them will never achieve full mutual understanding, and will finally die, there arises a poignant experience of exile. When we are arrested by the beauty of a flower or a work of art and recognize how unbidden and evanescent the appearance of beauty is, we feel like outcasts from the primal glory of the created universe. And in the realization that a particular act is incumbent on us, simply because it is right, we sense the power of the unconditional, of something that cannot be readily accomodated within the endless conditionalities of the world. Such experiences arouse an urge toward transcendence, toward realities that are not mere objects, usable and disposable. This urge is often called *eros* and is a major theme in the philosophy of Plato. *Eros* is love of the absolute. It drives us beyond the world, in the direction of whatever is real, good, and beautiful without qualification. It drives us, in short, toward God.

Eros tends to evoke a spirituality of ascent. The purpose of life is to transcend the world, the scene of our exile, and to enter the realm of authentic being. In Plato this realm was an order of pure ideas, or essences, and access to it was gained primarily through philosophical discipline and reasoning, although irrational forms of ascent ("madness") were also affirmed in Plato's thought. Such a vision can have great beauty and spiritual nobility. Yet it contains a degree of pessimism, for the lower realms of being are as eternal, even if not as real, as the higher realms of being. Evil, understood by a follower of Plato—Plotinus—as the matter on which pure ideas depend for attaining actual existence, has a permanent place in the structure of the universe. The sombreness of such a view can best be seen, perhaps, in its political overtones. Since ascent into the higher realms is an arduous undertaking, and requires exceptional intelligence and long training, a spirituality of ascent is likely to be elitist. Only a small aristocracy, like Plato's philosophical rulers, inhabits the heaven of ideas. The multitudes of ordinary human beings must dwell far below, where what seem to be realities are in truth only shadows, as in Plato's Cave.

Hope betokens a different kind of spirituality. The spirituality of ascent rests on a spatial vision of the universe, with the world and being-itself related in terms of below and above. Granted, space is only a metaphor; yet it is a virtually inevitable metaphor. The time required for ascent is not integral to reality, and the universe is envisioned, accordingly, as an eternal and changeless cosmos. In contrast, the spirituality of hope involves a temporal vision of reality. Man passes beyond the world and approaches being-itself by living in time. Hope reflects a spirituality of expectancy, or, one might say, of personal and historical progress. Erotic spirituality comes to us primarily from the Greeks, a people who inhabited dramatic natural settings, ordinarily illuminated by brilliant sunlight, and who thus readily conceived of reality in spatial terms. The spirituality of hope comes to us mainly from the ancient Hebrews. Believing above all in the sovereignty and freedom of God, who created a spatial universe, yet created time as well, and in time inaugurated the recreation of the universe in response to human disorder, the Hebrews looked to God's words and deeds, in the past and the present, in order to work out the proper form of their lives. They thought of reality, accordingly, less as hierarchy than as history.

The temporality pervading the Jewish—and, by inheritance, the Christian—outlook is particularly striking in the expectation that the created universe itself will finally be dissolved by God. When the Greeks looked out on the natural world, they saw reflections of an eternal order. Jews and Christians see heavens that at the end of the ages will be rolled up like a scroll, mountains that will become a level plain, and a sun, a moon, and stars that will be extinguished and replaced by the light of God. They see new heavens and a new earth, an earth where there will be no more night and no more sea. Such images, drawn from Jewish apocalyptic and from the New Testament, suggest how radically different an ontology compared with that of the Greeks, Christian hope rests on.

The Christian world exists in time and is carried along by time, like a raft on a river. The raft can be steered, but the course of the river cannot be known or changed. There are rapids and falls in the river, and sooner or later the raft will inevitably break apart and be lost. In such metaphors the Christian vision of the world in time can be expressed. The stream of time does not flow accidentally but is governed by an omnipotent and righteous God and therefore is subordinate throughout to a divine, merciful intent. God wills the end of worldliness and of the world it sustains (hence the destined breaking apart and loss of the raft). The purpose of history is the replacement of the world with the kingdom of God. Spatial metaphors do not altogether disappear, of course; God occupies the heavens above as well as the future ahead. Still, spirituality is understood as the task not of rising above, but as living within, time and history.

Time thus is prior to space, history to cosmos. It must be particularly noted, however, that time and history are not affirmed absolutely. Although historical happenings are entirely real, and will be part of the eternal order of things within the memory and mind of God, they are signs of human fallenness. We live in history because we must, and not because living in history is good in itself. Correspondingly, we entertain hope because we do not now inhabit the kingdom of God. Hope is a sign that all is not well. We hope for a state of things in which hope will give way to present realization of all we have hoped for. In short, we live in history toward the end of history.

When Christians speak of the flow of time and the course of history, however, they are not speaking of random currents and tendencies, such as any careful observer might note, but of directions established and revealed by God in decisive historical events, and in one climactic event: the life, death, and resurrection of Jesus. Here the creator of the heavens and the earth set on foot the creation of a new humanity, undeformed by worldliness and the world. The crucifixion of Jesus laid bare the perversity of human beings. At the same time, by crucifying the world to human beings, and human beings to the world (as Paul put it), the Crucifixion became the decisive divine act reconciling God and fallen humanity. God in his mercy was ingenious, so to speak; human perversity was used to the end of human salvation. This means that the work of transforming human beings to make them fit for the kingdom of God—crucifying them in their worldliness, recreating them for life beyond the world—was written into the divine narrative determining the unfoldment of temporal events. Here again we gain a revealing glimpse of the spirituality of time. The absolute has entered into history; to approach the absolute we too must enter into history. Living responsibly in time we will be carried beyond time and into eternity.

This, in bare outline, is the faith on which Christian hope is based. Hope is the virtue by which we live in time. As we have already seen, faith and love are more basic than hope in that hope could not exist without them. Only through hope, however, are faith and love engaged in the life we lead in time. The greatest works of pagan spirituality, such as the *Phaedrus* of Plato or the *Enneads* of Plotinus, are in a sense hopeless. They are intended to show what a few human beings can accomplish, given the disciplined intelligence which, although possessed by only a small minority, defines the human essence. But these works do not speak to most human beings; and they do not engage even those they speak to in history or in the temporal unfoldment of life, except for the accidental circumstance that time is required for ascending to the absolute. Time is a hindrance rather than the form of grace and a pathway to God. Not the pagan classics but the New Testament, and the Hebrew scriptures from which the New Testament arose, engage us in history. And they do this by construing history as the shape given by God to human life in its movement out of the world toward God. By taking part in the history ordained and revealed in Christ, we are led to the place where we shall know God, one another, and the self. Hope is the spirit that upholds us in this journey.

The life of Christ enables us to see time in its true character—as not merely the kind of time we chart with watches and calendars but as God's time. Such time serves in every detail of its unfoldment to carry us nearer to God and thus nearer to ourselves and one another in a discerning love. It leads us out of the world, it divests us of our selfishness and in this way leads us toward the spiritual perfection in which our true identities are found. In sum, it is sanctifying time. Only now and then, through grace, do we see time in its full spiritual force; yet time in its essence and in its depths is nothing other than a deployment of the divine power which is often called providence. Hope might be described as living in openness to the truth of time.

Let us call the truth of time "destiny." This word is sometimes used interchangeably with the word "fate," but that is a usage which obscures the nature of destiny. The providential character of time does not consist in the kind of implacable necessity, indifferent to the well-being of individuals, which we have in mind when we speak of fate. Your destiny is your utmost fulfillment, an unfoldment of your very being. It does not just come upon you from without nor can it destroy you. The danger inherent in your destiny is that you can fail to recognize it and live it. In some degree we are all guilty of such a failure; we do not live the lives we were intended to live. While your destiny is not an alien force that comes upon you from without, however, and in that sense comes from deeply within you, it is not, as popular rhetoric often suggests, something you simply choose. It is the life given to you by transcendence, or God. Thus, in Dostoevsky's *Crime and Punishment,* when the detective Porfiry urged the murderer Raskolnikov to give himself up to the police, and referred to this act as "plunging into life," he was not telling him simply to recognize what fate was going to do to him whether he liked it or not; nor was he calling on him to abandon all concern for his own ultimate good. Rather, he was speaking to him of the life which had been given him to live but which he had betrayed by committing murder. As the example of Raskolnikov indicates, however, even a grave betrayal of destiny does not mean that one's destiny is eternally forfeited. A Christian may think, as did Dostoevsky, that a merciful God continually refashions human destinies in response to human misdeeds and betrayals, and that only when this divine work ends (whether, for one individual, with the commission of an unforgivable sin, or, for humankind, with the end of history) will there come into effect the final loss of destiny symbolized as Hell.

The idea of destiny is at the core of Christianity. The life, death, and resurrection of Jesus disclose the eternal destiny that renders the whole course of earthly events, incalculably complex and seemingly random as it is, a single story, with a structure and a meaningful end. The destiny of a single person is a unique act of participation in a destiny which is universally human. Every detail of every human being's life enters into the architecture of a providential order which at last will do away with all darkness and estrangement. Such claims are unquestionably extreme. But so are the concepts of divine omnipotence and goodness. Only one who believes that all occurrences, among them both the most trifling and the most shocking, play a part in the final reunion of creation believes in the might and mercy of God. If we say, as common sense suggests, that some things, such as the agonizing death of a small child or the Holocaust, can never in all eternity be justified (as Alyosha Karamazov came within a hair's breadth of saying), we have tacitly granted the reality of an evil force existing independently of God. We have nullified one of the decisive events in the development of Christian understanding—the overthrow of Gnostic and Manichean dualism and the affirmation of the omnipotence of God.

We have also, in affirming the occurrence of meaningless events, struck at the Christian interpretation of Jesus' life. If one tried to think of a happening that could never, in all eternity, be justified—shown to be meaningful—one might think of the death by torture of an innocent young man. Such would have the look of an irredeemable evil. But of course it was precisely this evil that befell Jesus. The cross, as everyone knows, was a device for rendering death slow and agonizing. In Christianity, however, it has become the symbol of God's merciful sovereignty and, in this way, of the ultimate beneficence of creation and history. What happened on the Cross seems to Christians not just meaningful in every detail but the key to the meaning of every past and future historical occurrence. It is understandable that the Church engaged Gnostic and Manichean dualists in a fight to the death. The dualistic universe has no place for Jesus' death as the saving act of a sovereign God.

The notion that everything has meaning, however, is not utterly in conflict with common sense. It is given a certain plausibility by an age-old human activity, one often engaged in by people of thoroughly secular views—that of story-telling. Whenever someone tells a story, the events recounted take on meaning. What kind of meaning? That depends on the kind of story told about them. But no story is meaningless. In every story events are understandably related to one another and thus shown as not entirely absurd. Novelists such as Louis-Ferdinand Céline and Joan Didion, who deny that temporal occurrences have meaning, necessarily deny also that it is possible to tell a true story about them. They try to display the accuracy of Sartre's maxim: "*Anything* can happen, *anything*."[3] It is sometimes claimed that some events, such as the Holocaust, are so irredeemably meaningless as to

---

3 Jean-Paul Sartre, *Nausea,* trans. Lloyd Alexander (New York: New Directions, 1964), p. 77.

defy the story-teller's art. This is questionable. The great novels of Western literature deal with murder, tyranny, and every other known evil. Personal memoirs that have come out of the concentration camps of the twentieth century suggest that there is nothing so vile or crushing in human experience that it cannot be recounted in a way that gives it a measure of meaning.

It must be acknowledged that stories adhering fully to manifest facts will often achieve only very limited meaning. In many stories—stories found far more often in newspapers than in novels—large masses of absurdity, unassimilated by the story, remain. This is the case in stories of tragic accidents and senseless crimes. Reports in the daily press contain many stories that are heavy with fate (that which is meaningless, inescapable, oppressive), as distinguished from destiny. Accordingly, stories that show us a world where no tragedies occur and all conflicts are happily resolved strike us as sentimental. We feel that the manifest facts that give life its twisted and angular appearance are ignored.

Every serious narrative, nevertheless, represents an effort to reduce the scale of absurdity. In that sense, a meaningful universe is the premise of all earnest story-telling, even though rarely, if ever, an explicit conclusion. Thinking along this line, we might imagine that there is one possible story, entirely true, recounting an archetypal event, and not only in itself meaningful throughout, but, in its archetypal character, showing forth the meaning in every terrible detail of every tragedy in human history. Such a story would be transparent to our destiny as individuals and peoples, that is, to the meaning inherent in every personal life and in all of human history. If a story of that kind were a real possibility, we could think of every narrative-effort as a search for that story. Obviously, the archetypal story could not contain an explicit account of everything that had ever happened. But, dealing with an archetypal event, it would not need to. The essence of Christian faith, of course, is the belief that Jesus' life, death, and resurrection constitute an event of this sort and therefore disclose the inner meaning of all events. Christianity seems to tell us that every story-teller who is not simply seeking diversion is trying, however unconsciously, to replicate the story told in the Gospels.

Search for the true and universal story which will reconcile us to all that has ever happened is, in effect, a search for personal reality and justification. There can be no peace or joy in my life until I have gained assurance concerning my identity (who or what I am) and my value. But these are not determined by objective qualities, as though I were a thing with a price, like an automobile or a piece of furniture. They are determined by my story—according to Christianity, by whether my story shows the incarnate God overcoming evil with good and death with life. When I wish to know who I am and what I am worth, I contemplate my past and present and, as far as I can, my future. Christianity claims that I can do this veraciously only by consulting the story of Christ.

The major form of story-telling in our time is probably the writing of novels. In the best novels, even though many have been written by authors professing no formal Christian faith, great ranges of human experience, comprising countless details, are shown to be suffused with meaning. It may be objected that novels are fictional—that is, untrue—and that the meaning displayed is equally fictional. But such an objection runs contrary to our intuitive understanding of the novels that move us most deeply. We do not finish reading works like *War and Peace, The Brothers Karamazov,* or *Moby Dick* feeling that we have been enjoying a temporary refuge from reality. We feel rather that we have journeyed into the depths of reality. We may feel even that we have gone more deeply into reality than we would have had the author given a purely factual account of some occurrence in the visible, palpable world. All of which suggests that what is really happening around us— the unfoldment of destiny—is not manifest in "facts," in public realities and occurrences of the sort anyone can see. Hence those who deliberately confine themselves to facts, such as historians and biographers, thereby commit themselves to the surface of things and eschew the depths accessible to novelists.

Hope is the capacity for carrying on one's life in the confidence that it will finally be seen as a story fashioned by an omnipotent and merciful God, a story therefore in which there are no unassimilated absurdities. As God's story, it contains all truth and it will never be forgotten. And not only is it my own personal story, displaying my identity and worth as well as my unity with God and the whole created world. It is the story of humankind, of everyone. If story-telling is implicitly a search for an ultimate and unsurpassable narrative, for what we have called "destiny," hope is based on the faith that such a search will not prove to be in vain or ill-founded.

Porfiry's advice to Raskolnikov illustrates how close the idea of destiny is to common sense. Porfiry is not depicted as a Christian, and he does not for the most part address Rakolnikov in Christian language. His advice centers simply on "life." Calling on Raskolnikov to surrender to the police and confess his crime, he urges him to "plunge straight into life, without deliberation." Although he says nothing explicitly of divine providence, the concept is very near the surface when Porfiry says that life "will carry you direct to the shore and set you on your feet." And he calls it "the sacred truth" that "life will sustain you."[4] Later Porfiry refers to Raskolnikov's life as "the life God destines you for." After the murder, Raskolnikov's worst torment lay in his feeling that he had cut himself off altogether from the human race. For Porfiry, the human race is represented by the order of justice which Raskolnikov had assaulted through his crime. By confessing and suffering punish-

---

[4] Feodor Dostoevsky, *Crime and Punishment,* trans. Jesse Coulson (New York: W. W. Norton & Co., 1964), p. 441.

ment, Raskolnikov would again become a participant in universal human life, a life carrying all of its participants to the "shore," which, for the deeply Christian Dostoevsky, was unquestionably the kingdom of God. Despite his predominantly secular language, then, Porfiry is urging Raskolnikov to rejoin humanity by entering into the universal destiny, or life-story, in which all common humanity, as well as every personal destiny, is found.

There is another truth implicit in Porfiry's words, one discussed earlier in this essay. Although Porfiry is looking toward the ultimate "shore" which is the kingdom of God, his mind is mainly on things that will happen within days or weeks, such as Raskolnikov's confession. He is aware that hope is temporal as well as eternal. As I have already said, not only may we hope for temporal values; if we are cognizant of God's infallible governance of all things (in the sense, not that God wills evil human deeds, but that he foresees and allows them, and determines their ultimate consequences), we must. This was expressed by Kierkegaard when he wrote that hope which is only for a future life is not reflective of true faith. It has only "a presentiment of its object at the extremest limit of the horizon, yet is separated from it by a yawning abyss within which despair carries on its game."[5] Hence, the discipline of hope requires that we hope for things which might occur next year, or next week, or even within the next hour. And this is because (as all story-telling presupposes) there is meaning in all temporal occurrences.

For Christians, however, temporal hope is conditioned by the Cross. It incorporates an awareness that anything we hope for in time may, in the mystery of the divine disposition of earthly affairs, be denied. The Cross symbolizes the principle not only that the worst happenings can be meaningful but also that disappointment and tribulation enter properly into the course of every "life," or destiny. Christian hope thus includes awareness of a risk; hope is not the same as absolute assurance. The proviso of the Cross, however, renders every risk acceptable. Hope precludes fear. This is because it is based, as we have seen, on love, and since love is a consciousness of the destiny embracing all whom we care for, "there is no fear in love." (I John 4:19 RSV) So even while we grant that temporal hope may be disappointed, we are confident that the omnipotent narrator of human destiny will weave every evil into a story which serves our ultimate welfare. Hope conditioned by the Cross is at once prepared for temporal disappointments and sure of eternity.

This points to a characteristic of hope so fundamental that it seems worth marking it with a particular term. I shall employ a term that is perhaps overused in modern theology but still effectively signalizes the tensions and surprises, the oppressive darkness and the unexpected light, which enter into human relations with

---

[5] Søren Kierkegaard, *Fear and Trembling: A Dialectical Lyric,* trans. Walter Lowrie (Princeton: Princeton University Press, 1941), p. 25.

the divine. The word is "dialectical." Hope is dialectical in the sense that it arises from conditions antithetical to those for which we hope. We hope for wisdom when we realize our ignorance. In the midst of moral degradation, we hope for righteousness. Overcome with weakness, we hope for strength. And, we enter into life, as the Crucifixion and Resurrection tell us unequivocally, by way of death. In the dialectic of destiny, we confront our folly, sinfulness, weakness, and mortality, and in doing this we also confront, through grace, the wisdom, and righteousness, and power, and everlastingness of God. This is the fundamental order of life.

Christians believe that this order is ordained and revealed in the Crucifixion and Resurrection. Christ in this way is the key to human destiny and the foundation of hope for the whole human race.

The dialectic embodied in Christ has been present in a variety of ways in the preceding discussion, although I have not used the word. The concept of revelation, for example, is dialectical, for it implies that reaching a knowledge of God depends on experiencing our ignorance and realizing the spiritual inadequacy of human faculties. And the Christian concept of love, underlying the idea of community, is dialectical, in that we do not love merely the human creature we perceive before us but rather our "neighbor," who is a mirror of transfigured humanity. Finally, a principle I particularly stressed—that hope is eschatological—is conspicuously dialectical. It implies that the whole of history, of human activities on earth, does not attain to God but rather reveals the humanly untraversable distance separating us from God. All that human beings have done needs to be brought under judgment and subjected to a divine completion. Human hope at its best looks toward this completion. The dialectic of hope will come before us in multifarious forms in the course of this essay.

The universe of hope might be described in sum as a universe that justifies our trust. In spite of the crises and the temptations to despair and rebellion that may be occasioned by the dialectic of destiny, it is a hospitable universe. It enables us to live in time without fear and in the course of our temporal lives to work out our relations with eternity. To understand this fully, we must understand how a single human being, so miniscule against the background of world history, and so flawed by the standards of divine righteousness, finds his destiny in the depths of that history.

Sin, Suffering, and Forgiveness

The idea that an individual's destiny is found in the depths of world history does not imply that one must comprehend world history in order to achieve a meaningful personal life. No doubt countless individuals have carried on more or less meaningful lives while knowing little or nothing of the history recounted by historians. But the idea that a single human destiny informs both individual lives and the life of the human race as a whole does imply that the study of history may contribute more directly than is often realized to the conduct of one's personal life. Also, it implies a reverse relationship. Anyone who succeeds in living a meaningful life, even in a state of complete historical ignorance, actualizes a particular and unique embodiment of the life destined for all human beings, and must thereby gain some kind of insight, however unsought and even unrealized, into human history. To speak very simply, there is just one human task, a task faced by all men and women, of all times and places, and that is overcoming human perversity and evil and in that way passing beyond all suffering. The immensity of the task has been made appallingly clear in the twentieth century. Such phenomena as totalitarianism and death camps have constituted lurid exhibitions of the iniquity and misery belonging to the human condition. It is not just states and their leaders, or observers such as historians and journalists, who are concerned with these terrible realities. Every person is concerned with them, for every person must, in one arena or another, face and struggle with the human forces that produced them.

How can this be done? By working out, and living, the archetypal story which delineates human destiny. This is a story of sin conquered and suffering left behind. Every person who achieves righteousness and a commensurate happiness does what the entire human race is called on by human nature and divine revelation to do. Of course, perfect righteousness and happiness are never achieved by anyone within the limits of earthly life. But as Thomas Aquinas suggests, in God's eternal accounting a fragmentary achievement may be taken as a full achievement and thus as a completion of earthly destiny. Still, how is even a partial achievement to be assuredly laid hold of by a being so fragile and fallible as a single human person? Christianity has a very clear and highly-refined answer to this question. It consists in the Christian version of the archetypal story and is designated by a phrase often associated with the Reformation, yet originating in Paul and accepted, with their own particular qualifications, by both Catholics and Protestants. The phrase is "justification by faith"—a phrase having an old-fashioned, and for some probably an antiquated, look yet pertaining to matters of deep and enduring significance.

As is known by anyone who has committed an irreparable wrong, to feel guilty is to feel the whole course of your life brought into question. You cannot simply declare that the past is past and go on as before; you cannot disregard your guilt. On the contrary, to continue with your life you need for justice to be done. In a word, you need to be justified. To feel unjustified is to feel unfit for life, that is, unfit for taking on a destiny. The issue of justification thus faces sinful human beings at the very moment they embark on their destinies. In this sense, it is a primordial issue.

Someone might say, however, that only for a few is it an issue—only for those who have committed an irreparable wrong. But Christianity claims that such a wrong has been—or, more precisely, is continually being—committed by each one of us. The wrong is simply that of rejecting God. The doctrine of justification by faith rests on the presupposition that we all tend irresistibly (except through grace) to concentrate on finite values to the exclusion of the one infinite value, the sum and source of all other values, God. As a result, even the finite values, like flowers torn up by the roots, wither and lose their glory. In this is our fallenness. We stand, as it were, with our backs to God. We refuse to acknowledge the one reality which has unconditional value and is the soil in which all other values grow and live. In this way we repudiate life itself. We are guilty of particular and observable misdeeds, too; these tend to follow from our primal guilt. But many people avoid the most horrifying infractions of the moral law, yet this does not make them innocent. Their primal orientation, freely affirmed in their individual patterns of existence, still is away from God and thus away from life and from hope. This is what Christians call "original sin."

The concept of original sin is offensive to most of us. It looks misanthropic, and it is seemingly falsified every day—for example, by the acts of kindness we frequently witness, or by the innocent faces of children. It goes against the grain of modern culture, with its commitment to human technological prowess and to the creation and enjoyment of material abundance. Worst of all, it forcefully challenges hope, telling us that without grace we are always in the wrong; that there is no pure vantage point within us, such as reason, from which we might survey, and thus gradually comprehend and control, our evil tendencies; and that every social institution and political program, however carefully constructed to circumvent our idolatrous inclinations, will in some degree be subverted by those very inclinations.

Yet the concept has much to be said for it. It is massively illustrated, if not conclusively demonstrated, by the violence and disorder of our times. It is strange to see people who live in the age of Hitler, Stalin, Mao, and Pol Pot become indignant at the supposedly unfair aspersions cast on human nature by the concept of original sin. The concept is corroborated also by common inner experiences; for example, the experience of falling prey to an irresistible temptation and then feeling personally at fault in spite of the irresistibility of the temptation.

And beyond all empirical considerations, the idea that the human race is affected by sin at so primal a level of its being that it cannot be saved by its own resources is upheld by Christian revelation. It is implied by the very appearance in the world of a Savior. And it is underscored by the violent death which ended the Savior's earthly ministry.

The most formidable obstacle to achieving justification, however, is probably not our reluctance to recognize our guilt but rather the guilt itself. How can it be set aside? According to age-old wisdom, strongly expressed in the Old Testament, guilt can be expiated only by punishment commensurate with the guilt. But for repudiating life and the source of all life, it would seem that the only fit punishment is loss of life, and this means, if life is eternal, as Christians maintain, the kind of everlasting loss traditionally called "damnation." Thus, as Paul stressed, the human race is ensnared in a profound dilemma. Before "the Law," the fundamental rules of right and wrong, we are guilty. Yet the Law knows no remedy for guilt—no means of effecting justification—but punishment. It knows only the rule of retribution, "eye for eye, tooth for tooth," unflinching application of which would be the end of us. It is not only the Old Testament which confronts us so implacably with the rule of retribution. So does Greek tragedy, and so does our own deepest conscience.

Christianity does not contest the retributive demand of the Law. Rather, it claims in behalf of every person—in this way justifying and exalting every person—that the demand has already been met. This was done in the inferno of suffering and death undergone by Christ and symbolized by the Cross. Since Christ was not merely one human being among all others, but was in some sense the primary human being—"the Son of Man," or the Word of God become flesh—justice has been done. If we accept this fact (which in the entirety of history is the fact of all facts) we accept our justification. The act of acceptance is "faith." Through faith, then, we are set free from guilt and thus set free for life, or destiny. This applies both to the guilt inherent in our orientation away from God and to the ensuing guilt, that contracted through particular acts. It is singularly inappropriate that the doctrine of justification by faith should be so draped, as it is in the eyes of secular society, in theological cobwebs. For it is fundamentally a doctrine of liberation, and it is fresh and relevant in every age.

The logic of the doctrine, and the nature of the liberation effected, becomes clear when we note that "justification" is tantamount to righteousness. The Cross brings liberation not only from the penal consequences of past sins, but from the sinfulness which underlay those sins. It spells the crucifixion and resurrection of the one who committed the sins. This is why it effects justification; if the sinner were merely released from penal debts, but left morally and spiritually unchanged, nothing would have been accomplished. According to the Christian doctrine of justification, however, God forgives us only in the process of changing us. In understanding how this comes about, the distinction between justification and sanctification can be helpful. We can think of justification not as identical with righteousness, or sanctity, but as opening the way to righteousness. To be justified is to be set on that way—to be released from the past and allowed to begin the work of sanctification. Carrying on this work is the substance of one's destiny.

The idea of justification by faith tells us what we probably want to hear more than anything else: that there can be new heavens and a new earth. Human historical records come close to being annals of negligence and criminality. Not that there have been no accomplishments. But even the greatest of these, like the culture of ancient Greece and the empire of Rome, are borne up by seas of blood. Reading history, one would not dream of asking whether most people have been good; a question far more likely to come to mind is whether *anyone* has been good. Hope founders, then, if not on the verdict of each one's conscience, on the written record. Is there no way of breaking the age-old grip of evil on the human spirit? Christianity, through the doctrine of justification by faith, answers that there is. It was accomplished on the Cross. For both individuals and peoples, hope is possible.

The phrase "justification by faith," however, invites oversimplification. If one needs merely to "accept" the Cross, then Christian life is easy. Yet there is perhaps not a single great Christian who has held that Christian life is easy. This is not primarily because one who accepts the Cross must then strive toward righteousness. Righteousness is given by grace, and anyone who sees righteousness as a goal to be reached only through painful human effort is apt to stumble over the same obstacle that held up the Jews in their spiritual progress, that of seeking justification in obedience to the law. Christian life is difficult because, to use a strong term, it is humiliating. One must give up every effort at self-justification—the kind of justification one might feel entitled to by virtue of visible accomplishments, such as books written, political causes fought for, or morally good acts carried out. One must acknowledge how far short of God's righteousness one's own righteousness is. This, at least in part, is what Dietrich Bonhoeffer had in mind in writing that "when God calls a man, he bids him come and die." The Cross does not offer (in Bonhoeffer's famous words) "cheap grace."[6] To accept the Cross means to give up not only every public claim but also every secret thought and every subtle pretense that I am justified by my own wisdom and righteousness. It is to cleanse my mind, so far as I can, of every thought that my own moral or intellectual deeds will justify me. It is to realize that neither the record of my past nor my own intrinsic qualities give me any right to life or to any of the goods of life. Emotionally and spiritually, I must "fall into the earth and die," I must be "crucified with Christ."

Yet the crucifixion I must undergo cannot be accomplished merely by a change of attitude. To think that it can is another of the oversimplifications often imposed on the doctrine of justification by faith. Crucifixion must be actual, and it must be mine as well as Christ's. I must actually experience evils which in one way or another bring about my own nullification—evils such as sickness, material inse-

---

6 See Dietrich Bonhoeffer, *The Cost of Discipleship,* trans. R. H. Fuller, revised and unabridged edition (New York: Macmillan, 1959).

curity, and persecution. And finally I must actually die. Christians who are shielded from such evils by what the world calls "good fortune" may in reality be unfortunate. People who are rich, powerful, healthy, and everywhere respected, may find it virtually impossible to live the life of the Cross. On the other hand, Christians whose lot it is to suffer greatly may, like Paul, come to rejoice in their sufferings; they may learn to "glory in their infirmities," and may discover that they are "content with infirmities, weaknesses, insults, hardships, persecutions, and calamities." (II Corinthians 12:10 RSV) The point, simply, is that faith in the Cross requires participation in the Cross. This is why Christian life is not easy.

Suffering is so essential to the destiny underlying hope that, in our temporal hopes, we have to be wary of hoping for a cessation of suffering. In many cases, it is surely legitimate to hope that suffering will be greatly alleviated. Yet reenactment of the redemption effected on the Cross is a lifetime task. We come down from the Cross only when we die. Hence, in forming our hopes, we should fix our minds not so much on the alleviation of suffering as on the spirit in which we bear it. We should hope that we can see the meaning in whatever suffering our destinies impose on us and can, in that way, be delivered from fear. In short, we should hope for a wiser and surer hope.

Today we are intolerant of suffering and hear impatiently those, like Paul, who advocate an ethic of the Cross. This is not entirely unreasonable. Technology has made it possible to relieve many kinds of suffering, and responsible people have a natural and laudable desire that society apply itself to the task of reducing suffering as far as possible. But our intolerance of suffering almost certainly derives also from less commendable sources, such as overestimating human power and innocence. Overestimating our power leads us to assume that most suffering can be done away with; overestimating our innocence blinds us to the possibility that suffering may be necessary to the development of moral strength and excellence. Modern advertising amounts to a highly-organized campaign to suppress any suspicion that suffering may be practically unavoidable or morally necessary. The pleasures of material abundance render the message of the advertisers superficially plausible. As a result, we have largely lost what might be called "the wisdom of suffering"— wisdom such as that expressed, not only in the Christian Cross, but in Greek tragedy and in the "suffering servant" passages in Hebrew Scripture. Hence, in present-day America, in spite of the overwhelming majorities who profess Christian faith, the symbol of the Cross stands in stark opposition to the prevailing culture. Accordingly, the idea implicit in the Christian doctrine of justification—that conquering sin requires suffering—is apt to be viewed with skepticism. How can suffering lead toward life or awaken hope? Isn't Paul's ethic of suffering deeply morbid? There are two answers to such questions.

The first is that only through the sweeping act of self-negation involved in living under and on the Cross is the glory of God fully acknowledged. If I think that my own goodness is such that it might impress and satisfy God, I demean God. I make far too little of God's righteousness. And if I think that my own wisdom, although less profound than God's wisdom, still is measurable on the same scale with that wisdom, again I demean God. The Cross has from the beginning been regarded by Christians as glorious. This is because it represents primarily not the abasement of man but the exaltation of God. Such is the difference and distance between man in his fallenness and God in his glory that one must taste the fallenness, in all of its bitterness, to gain a due sense of the glory. To refuse my own abasement is to blind myself to God's exaltedness.

To accept the self-negation implied by the Cross, however, is to rise from my abasement. God is gracious, as Christians say, and shares his glory with those willing to recognize their own lack of glory. This is the second answer which Christians make to non-Christians who see the ethic of the Cross as life-defeating and morbid. With the recognition of God's glory, life can begin. Following the Crucifixion comes the Resurrection; through death comes life. The divine act of justification, accomplished through the Cross, frees everyone who accepts it for entry into an authentic destiny. This destiny consists in sanctification. One is not simply seen by God as good, which is what occurs through justification; one actually becomes good. The Catholic tendency to conflate justification and sanctification is valid in that if God sees that you are good, you must indeed be good. The Protestant tendency to separate the two, with sanctification coming about gradually and only after justification, arguably adheres more closely than the Catholic view to human experience. According to both views, however, the Cross raises those who faithfully accept it and center their lives on it into the glory of being the ones they were intended by their Creator to be.

As everyone knows, however, suffering does not always and necessarily bring spiritual benefits. So far as we can judge by observation, there is suffering that is destructive of the sufferer and leads toward despair rather than hope. What makes the difference between redemptive and injurious suffering? Paul provides a clue. In his great hymn to love, he declares that even though you give your body to be burned, you will gain nothing if you are lacking in charity. This seems to be true of suffering in general; divorced from charity, it is sterile or worse than sterile. When the end sought is justification, however, one particular form of charity seems essential. That is forgiveness. To be justified is to be forgiven by God, and the Gospels say unequivocally that the unforgiving cannot be forgiven. You cannot withhold forgiveness from others, then look for forgiveness from God. It follows that suffering is spiritually fruitless when accompanied by hatred, even when those hated are truly culpable. The defining image of suffering borne in a merciful spirit is provided by Jesus when in the very course of being crucified he asked God to forgive his crucifiers. Whether there are times when forgiveness is inappropriate (Jesus asked forgiveness for his crucifiers on the grounds that they didn't realize what they were doing) is too complex a question to be dealt with here. At the very least, however, it can be said that suffering must be endured with a mind governed by mercy, and that withholding forgiveness is spiritually dangerous, defensible perhaps only when done out of charity and dictated by conscience.

It may be argued accordingly that forgiveness in the midst of suffering is the means by which we situate our lives in God's time and undertake to carry on our destinies. By suffering, willingly and with minds free of malice, we take part with Christ in the Crucifixion. Suffering becomes, in a manner of speaking, ecstatic— not in mood, but in raising us out of a degraded past and above a degraded self. It does this by forging the kind of faith which enables us to accept justification. We place sin—both our own and that of our enemies—behind us and dispose ourselves receptively toward righteousness. This means that we become accessible to self, community, and God. Thus forgiveness, in the company of suffering, is the decisive act of hope. There are times, as in the state's organized suppression of crime, when retribution is inevitable. But anyone who carries out retributive acts in a vengeful spirit, and in place of forgiveness, is playing fast and loose with human destiny and flirting with despair.

It is worth noticing that the standard of forgiveness amid suffering is not unrelated to twentieth-century realities. One of the most conspicuous fruits of sudden historical change is enmity. Wherever civil conflict and rebellion occur, fervent hatreds are sure to arise. All revolutions, even those that are relatively peaceful, leave simmering reservoirs of resentment. If every aggrieved party insists on settling old scores, historical progress becomes impossible. Illustrative is France—for all its creativity and genius, a nation divided and handicapped for over two hundred years by the hostilities produced in the destruction of the *ancien régime*. In the latter part of our century swift and violent change has been commonplace. Hence in dozens of nations, killers, torturers, informers, and other servants of tyranny have suddenly become ordinary citizens, living and working side-by-side with former victims. Efforts to achieve a strict accounting of all crimes and a just apportionment of punishments would not only fail, given the obscurity and complexity of past circumstances; such efforts would provoke dangerous passions among both those administering, and those perforce submitting to, the claims of justice. Such nations can gain a future—that is, hope—only through forgiveness.

With the concept of forgiveness, we have gained a vantage point from which we can see more clearly than before certain important aspects of hope. First of all, we can see that the faith through which justification is gained is crucial to hope not just because it renders the self acceptable but because it renders the other acceptable as well. That is, it makes love, and thereby the eternal and all-embracing community we hope for, possible. We have already discussed the Biblical command that you love not just those you find appealing but anyone you happen to encounter—your neighbor. The difficulty in loving your neighbor, however, is not mainly that he may happen not to share your interests or not to be the sort of person whose company you enjoy. It is rather that of original sin. Your neighbor is involved (as you are yourself) in the universal human repudiation of God and in that way obscures the divine image engraved in every person in the original act of creation. Neighborly love becomes possible only as the neighbor is seen as one who is, or at least through faith might be, justified. Seen in that way, the person before you, perhaps someone not very appealing or admirable, someone you have merely stumbled upon in the course of your daily life, is suddenly touched with a transcendental light. There is love, and the desire for community.

If hope is for God, community, and self, then it becomes possible only by entering into and accepting the divine act of justification accomplished on the Cross. Hope that ignores human sin and the need for justification is apt to become something very different from hope as here understood. Thus the apparently sublime hope that inspired communism turned in every instance into fury. Instead of community there arose a terrible caricature of human unity, totalitarianism. If human beings are not justified and transfigured by God then—at least so it will seem to those who long for human perfection—they must be transformed by human beings themselves. Now, looking back on the communist revolutions, we know how tragic an enterprise this is bound to be.

Contemplating hope from the vantage point of the concept of justification by faith we can see the deepest reason why hope must be in as well as for God. If hope is not in God, then it must be in man. But man, having mutilated his own being by separating himself from God, cannot sustain hope. Hope in man becomes proud intransigence, then fury. Instead of the attentiveness, and occasional dialogue, that comes out of genuine hope, there is propaganda and terror. One of the signal facts of human life, a fact too conspicuous to be missed or questioned except by those who refuse in their pride to acknowledge it, is that every human being is stubbornly inclined to seek things, like power, prestige, and pleasure, that bring forgetfulness of our finitude and mortality. Unless life has a transcendental dimension, in which that inclination is uprooted and its consequences forgiven, true hope is doomed. The Crucifixion is the breaking in of that dimension. It is consequently the fountain of hope. Needless to say, non-Christians can be merciful. But not easily: vengefulness is, in most minds, much nearer at hand than mercy. For a non-Christian to achieve mercy, and the consequent capacity for hope, transcendence must in some form break in and block the impulse to respond to every wrong through revenge. The event of justification can occur in the hearts even of those who do not recognize the Cross.

The doctrine of justification by faith makes the dialectical character of hope particularly apparent. Hope subsists among polarities such as abasement and exaltation, weakness and strength, folly and wisdom. The great polarity in which all others originate, according to Christianity, is that of fallen humanity and holy God, and the corresponding polarity in history is that of the Crucifixion and Resurrection. The former, effecting the condemnation and death of fallen man, the latter the raising of the dead into righteousness, or life, signify that God in his holiness does not allow his confrontation with man in his selfishness and ignorance to create an impasse. The road to God, community, and self is kept open for us all.

The dialectic becomes particularly clear in the notion that suffering can be "ecstatic." This does not mean that it can be a joyful thing to suffer, although some of Paul's words, as when he speaks of rejoicing in his suffering, or glorying in his infirmities, indicate that it can. It means rather that, as much as we hate it, it can raise us up. It can be experienced as participation in the Crucifixion and in that way as a medium of justification. When that happens, suffering can create a scene of hope. Sin and suffering, even in their most massive and frightening forms, are not allowed to disrupt the journey in which destiny is accomplished. Hope is always possible.

I have tried to sketch out the truth of time, the archetypal story. Such truth, however, is fragile. A story is such a simple, everyday thing that we are tempted, in our inveterate worldliness, to eliminate the inherent mystery not only of ordinary stories but even of the primal story, that of Christ. We tend to engage in objectification. In the twentieth century, the prestige of science and the spectacular achievements of technology have encouraged this tendency. The upshot, often in spite of ardent attachment to an imagined future, has been the loss of all true hope.

The Mystery of Hope

One reason hope is a mystery is that the end we hope for, God, is humanly incomprehensible. We know many things about God; at least, so Christians believe. We know, for example, that God is infinite and eternal. Such terms, however, are purely negative. By "infinite," we mean *not* finite, and by "eternal," *not* temporal. Since everything we experience is finite and temporal, the terms "infinite" and "eternal" convey no image to our minds. When we use such terms we define God only to the extent of specifying what God is not. We do, to be sure, know some things about God that are not merely negative. We know, for example, that God is righteous and merciful. Since we also know people who are righteous and merciful—in some degree—these terms convey positive images to our minds. But God is not righteous and merciful *in some degree;* we cannot even say that righteousness and mercy are qualities that pertain to God in the same way they do to human beings. God is righteousness and is mercy. Substance and attribute are identical. But for us, that is a paradox, not an understandable concept. Hence the human qualities provide us only with a rough idea of—an analogy to—the divine qualities. The upshot is that we can make true statements about God (hence the possibility of theology) but cannot comprehend God as we comprehend the things making up the world around us.

A similar incomprehensibility characterizes both community and self. At first glance, this may seem untrue, since I have immediate and daily experience of others and of myself. Little reflection is needed, however, to see that even close friends, indeed even the self, although in some aspects vividly known, defy comprehension. We explore them as though they were strange countries, or deep and intricate caverns. We are repeatedly surprised, and even come upon our own reactions and feelings unexpectedly. The whole world of literature—poetry, novels, memoirs, biographies—testifies to the inexhaustible depths of a human being. In Christian terms, these are the depths of the human soul. Community is a congregation of souls and the self is a soul. The incomprehensibility of community and self lie in this, that a soul is a creature and image of God. As with God, we can make true statements about them (for example, community involves shared truth, and a self is free) but we cannot add up such statements to reach a comprehensible total.

The mystery of God, community, and self does not lie altogether in their incomprehensibility, however. They are not simply unknown and unknowable; if that were so, we would be inclined to forget about them, and would probably be justified in doing so. As it is, however, we can search into them, even though we do this with a sense that their depths are infinite and thus beyond understanding. Moreover, these depths are powerfully alluring; they arouse in us a feeling that they contain something of limitless significance. Thus the idea of God, even for someone who denies the reality of God, is of a being who is numinous, majestic, and holy; the sense of community, as in the feeling one may have for a nation or a people, is of something transcendentally important; and many have felt, even if mistakenly, that if they could see deeply enough into their own souls they would perceive things of supreme significance. God, community, and self, then, are mysterious partly because they lure us into voyages of exploration—thus becoming the ends of hope.

Since mystery does not consist entirely in incomprehensibility, it is not necessarily reduced as comprehension increases. The concept of the beatific vision does not imply that God will in the end no longer be mysterious. It does not point to a time when God will be known as clearly and thoroughly as we know the things that we study in the physical sciences. If such a time were ever to come, the very idea of God would disappear like smoke from a snuffed-out candle. We would see that God, after all, is not God but only a hitherto uncomprehended aspect of a comprehensible—and controllable—universe. We would realize that "community" is only an edifying name for cohesive groups, in principle no different from other things in the world surrounding us. The soul would become merely the psyche, with complexities, no doubt, but not with impenetrable depths. Community and self would lose their allure. Hope would give way to sovereign intentions. As it is, however, knowledge may be widened indefinitely without encroaching on the encompassing mystery.

Hope looks beyond space and time. The things we hope for—God, community, self—are not spatial and temporal realities, even though they enter sufficiently into space and time for us to experience them. This means they do not wholly belong in the framework of knowledge. God, as the Creator, is reflected in the created universe that is sensually present in space and time; yet God is necessarily beyond space and time since these are elements of the universe he created. As for community, the transcendental dimension of a person known in community—the other—is brought out in Martin Buber's concept of the Thou. A Thou is essentially different from an It, which is a comprehensible and usable object in space and time. A Thou, by contrast, is not objectively knowable but rather must be encountered— addressed and heard in dialogue. A Thou, Buber remarks, "fills the heavens," a metaphor suggesting that a Thou constitutes space, through dialogic acts, but does not occupy space. The I, as distinguished from the other, can, in Buber, be either of two different entities. One is the I which inhabits an "I-It" relationship, the other is the I within an "I-Thou" relationship.[7] It accords with Buber's thought, I believe, although not with his terminology, to say that the former is a spatial and temporal, the latter a transcendental, self. In sum, the depths of God, others, and self, are not spatial depths but ranges of being that lie outside ordinary experience and objective knowledge. To live with hope is to tread the pathway of time in the direction of these ranges.

The consciousness of transcendence, and thereby the mystery of the things we hope for, is powerfully evoked in the writings of Kant. For Kant, all experience in the everyday sense of the term is of spatial and temporal entities. Yet various aspects of experience remind us continually that these entities subsist beyond space and time, and, accordingly, that we must think of them not just as they appear to us but as they are in themselves. For example, when we meet another person we are conscious of facing a unique entity—one that can freely act in conformity with a universal moral law and must therefore not be used solely in the expediential ways we use the things around us. We have an intuition of transcendence, not as an object of experience but as something shining through experience. Further, reason

---

[7] Martin Buber, *I and Thou,* 2nd ed., trans. Ronald Gregor Smith (New York: Charles Scribner's Sons, 1958).

strives continually toward a fullness of knowledge which cannot be simply knowl-edge of the totality of knowable things, for such a totality is inconceivable; we cannot get outside the universe and make it an object of investigation. The natu-ral thrust of reason, then, is toward things beyond space and time. Finally, beauty enables us to gain an inner sense of freedom even though freedom cannot be an object of experience; and sublimity, like that of the sea or of mountains, provides an intuition of the infinite in spite of the fact that the infinite, like freedom, is be-yond objective knowledge. For Kant, realities transcending space and time are both known and unknown: known in that they enter human awareness, unknown in that they cannot be assimilated into the world of objects.

Daily consciousness is pervaded by dualities either explicitly posed by Kant or suggested, in one way or another, in his writings. One of the most familiar of these is that of causality and freedom, the former treated mainly in the *Critique of Pure Reason,* the latter in the writings on morality. Closely linked with these, and famil-iar in modern discourse but not developed by Kant, are dualities such as subjective and objective, and inward and outward. Other dualities, more or less peripheral in Kant but central in modern theological discourse, are freedom and grace, time and eternity, and reason and faith. Modern philosophical and theological discussions are almost inevitably structured by these dualities, although the terms employed vary widely. Hence they have been exhaustively examined in innumerable theo-ries. In spite of these theories, however, we still do not know how to resolve the antitheses they pose. For example, we do not know, demonstrably and surely, how causality and freedom are related. Nor do we possess any apodictic, as distin-guished from merely hypothetical, concept of the universe that would enable us to synthesize such dualities as reason and faith, and time and eternity.

In short, we are profoundly ignorant—not culpably, as though we had failed to study and master knowable realities, but, so to speak, ontologically. We are helplessly immersed in realities that are beyond our grasp. We lack categories that might provide us with a coherent view of the universe we inhabit. We continue of course to frame theories, but the inconclusive history of philosophy shows that such theories are never demonstrable or even satisfactory to most thinkers. In some cases this is a very practical matter; witness, for example, our inability to judge with assurance degrees of guilt involved in the commission of crimes. In criminal pro-ceedings, judges and juries must always consider the circumstances surround-ing a crime and the relationship of circumstances to culpability. To what degree do circumstances extenuate guilt? For a determinist there is no guilt at all; for a radical protagonist of freedom every misdeed is simply inexcusable. Judges and juries at their best settle on the rough compromises of common sense—compromises with little or no philosophical validity. It is striking that one is immediately shrouded in such ignorance even in trying to estimate the range of one's own responsibility. In a generous mood, I can excuse almost any reprehensible act I have committed, in a less generous mood I drown in shame. Such uncertainties are particularly acute in the lives of Christians and of other religious people. Not only are they unable to assess their own guilt and righteousness. They must continually make highly debatable assumptions about the relations of freedom and grace, of time and eternity, of reason and faith. These assumptions may be inspired by revelation, but never are they drawn from a store of knowledge.

This, of course, is just one of numerous ways of characterizing our ignorance. We do not know where we have come from or where we are going—whether we have spring from biological accidents or from a divine creative intent, whether our ultimate destination is an everlasting night and void, without trace of human life and history, or the splendor of eternal light and amity. We do not know of the final disposition of evil. We see evil transfigured—as it were made into nothing—in the ephemeral pains and crises of childhood and in the way dissonance in music is resolved into exultant harmony. But whether anything of this sort can happen with the agonies of personal life and the horrors of collective history, we do not know. We do not know, indeed, what will happen to us, either as individuals or as societies, next week or tomorrow morning. Many of us have faith concerning such matters, faith even that provides all the assurance knowledge could provide. But we do not have knowledge.

It is disturbing that we do not, so disturbing indeed that occasionally it could drive us nearly to insanity were we not so habituated to the darkness. At the same time, the darkness is alluring and stimulates hope. Our ignorance evokes despair only as an occasional mood. The history of philosophy and religion is replete with signs of an intuition that the shadows around us conceal things we should not dread but rather should seek and that the deepest currents of life, if we enter trustfully into them, will carry us toward those things.

For the sake of hope, we should guard our ignorance. We should be wary of philosophies and ostensible sciences in which everything is explained. We should be especially wary of thinkers and leaders who claim that a particular leader or party, through the power of a pure and concerted will, can unify life and render all things clear and certain. It is noteworthy that some of the greatest theologies— Thomas Aquinas's, for example, and Karl Barth's—were deliberately left unfinished. There is something deeply right about the sketchy and unfinished character of the dialogues making up the body of Plato's life-work, and something dangerously wrong (as shown in the Marxist sequel) about the systematic all-inclusiveness of Hegel's philosophy. When human beings embark on enterprises of unification and completion, whether in thought or action, they are likely to undermine hope.

Our ignorance not only leaves room for hope and draws us toward hope; it also suggests the nature of our hope. We hope for light. This we are told not only by common sense but by Christianity as well. God is light, as John says, and the Word of God, Christ, was God's light sent into the world to be a light for all humanity. In this light, the dissonance of daily experience will disappear. Freedom will not clash with causality, nor faith with reason. The unity of all things will be plainly seen. The symbol of the Last Judgment is often treated as terrifying. Perhaps in some ways it is. But it is also alluring; it is a promise of ultimate clarification. The shadows of human ignorance will be finally dissipated, and if this is done by a merciful God, we can only look forward to its happening.

The mystery of hope is that it spans the chasm between the things we know and the things we do not know, between the world and transcendence. Hope is a way of thinking of time, and of living in time, in anticipation of things beyond time—things we desire above all else but cannot comprehend. As I have already argued, it is written into our original (but now in some measure defaced and abandoned) nature that we hope above all to see God; yet we cannot know what it would mean to do this. We hope also to see God in company with our fellow human beings, and we hope to discover our own selves when we do this. But hoping for these things is not like hoping for good weather on a coming day. We can imagine the latter, but not the former. Hope is a disconcerting passion, for it enters into us inevitably, yet it causes us to think of things that, strictly speaking, are unthinkable.

Let me put this more bluntly. We cannot know what we hope for. When I argue that we hope for God, community, and self I am trying to mark out directions rather than specify comprehensible ends. Nescience is one of the main marks distinguishing true hope from the various kinds of false hope that fill and confuse the world. The false hopes provide glowing pictures; true hope only points to the road we should travel. The ends of true hope are necessarily expressed in words, but the words do not provide images of the sort that we have when someone talks about their hopes for coming days and weeks. The reunion of all creation in God cannot be conceived of literally as a set of worldly circumstances, and the absorption of time into eternity cannot be thought of, except metphorically, as a temporal event. When hope is authentic, and not a form of resignation to the supposed finality of the world, it withholds glowing pictures. It calls on us to walk in darkness.

Admittedly, this assertion must be qualified. The darkness is not absolute. If it makes any sense at all to speak of the kingdom of God, then that kingdom must have something in common with the earthly entities to which we give the name of kingdom. There must be an analogy between earthly kingdoms and the heavenly kingdom. If that is so, then our knowledge of earthly societies and polities must offer insight of some sort, however vague and imperfect, into the city of God. When we see justice momentarily achieved somewhere on earth, we must gain a glimpse of celestial harmony. When we apprehend a significant truth in common with two or three others ("Where two or three are gathered in my name, there am I in the midst of them." Matthew 18:20 RSV), we must gain a fragmentary perception of transcendental communion. And when we see with our eyes the beauty of an earthly metropolis such as Paris, we must see something of the beauty awaiting the human race at the end of time. Hence a very few works, like The Revelation to John in *The New Testament* and Dante's *Paradiso,* provide compelling images of the end of history and of realities beyond time.

Indeed, we have seen already, in discussing the legitimacy and necessity of temporal hope, that the darkness we walk in is occasionally and momentarily dissipated. This happens whenever we experience an authentic value, such as truth or beauty. That true hope is eschatological does not mean that hope is anticipation of things that lie exclusively beyond the end of history. We can hope to see foreshadowings of the eschaton. The "last things" break recurrently into history, albeit only fragmentarily and ephemerally. When they do break in, we cannot seize them and save them. But by means of them, God carries those who are attentive through the crucifixions inherent in temporal life. One can hope that the next year, the next day, or even the very next hour will bring a glimpse of the heavenly city.

The things thus glimpsed, however, are always deep in the shadows of worldly existence. The beauty and intellectual vitality of ancient Athens can be, for a Christian, a pagan analogue to the kingdom of heaven; but the slavery and the harsh imperialism practiced by the Attic city tell us unmistakably that we perceive an analogue and nothing more. The range and impartiality of the Roman Law are, for a watchful mind, a foreshadowing of the universality of the kingdom of God; but the savagery of emperors like Caligula and Commodus shows us with dreadful clarity that we are not contemplating a heavenly reality. Moreover, we cannot speak of such analogues without awareness of their rarity. In most times and places, there is far less light than Athens and Rome provided. History unfolds in shadows and darkness. This is why hoping for temporal things, in all of their ambiguity and uncertainty, is reasonable only because they are intimations of eternal things—things humanly incomprehensible—that are yet to come.

The mystery of hope is fully apprehended, however, only when we realize that it is not only the ends that are mysterious but also the temporal course of affairs that leads to them. If we cannot comprehend the eternal ends we hope for, neither can we comprehend the temporal ways by which we reach them. Thus it is a commonplace of spiritual literature that circumstances we dread can turn out to be salutary, and that situations causing us great pain can prepare us for satisfactions we could never have imagined. Unable to grasp our eternal goals, neither can we grasp the temporal conditions that will lead us toward them. For Christians, all of this is exemplified in the Crucifixion and Resurrection. When the apostles saw Jesus on the Cross, they had to feel that the very worst they could fear had come to pass. As

Christians looking back on the Crucifixion, however, we feel measureless gratitude for its occurrence. The darkness in which we must walk conceals from our eyes not just the goal but every step along the way.

It becomes apparent how deeply in error are all efforts to gain objective knowledge of the basic patterns of history. Hence the significance of the difference between Augustine's writings on history, in which he refrains from any attempt to show the shape that the course of historical affairs must have in the mind of God, and the writings of Hegel and Marx. Hegel asserted explicitly that his philosophy of history exhibited the divine intellect. And Marx, dethroning God, tacitly claimed for human beings enlightened by his own science of history the status of infinite intellects and omnipotent sovereigns. The issue symbolized by Augustine on one side and by Hegel and Marx on the other is simple; it is whether we fully acknowledge our finitude and moral fallibility. To take the side of Hegel and Marx is, in effect, to repudiate true hope and to put in place of it a tacit claim, rendered plausible by the genius of its authors, yet utterly false, to human omniscience and omnipotence.

It becomes apparent also how difficult it is to practice temporal hope in the right way. As already argued, to live entirely without temporal hope is to exclude God from history. As a failure of faith, it imperils all hope. To stake one's peace of mind on the attainment of any of the objects of temporal hope, however, is to slip into the error of Hegel and Marx. It is to assume that we understand in some degree the proper pattern of earthly events. More simply stated, it is to assume that we know the eventual upshot of the earthly circumstances we hope for. But of course we don't. And that is what marks off the titanic self-assurance of modern philosophers of history from the humility underlying authentic hope. Recognition of the mystery of hope expresses that humility.

It is hard for us to bear the pervasive uncertainty imposed on us by the mystery of hope, yet that is what we must do. In the same passages in which God, through the prophet Isaiah, commands that we walk in darkness, we are warned against "kindling a fire," or "setting brands alight," in order to illuminate the way ahead. "Walk by the light of your fire, and by the brands which you have kindled!" we are admonished, "This shall you have from my hand: you shall lie down in torment." (Isaiah 50:11 RSV) To rebel against the darkness is to repudiate the mystery of hope. This, in turn, is to forsake those things toward which we are impelled by the deepest forces of our created nature—God, our fellow creatures, and ourselves.

Hope thus is not a way of vaulting beyond time into a future secured against all of the perils that time entails. It is a way of dwelling within time—in our present situation, in the face of present constraints, sufferings, and responsibilities. By submitting to the darkness inherent in the mystery of hope, we safeguard at once the transcendental character of our hopes and their temporal bearing. Acknowledging that we cannot rationally grasp or clearly imagine what we hope for ultimately, we also acknowledge our ignorance, our weakness, and our dependence on God; we confess the faith on which hope rests. Yet we continue to walk in time, counting on God to keep us from stumbling. We are at once open to eschatological glimpses and wary of misconstruing them, as is done, for example, by those who make science or art the center of life, thus turning true values into false gods.

Living in the darkness of time is required not only by our patent inability to envision the eschatological future but also by scriptural revelation. We human beings must live in time because God, incarnate in Christ, lived in time. Eternity and time are not incompatible. This truth is expressed not only in the doctrine of the Incarnation but also in the ancient principle that in the mind of God history is not an unfoldment but a finished harmony. It follows that eternity is not reached by transcending time, as in the philosophy of Plato, but by living in time with a readiness for encountering God, other, and self—that is, with hope. God's own temporality makes it incumbent on us to live in time. And while we must live in space also, space must be subordinated to time, which happens when we perceive our place of habitation—home, city, nation—as an historical situation. In short, we must define ourselves historically rather than geographically.

If it seems harsh to say that hope requires us to walk in darkness, let us remember that it is not so much blind hope that has misled us in the twentieth century as it is hope that is ostensibly clear-sighted. The worst tragedies have come where hope was earthly, specific, and confident. Marxists in the Soviet Union, China, and elsewhere did not believe that they were walking in darkness nor did they feel themselves ignorant of the object of their hopes. Yet they walked into an abyss. If their hope was the final and complete fulfillment of the modern revolutionary impulse—"liberty, equality, and fraternity"—the culmination of their historical efforts, so far as we can tell, was the precise opposite of what they had hoped for. Paradoxically, rebelling against the darkness deepens it, whereas light is gained by accepting the darkness. Thus the God who warns men against "kindling a fire" and "setting brands alight" promises in another passage that he will care for "the blind." "I will turn the darkness before them into light, and the rough places into level ground." (Isaiah 42:16 RSV) The necessity of walking in *God's* darkness, it seems, is not as onerous as it looks.

Hope as Exaltation

Hope is essentially ambiguous. By its very nature, it is a state of deprivation—of what is hoped for. But as everyone knows, it is not simply a state of misery; it is a foreshadowing of happiness. In the Christian vision, living with hope is journeying toward God. In this metaphor, we can see hope's ambiguity. A journey implies a destination as yet unattained; in the present case, that means separation from God.

Yet a human journey toward God is possible, and can be resolutely embarked on, only because God, through grace, is present throughout the journey, not merely at the end of it. This accords with primary Christian symbols. The Incarnation and Crucifixion reveal God as fully engaged in human life, even in the worst of times. To have hope, then, is to be not only away from God but also with God, cast down but simultaneously lifted up. These two dimensions of hope are mixed together, in proportions varying with moods and circumstances, in the experience of everyone who lives with hope. When we are cast down, conscious mainly of deprivation, then, so to speak, hope is disciplinary; living with hope means submitting—necessarily with a modicum of hope, but also with pain—to conditions of fallen existence which present themselves as divine requirements. When we are lifted up, we experience "tremors of bliss" (a phrase from T. S. Eliot); we feel ourselves on the boundary line of the eternal country where we belong.

Hope is far oftener disciplinary than exalting. This is because of its mystery. Given our incapacity for comprehending the things we hope for, embracing hope does not transport us into the future, normally, but throws us back into our present circumstances. With hope, we will do and bear, with more or less serene spirits, what these circumstances require of us. Hope will take the form of obedience. Occasionally, however, the sun will break through the clouds and give us a momentary sense of our destiny. It is then that hope becomes exaltation. We shall consider the disciplinary aspects of hope in the following section of this chapter. In the present section our concern is mainly with the other, and far rarer, dimension of hope, that which exalts us.

Hope, as we have already seen, is not only *for* God; it is *in* God as well. It is the spirit in which we journey not only *toward* God but *in the company of* God. To speak of hoping in God, and journeying in the company of God, is to speak of trust in God. It is this trust that determines the degree to which hope lifts us up. There is a measure of trust in all hope, for Christianity affirms in the most uncompromising terms that God is worthy of trust; he is pure love possessed of sovereign power. Hence a god in whom you have no trust is not God but a figment of a frightened imagination. Hope must consequently be *in* God or it is not *for* God either. Nevertheless, trust waxes and wanes, and when it wanes hope will not exalt us. On the other hand, when trust is great, we feel that nothing can defeat us.

Rather than saying that trust waxes and wanes, however, it would be more accurate to say that it comes to us sometimes as an emotion that fills our spirits and minds and sometimes as a mere possibility, which we must seize and adhere to. In the latter case, we *entrust ourselves* to God and our destinies, and we live in obedience rather than exaltation. It is when the sun breaks through, and we see into the mystery of hope, that we are lifted up. A particularly eloquent expression of the exaltation that comes with trust-filled hope can be heard in familiar words of Paul.

"Who shall separate us from the love of Christ?" Paul asks. "Shall tribulation, or distress, or persecution, or famine, or nakedness, or peril, or sword? . . . No, in all these things we are more than conquerors through him who loved us." (Romans 8:35 & 37 RSV)

Trust which counts on God to arrange temporal circumstances to our satisfaction is manifestly misplaced. The only hope sure of fulfillment is for eternal life, that is, God. Every temporal hope should be tentative, entertained with the knowledge that it may be disappointed. It should, moreover, be accompanied by a readiness to incur disappointment without falling into despair. The Crucifixion, in the Christian vision, has a twofold import. It is a sign that God has at heart the ultimate interest of every human being, in spite of human sin; in some sense, God goes through death for the sake of each one of us. But the Crucifixion is also a sign that God often works in ways that confound human expectations and desires. Hence, when we hope for temporal ends, we hope amiss unless we remember that what we hope for may not serve our eternal ends, and that something different, even dismayingly different, may. Our hopes thus must be rectified as we move through our individual lives and our common history. Faith and righteousness provide no exemptions from this condition. Thus in the Gospel of John Jesus warns Peter that the temporal future that lies before him is not one he will like. "When you were young," Jesus says, "you girded yourself and walked where you would. But when you are old, you will stretch out your hands, and another will gird you and will carry you where you do not wish to go." (John 21:18 RSV) This was said, it was added, in reference to something distant from ordinary hope, that is, death—in this case, the death by which Peter was, according to Jesus, to glorify God.

In a word, trust must be wise, that is, aware that God is concerned with our eternal interests, but that these may be in conflict sometimes with our temporal desires. Hope inspired by a wise trust can provide a certain transcendence over the worst of circumstances. It can mean exaltation, even in the midst of tribulation. There is of course much in life that seems dreadful. Illness, poverty, loneliness, death: all of the well-known evils of human existence prompt dread. But there is nothing that renders dread fitting and inevitable. God in his infinite power can make the greatest evils serve the end of human redemption. "All things work for good to them that love God." (Romans 8:28 KJV) There is no terror or absurdity that can stand out forever against the divine providential order we have called destiny. Hope is the consciousness that this is so. Such statements often inspire incredulity and even anger, particularly when applied to gross and particular evils, like disease and death among the young. But such reactions presuppose a knowledge of our eternal interests, and of the temporal conditions furthering them, that we simply do not possess. Hence, although often clothed in garments of compassion, or of resolute rationality, they reflect a proud unwillingness to defer to the mercy and power of God. Not that asking Why? in the face of tragedy is wrong. On the contrary, it is quite in order and can lead to deeper understanding. We must take care, however, not to ask in a fashion that is merely rhetorical, as though no answer is possible; and, finding no answer, we must not assume that no answer, in time or eternity, can ever be found. God could not spare us all suffering and tragedy without making puppets of us. Christian faith, grounded on the Incarnation, Crucifixion, and Resurrection, is that God teaches us in all we suffer, and that in doing this he exalts us.

To trust in God, then, is to trust in the universe of hope—in destiny. It is to trust in time and in the whole course of events within which one's life is carried on. So, at least, is the case in Christianity, with its faith in a God who is Lord of all time yet is not indifferent even to the fall of a sparrow. Life can carry you to the shore and set you on your feet because it is not a chaotic outpouring of purposeless vitality. As a great novel is organized in every detail according to the intent of the author, so human life is pervaded by the artistry of God. Of course many happenings seem like fate—deadly and irresistible—rather than like destiny; often, too, events seem merely accidental, unconnected with the past or the future in any way that gives them meaning. However, trust and the hope it inspires place the necessities and contingencies of temporal existence under the light of faith, where they take on the contours of destiny. Trust, and trustful hope, are in essence metaphysical affirmations. They imply that in spite of all appearances there is nothing to fear in life, and nothing we need to dread.

The way in which we are exalted by destiny can be clearly seen if we recall that destiny is selfhood. To live your destiny is to be raised above accidental circumstances to the level of your essential being. This is not merely because destiny precludes accidents and thus provides a propitious life-environment. The relationship between destiny and self is more intimate than that. Destiny defines the self: you *are* your destiny. To speak of destiny as though it is merely something that happens to you is to assume that a person is in essence always the same, changeless at the core amid the ceaseless changes of life and history. But the truth is that what happens to you—including in this category the ideas and impulses that arise within you in response to outward events—defines your identity. The only way you could be fully identified would be by a story—of the kind God alone could tell—of the unfolding of your life in all of its depths and complexities. Thus living your destiny is carrying on your life as the one you really are. To be exalted by hope is to be conscious momentarily of the authentic selfhood that unfolds in time. In this consciousness there is trust in the God in which selfhood is grounded.

The experience of hope as exaltation is one of the eschatological moments in which, in the course of the temporal journey, there is an occasional glimpse of the end of the journey. When spiritual figures such as Paul the Apostle, or secular figures of transcendent greatness such as Abraham Lincoln, appear in history; when someone gives up his life for others, as when a soldier casts himself on a hand grenade in order to save the lives of his comrades (a feat of self-sacrificial love which has occurred countless times in modern warfare), there is a glimmering of heaven. Even when there is merely an unexpected sparkle of truth in a conversation; or when the grandeur of a philosophical system, such as St. Thomas's or Kant's, is suddenly perceived; or when the countenance of a beloved person seems for an instant radiant with a transcendental light, we find ourselves momentarily lifted above the transitory events in which our lives for the most part are spent.

Eschatological moments show us values that are not limited or fleeting. From a purely secular standpoint, every good and beautiful thing arouses nostalgia, for at the very moment of enjoyment one senses (given a secular standpoint) that it is disappearing forever. Seen under the light of hope, however, values take on a very different aspect. They emerge as intimations of things yet to come and reveal a mysterious invulnerability to the ravaging power of time. My love for another human being—where there is hope—is not pervaded by the anguish of knowing that both of us must die, but rather prefigures a love less exclusive and less liable to interruption. Through trustful hope, we may surmise, John Locke (a more serious Christian than many realize) was moved on his deathbed to drink toasts in a teaspoon with his friends, and William Blake, in like circumstances, to sing hymns. Where there is hope, the splendors of earthly things—of light, of firmament, of sea and land, of sun, moon, and stars—are not transient glories but are analogues of God and the heavenly company which is destined finally to be as visible and present as mountains and trees are now. With hope, an evanescent era of splendor like Periclean Athens is remembered as a sign, not of the fragility of human achievements, but of the translucence of the kingdom brought near through Christ. In eschatological moments, we are exalted by glimpsing the "last things" we hope for and are imbued with the trust that enables us to continue the journey toward these things.

Hope is anticipatory membership in the kingdom of God, and as such it provides the only real security we can know on earth. This is one reason why the kingdom of God is the pearl of great price, for the sake of which it is worth sacrificing every other possession. Thus Paul pronounced all that he had given up for Christ, which comprised practically everything that most of us today would consider essential to a decent existence, to be "dung." (Philippians 3:8 KJV) The world attracts us because it apparently offers the possibility of security. We can fill our barns with grain and then exult in our prospects of pleasure and our apparent invulnerability. The moment we do that, however, we become in truth highly vulnerable, as the Biblical parable brings out when God tells the man glorying in his stock of grain that he will die that very night, leaving behind all that he possesses. And hope vanishes, when our barns are full of grain, for we have abandoned all thought of the future, enclosing ourselves in the present pleasurable, and sup-posedly invulnerable, moment. In Augustinian terms, the City of God is our one unassailable fortress. Only by living as members of that city, through hope, can we live righteously and wisely, which is to say securely and trustfully, amid the insecu-rities of time and history. Trustful hope exalts us by making us unafraid.

We see again, in thinking of the exaltation hope can bring and of the transcen-dental trust on which it is founded, the strange disproportion between hope and fear. Hope presupposes suspenseful circumstances yet in large measure precludes inward suspense and instead brings serenity. This happens, as we have already seen, because hope is *in,* as well as *for,* God. The journey toward God is made in the company of God. The power of hope is seen at its fullest when it lifts us up. But even when it consigns us to obeying the necessities of our destiny, it does not aban-don us to fear.

Although the trust which exalts us is implicitly religious, it is not necessarily inaccessible to secular minds. It happens sometimes that people adhering to no ex-plicit faith nevertheless feel that reality in its depths somehow justifies their trust. Such people in some cases are no doubt moved merely by optimism, which, as a mere temperamental propensity—an insensitivity perhaps to the perils of life—is not at all equivalent to hope. The spontaneous trust I am speaking of is deeper than optimism. It does not preclude an awareness that tragic events often occur; it rests, simply, on the confidence that such events need never be conclusive. Life can surmount them. Such an attitude, I believe, is tacitly religious and would be impos-sible for an absolutely logical and uncompromising atheist. Secular minds are of various sorts, however, and in some of them trust in life, such as that which Porfiry expressed, can find a lodging place. The possibility of hope that has the compo-sure—the exaltedness—given it by trust, therefore, is not confined to Christians.

Such is the value of hope that the primary object of hope here on earth, it might be said, is hope itself. More precisely, hope reduced to a state of obedience aspires to become hope as exaltation. This is not very different from saying that the object of hope is life. Hope is strength for living in time, with all of the dangers and defeats that entails. As strength, hope involves joy, even when such joy is only of the kind Paul spoke of when he said that "we rejoice in our sufferings."

It is not a mere misfortune, however, when hope fails. It is one of the mysteries of destiny that divine grace does not remove human responsibility. Hopelessness bespeaks an unreadiness for God and a mistrust of God. It is therefore a culpable state. A person in despair is locked up within the world. It follows that hopeless-ness is not merely to be endured. It must be resisted. To resist despair is to strive toward hope, and that is to strive toward God. One cannot do this, however, if hope is lacking altogether. One cannot strive toward hope without hope. What is the source of this last vital remnant of hope? The answer is one we have already touched on: grace. Here we reach the ultimate foundations of hope. We can hope for hope only if God enables us to. When God gives us this ability, however, we immediately become responsible for using it. Reduced to the state of hoping for hope, we are not lifted up by hope. Rather, we are constrained to submit to the claims of hope.

Hope as Obedience

The two main dimensions of life with hope, exaltation and obedience, consist of two contrasting relationships with destiny. In its fullness, hope is a consciousness of being lifted above chance and fate by auspicious tides of life. When hope is small, however, and verges on despair, destiny becomes something to which we must submit. It becomes a discipline. In the former case, it spells happiness; in the latter case, endurance. As exaltation, living with hope means rejoicing in the Lord; as obedience it involves a certain alienation from the Lord, who becomes manifest as command and constraint. In discussing hope as exaltation, we viewed it when it is flourishing; in discussing hope as obedience, we see it when it is only an ember, giving just enough light to enable us to see the things we must do and suffer, and to realize, given the authority with which these necessities speak to us, that our lives and history are not meaningless. It may seem that submitting to such constraints hardly deserves the name of hope. The name is not inappropriate, however, because we submit in the faith that an obedient life is fashioned by grace and will bring us finally to the fullness of being we understand as God.

It must be borne in mind, however, that God's commands do not come to us simply as abstract rules. They come as the fused moral and practical necessities inherent in our diverse situations, personal and historical. Often these necessities require us to act; sometimes they require us merely to endure. But in neither case do they lift us above the circumstances of worldly life. Rather, they constrain us to face and respond to those circumstances, and to do this in a spirit of trust and fidelity toward God. To forget the situational form of God's rule over us is to place ourselves in an abstract and unreal universe—perhaps starkly moral, perhaps stringently practical—and thus to lose touch with the commands themselves (which an omnipotent and providential God embodies in circumstances) and with the destiny they represent. In order to designate accurately the hope moving those who seek God by living the concrete lives given them to live, let us use the term "situational obedience."

When destiny is experienced as constraint rather than exaltation, this must be understood in relation to grace. Grace is not withdrawn, for in that case we would enter into a nighttime of despair in which we could neither see nor care about the moral and practical necessities bearing on us. But grace does not spare us a full experience of our fallen state. It may come to us in the form of what worldly understanding calls misfortune; it may even come to us as a sin we commit (David and Bathsheba, Paul and the persecution of the Christians) and then recoil from in repentance. Grace here takes on a certain severity. Although there is faith that circumstances are providential, there is lacking the full inward assurance which exalts us. One's personal and historical situation is inhabited resolutely rather than joyfully. For most of us, life is far more often constraint than exaltation—as acknowledged in the wry exclamation, "That's life!" Nonetheless, when constraint is experienced as obligatory, and as originating ultimately in God, then it still is a medium of grace and will sooner or later be seen as destined and not merely accidental. Even a life that puts harsh demands on us can be a life of hope.

The mysterious disproportion we have already noted between hope and fear is particularly significant in relation to hope as obedience. When hope is experienced as exaltation it fills the mind and spirit; there is little room for fear. When hope is reduced to claims on our obedience, however, it leaves large areas of the self open to the invasion of other emotions, even to impulses of rebellion, such as the "murmuring" of the Israelites in the wilderness. Here the grace which gives us hope also gives us the perilous opportunity of rejecting hope, and either rising up in pride to meet with our own powers whatever misfortunes we face or else plunging into despair. If we seize this opportunity, we expose ourselves to fear and will eventually be overwhelmed with fear. Hope will vanish. As long as hope remains, however, fear is held at bay. In spite of suspenseful circumstances, there remains the inexplicable certainty that eventually (as Julian of Norwich assures us) "all will be well, and every kind of thing will be well."[8]

When hope becomes obedience we are made acutely aware of a somber truth about hope: it is occasioned by our fallenness. We hope for God because we are separated from God, and we anticipate the City of God, as Augustine so dramatically maintained, because we inhabit the city of man. In a word, we are exiles. If we forget this, hope fades. We may then come to suppose that we ourselves possess the power and goodness needed for setting right the injustices and other derangements of life; this, in substance, was the delusion of Communism. Hope is replaced by pride. We may, on the other hand, assuming that all things are governed by a law of improvement, entrust ourselves to the spontaneous course of events. The American belief in progress illustrates this agreeable but dangerous possibility. Here historical idolatry, rather than pride, takes the place of hope. A final option is that of deciding that everything is largely satisfactory as is and thus indulging in a supposition condemned in the Bible: that today all is working for the best and that tomorrow will

---

8 Julian of Norwich, *Showings*, trans. Edmund Colledge and James Walsh (New York: Paulist Press, 1978), p. 149.

be just like today. Again, hope is uprooted—deprived of the only soil in which it can live and grow. Just as hope is for God, so it can inhabit the lives only of those who know that they are apart from God, and that this reflects not a slight derangement of their circumstances but a profound disorientation of their being.

In short, when we examine hope as obedience, we again realize that hope is dialectical, presupposing a polarization of man and God. This is dramatized in that great song of hope, the Beatitudes. Those who are poor in spirit, who are sorrowful and meek, who hunger and thirst for righteousness, know they are fallen; grace responds, and they are promised the kingdom of heaven. They are given hope. Those who are merciful and pure in heart are those who hunger for God; grace tells them that they shall see God. The Beatitudes teach us that hope is not simple and harmonious but a state of spiritual tension. We are truly hopeful only when we are painfully conscious of not possessing the good we hope for. When Paul speaks of rejoicing in his sufferings, or of glorying in his infirmities, he is not speaking of a rare or strange spiritual condition. In the tone of the Beatitudes, he is speaking simply of hope—the dialectical hope inherent in the Crucifixion and the Resurrection.

As fallen creatures, however, we cannot clearly envision the ultimate realities from which we are fallen. As Plato saw, we live in a realm of shadows, a cave. Sunlight, and the appearance of things when bathed in sunlight, are inconceivable to us and repel us when we first experience them. This is why living with hope is walking in darkness. We cannot clearly envision what it is we hope for. Our very fallenness—even though it occasions hope—obstructs our view of the future for which we hope. Although we can know that something of absolute significance is lacking from our lives and can even, through revelation and natural reason, know in a general way what it is, we cannot imagine or rationally comprehend what our lives would be like were the missing good regained.

Collective life, too, no less than personal life, is carried on in darkness. The ultimate end of collective life is the kingdom of God, which will presumably be analogous to earthly communities, yet so different from them as to be unimaginable. We can of course specify valid standards applying to collective existence in the world, such as constitutional government and popular representation. These, however, concern worldly polities, not the kingdom of God. At best they mark pathways leading through the darkness toward God's kingdom. If we try to outline an ideal society in which these pathways might terminate, we find ourselves involved in the self-contradictory enterprise of trying to delineate the worldly form of something essentially otherworldly. And when, like Hegel and Marx, we try to mark out the general direction of the path we will follow—that is, the basic patterns of history—we undertake a task entirely beyond human capacities. In sum, we can see, in our fallenness, only the realities immediately before us. We retain faculties of immediate perception, but not of foresight.

It follows that possessing hope does not mean, either for societies or individuals, living in an imagined future; we do not have the spiritual insight—the depth of imagination—to do that. Rather, possessing hope means living, often with pain and therefore with resolution, in the present time. This is true even of hope as exaltation. Never are we allowed to leave the present and live in the future. Even the great prophets of the Old Testament do not provide us with visions of the last things. It is true that the Book of Revelation touches on the *eschaton*, and one great poem, Dante's *Paradiso*, contains scintillating images of the kingdom of God. But these are highly exceptional works, and to suppose that they describe the proper state of mind of a hopeful person would be to misapply them. Hope is maintaining the humility of trying simply to be adequate to the circumstances in which God has placed us. When we are threatened by despair, hope will not be recovered by strenuous acts of imagination, disclosing things to come, but only by doing and suffering what we have to do and suffer. This was all perfectly expressed by Cardinal Newman in the well-known words of the hymn he wrote with the opening refrain, "Lead, Kindly Light, amid the encircling gloom." Newman exclaims that "the night is dark, and I am far from home." Yet his plea to God is notable for its restraint. "Keep Thou my feet; I do not ask to see the distant scene,—one step enough for me."[9]

In the Book of Isaiah God says that he will lead the blind "in paths they they have not known." He declares that he will "turn the darkness before them into light, and the rough places into level ground." (Isaiah 42:16) Jesus, too, alludes to the darkness that enshrouds the future. The kingdom of God will come like a thief in the night, silently and unexpectedly. We cannot know how or when and therefore can only "watch and pray." In such ways as these, the Bible exhibits the spirituality informing the lives of those who do not try to see into the future but try only to respond to the moral and practical necessities inherent in the situations they inhabit. To attend to the personal and historical circumstances surrounding us, without trying to see where they are ultimately carrying us, and to do whatever these circumstances require and to acquiesce in whatever sufferings they involve, is to rely on God even though assailed by temptations of mistrust. And to rely on the God whose kingdom is at hand is necessarily to watch for God. Such is the nature of the hope sustaining us in the darkness of time and history.

Our fantasies of the future and images of paradise are practically always far too human, shaped by earthly desires, personal preoccupations, and pride in human power. Since we cannot conceive of or picture the state of things when history has merged into eternity, the result of trying to live toward an imaginary kingdom of God is that of immuring ourselves in an imaginary kingdom of man. Hope is not

---

9 See Ian Ker, *John Henry Newman: A Biography* (New York: Oxford University Press, 1988), pp. 79–80.

liberated but secretly constricted. In late twentieth-century America, it is common to speak fondly of the "dreams" people harbor, of how tragic it is when they are disappointed, and how wonderful it is when they are realized. Notice is seldom taken of the fact that our dreams often arise from profound misunderstandings, not only of our abilities but even of our real desires; nor is notice taken of the fact that the failure of our dreams may bring us nearer to maturity. Human dreams are dubious because human beings are sinful and their dreams not only reflect this—for example, when they are shaped mainly by personal ambition—but they spur those who indulge in them to sinful acts. Dreams concerning the welfare of others are not exempt from these strictures. They are rarely as unselfish as we suppose and often they manifest a proud assurance that we know—as in truth only God can know—what others need. When dreams are political, they are obviously not less dangerous than when they are personal; the lives of countless millions have been lost through the acts of political dreamers. Christians themselves have misconstrued and trivialized hope by trying to imagine life in heaven; the insipid images thus created—throngs of the redeemed, clothed in white robes, and singing and playing on harps among the clouds—illustrate the vanity of the effort. In sum, hope is not glorying in a purely human future, for that would be cultivating a spurious hope; nor, strictly speaking, is it glorying in God's future, for that is beyond our comprehension.

The requirements which circumstances impose are measured both by practical intelligence and moral conscience. The question is always, "What must I, and all of us together, do?" and the answer depends on understanding both what is possible and what is obligatory. As a theory this may sound excessively vague; it is, however, a commonplace of daily life, both in the private and the public sphere. The duality of practical and moral necessity, in quite definite forms, repeatedly faces, and must be resolved by, every individual and every political leader. Thus George Washington, in commanding America's revolutionary forces, in presiding over the constitutional convention, and in serving as President responded to circumstances which were simultaneously historical and personal. And his responses depended equally on practical sagacity and moral fortitude. He had to be cognizant at once of the often-straitened military, economic, and political circumstances of the nation and of its moral significance as the main protagonist of republican government in the world.

Another example of situational obedience, carried out in circumstances clearly political and historical, yet requiring great personal resolution, has been provided in our own time by the French village of Le Chambon-sur-Lignon. During World War II, and the occupation of France by the Nazis, the citizens of Le Chambon devoted themselves to sheltering, and transporting to safety, thousands of Jewish refugees. Although Le Chambon was not in the occupied zone, there was an SS camp nearby and the policy of the government over them—the Vichy government—was emphatically anti-Semitic. The Nazis were quite capable not only of killing individuals who resisted their will but of razing entire villages suspected of conspiring against them. So the citizens of Le Chambon were risking everything in their efforts to save Jews from the Holocaust. Yet these efforts were pursued over a period of years, without betrayal or open dissent on the part of any of the villagers. Leadership was provided by a Christian pastor, and most of those immediately involved were apparently Christians; for them, the Jews were God's own people. What is most striking in the present context, however, is that on being asked in later years to explain their heroism, most of them answered that they simply did what obviously had to be done. They responded to the necessities of their situation. If one word were used to describe their deeds, the most precise would be, not loving or heroic or moral (even though any of these words would be appropriate), but obedient. They lived up to the demands of their circumstances.[10]

It must be noted, however, that situational obedience does not invariably involve either action or suffering in the usual sense of these terms. It may require waiting—a theme touched on earlier. One may not be called on either to act very decisively or to suffer very greatly. One may merely have to bear feelings of futility—that nothing is being accomplished, not even the moral purification one can hope for in suffering. One is, so to speak, assigned by God to a station, and may have to live for years like a solitary sentinel at an outpost where little ever happens. Immobilized by darkness, one waits for light.

Our situations often are simultaneously private and historical—and as historical also political. Granted, for many of those living in "normal" times, the historical and political dimensions of their lives may be more less unstated and even unrecognized; their struggles with necessity seem intimate and private. And this impression is not wholly false. Some of our major responsibilities, such as those to other family-members, have to be met, singly and separately, by each individual. In this sense, the intimate and private dimension of obedient hope is quite fundamental. Nonetheless, even the most personal pursuits, such as following one's vocation or educating one's children, are practically always structured by national and global circumstances and thus are historical and, at least in a broad sense, political. The public structures of our private lives are apt to become particularly visible in times of common crisis, such as war or revolution. Then the historical and political necessities implicit in a personal situation may suddenly become clear and pressing. Such was the case with Dietrich Bonhoeffer, a profound Christian, executed by the Nazis at the end of World War II for his resistance activities. A man of somewhat

---

10 See Philip P. Hallie, *Lest Innocent Blood Be Shed: The Story of Le Chambon and How Goodness Happened There* (New York: Harper Collins, 1979).

conservative and non-political inclinations, he discovered that simply to be fully human, in the Christian sense, he had to be a conspirator against the established government of his nation.

Obedience has unique importance in Christian ethics. The fall of the human race is understood in terms of a primal act of disobedience to God. The redemption of the human race, correspondingly, is conceived of as a cosmically-significant act of obedience—that which brought Christ to the Cross. Possibilities of obedience, by which we set ourselves against our fallenness, and strive to gain a fuller and sounder hope, face us every day. This is implied by the concept of situational obedience. If the whole of history and every detail of every human life reflect a destiny ordained by God, then divine commands are implicit in all occurrences and all circumstances.

The ethic of situational obedience is by no means bound indissolubly to a Christian, .or even to a broadly religious, worldview. The idea of necessities that are simultaneously moral and practical, and imposed on us by circumstances we cannot readily evade, is comprehensible to almost everyone. Believers and non-believers alike can shape their lives in response to such necessities. Moreover, non-believers can understand them broadly in the same way as do believers: through conscience, informed with practical intelligence. Thus, surveying the world in a mood of moral concern will often lead both the religious and the irreligious to answer in similar ways the ancient question, "What then must we do?"—even though sometimes there may be nothing we can do but wait. And the irreligious, in spite of their metaphysical premises, may sense, through conscience, that the things they feel bound to do, or forbear doing, carry inexplicable authority, reflective somehow of the encompassing mystery of being. This will not necessarily strike Christians as strange. People who strive, without pride, to meet the responsibilities they encounter in their historical and personal situations will, albeit unconsciously, encounter Christ—God's Word and mind, and the form of God's lordship in history.

The most dramatic expression of hope in the Bible is probably Jesus' proclamation that the kingdom of God is at hand. It is a puzzling utterance, however, for it seems to show that Jesus expected history to end within a few years or decades, and of course that didn't happen. Must we then set it aside—*that is, set aside Christ's main words on hope*—as based on an illusory historical perspective? That is doubtful. As I have already argued, authentic hope looks beyond history and anticipates eternal life; but to envision the coming of eternal life as a purely historical event, having a date like other historical events, reduces eternity to temporal terms and measures. This suggests that Jesus did not mean, in proclaiming the imminence of the kingdom of God, that it was coming soon, for "soon" would place the eschaton

in historical time. But if Jesus' proclamation does not foretell an imminent historical event, what is it all about?

To speak first in the broadest terms, it obviously expresses God's purpose
in history, that of recreating sinful humanity and effecting the definitive triumph,
in spite of all evil, of God's original creative intent. In Isaiah's concise formula, the
divine purpose is the creation of "new heavens and a new earth." Although we
cannot objectively comprehend the fulfillment of this purpose, nothing else concerns us as deeply, unceasingly, and unconditionally. Everything else in our lives
and surroundings has reality and significance only insofar as it is validated by that
purpose. In other words, we must view our lives and circumstances as relativized
by a mystery surpassing our powers of rational comprehension and literal speech,
yet having an all-determining relationship to everything we do and suffer and
think. Still, why should Jesus proclaim God's ultimate purpose as though its fulfillment were imminent?

The answer, surely, is because that purpose, here and now, is our supreme concern. We cannot say *when* that purpose will be realized for doing that would place
it in a temporal framework. If we say *soon,* eternity is subordinated to time. But the
same thing happens if we say *later on.* We enclose in a temporal framework personal and historical lives which lead into eternity. Yet, refusing to situate the kingdom of God in time, we must fix our minds upon it with the same undivided and
unqualified interest we would feel if we knew it would be upon us before the sun
goes down. We are not permitted to separate ourselves from the kingdom of God
by establishing a comfortable interval—of, say, a thousand years, or even a hundred
years—between ourselves and its onset.

These comments are in part simply reminders of the point and necessity of
situational obedience. Impending over our lives, the kingdom of God allows us
neither to idealize nor to escape from the worldly circumstances surrounding us.
Out of loyalty to our ultimate communal destiny, we must inhabit them faithfully
and lucidly. This means adhering to the transcendental standards inherent in the
idea of the kingdom of God: cherishing the truth in all of its various forms; and regarding every other human being as a fellow citizen—as one destined to share the
truth in an everlasting community, and as thereby ennobled and brought near to us
in our worldly exile and our common destiny. And it means doing this with attention to the temporal conditions in which such standards must be carried out.

In reminding us of the point and necessity of situational obedience, however, Jesus' proclamation calls forth the spirit without which such obedience is
mere worldliness and despair. It calls forth attentiveness. We must be watchful
and prayerful, alert to a happening which will set at nought all anticipations and
precautions—an event that will come like a thief in the night. Since we cannot con-

ceptualize the coming of the kingdom of God, however, neither can we control it. We can only wait for it, thinking of it as an imminent possibility. All of this is inherent in the mystery of hope. The universe must not be treated as a city in which human beings are masters. It is more in the nature of a desert open to the sun and wind—open to the light of eternity and the power of the Holy Spirit. It is where, in hope, we wait for God.

My argument in this section is simply that by heeding the necessities imposed by our personal and historical circumstances, we live in obedience to destiny; and in doing this we live according to the limited measure of hope normally allotted us. God wills in Christ a gathering together of all creation in the divine presence. This purpose is written into the whole course of history, both as its climax and as the hidden meaning of every occurrence; it is written also into the course of every individual's life. All circumstances and happenings, however absurd or unbearable they may seem at the moment, will serve God's ends. Hence we who have lived in the twentieth century will see that the numberless millions of lives lost in political atrocities and needless wars were not wasted. And we will see that the lives we carried on, in responding to the requirements of our personal and common situations, were not without meaning.

---────────── ❧ chapter three ☙ ──────────

THE SPIRITUALITY OF HOPE

T he spirituality of hope consists, as I understand it, in disciplines calculated
to call forth hope. It is attempting to attain the exaltation of hope in its
fullness and to keep alive and fan into flames the spark of hope that remains when
hope has become obedience. This can only be done, since hope is directed ultimately toward God, by cultivating love for God. Such love takes on life in various
ways. It does so through faith and through love for other human beings, for example, and the spirituality of hope therefore consists partly in cultivating faith and
love; God is sought through prayer, philosophy, and meditation and these accordingly have a place among the spiritual disciplines which nurture hope; those who
love God are often challenged by a past that seems to demonstrate the power-
lessness or malice of God and thus are moved to acts of remembrance that strive to
perceive the past as providential; and since suffering seems to signify divine neglect, and death to foreclose every ultimate hope, those who love God and struggle
toward hope inevitably try to understand suffering and death as gateways to the
kingdom of God. These are the main tasks involved in cultivating hope.

The first question we encounter in taking up the spirituality of hope concerns its proper setting. By setting I mean human context, or social environment—
church, hermitage, monastery. But need we ask about social setting? Can't spirituality be carried on in solitude? Indeed, isn't spirituality essentially solitary?

Solitude, Church, Dialogue

Spirituality no doubt always has a solitary aspect. This can be seen in the main
forms of the spirituality of hope. The faith that links one with God is apt to be

experienced as intimately personal, so that we speak of *my* God and *your* God; likewise, love for another person is my love, or your love, and not anyone else's. As for prayer, someone who prayed always with others and never alone would hardly know prayer; and a philosopher incapable of solitude is very nearly a contradiction in terms. Remembrance is sometimes collective, as when a nation commemorates a significant event in its past or a scholar writes the history of a people; yet with every individual, remembrance takes the form of singular personal reminiscence. Suffering typically sets one apart from others, for even suffering that is owing to some common condition, such as war or famine, still belongs poignantly to the sufferer in a way that it belongs to no one else. Finally, concerning death, it is a commonplace, but nonetheless true, that one dies alone; the sense of mortality underlying all serious spirituality therefore brings an atmosphere of solitude into all spiritual activities. Social thought in our time is pervasively hostile to individualism. Such hostility is in some ways justified, for it is not the destiny of any individual to be forever alone. In our fallenness, however, we are very often alone, and this is seen in the fact that our major spiritual experiences occur deeply within us and cannot be easily or completely shared.

The solitude inherent in spirituality derives partly from the element of personal responsibility that is central in all spiritual efforts. Solitary resolution and sustained exertion are indispensable. Whether I live compassionately, prayerfully, thoughtfully, and so forth is decided largely by my own choices; even how I suffer and die depends in some measure on my own choices. Since a society is organized mainly for meeting economic and military needs it is not the kind of entity that can relieve a person of spiritual responsibilities. As Aristotle noted, even though the ultimate aim of society is the *good* life, its immediate aim is mere life. This is an intensely practical aim, requiring practical intelligence. Political philosophies which stress the spiritual character of the social order risk obscuring the stubbornly expediential and impersonal qualities which inevitably attach themselves to any working society. These force on every spiritually-serious person a measure of withdrawal.

But isn't withdrawal in conflict with spirituality? Or, to ask the same question in another way, isn't spirituality essentially communal—situated in a context of truth-seeking relationships with other people? The answer to these questions is not in doubt: it is affirmative. Spirituality cannot be destructive of true relationships—of love and shared truth. It must be in some way communal. What this tells us, however, is not that spirituality bars solitude but that solitude, paradoxically, is a communal state.

The withdrawal required by the imperative of solitude is not from community but from society. It is *for the sake of* community and is *from* society insofar as society is impersonal, hence obstructive of community. You are forced, so to speak, to be communal alone. Dwelling in true solitude, then, means sustaining a readiness for communication—continually attentive, and ready to speak. If the true purpose of solitude is forgotten, however, what people refer to as "solitude" will become mere indulgence in the pleasures of a seemingly-impregnable private world. Such a state as that might better be called "self-absorption" or "disengagement" than "solitude."

The communality of solitude is a principle highly relevant to the state of society in the twentieth century. We are lured from all sides into forms of social unity, such as business organizations, governmental bureaucracies, and common diversions like those offered on television. Supposedly these are participatory and communal. But in fact, by habituating us to impersonal relationships and the pursuit of unspiritual purposes, they incapacitate us for authentic communication. They are not communal but merely social. They are sometimes designated, in their all-pervasive and alluring impersonality, by a term already discussed: "mass society." Anyone pursuing the spirituality of hope in our time is forced to stand apart from mass society and to nurture the solitary communality in which spirituality is possible.

Still, solitude is only an earthly necessity and not an absolute good. The one absolute good is God, hence the enjoyment of God and of God's creation in perfect and eternal communion. Only because of the rarity and ephemerality of such communion on earth is solitude necessary. It is an earthly expedient, not an eschatological goal.

Moreover, since solitude is communal it normally requires, along with a certain critical detachment from society, a continuing involvement in society. Solitude cannot be equated with isolation. Someone sentenced to solitary confinement might be able to sustain a communal spirit, but no one with a communal spirit would choose solitary confinement. Communality consists in trying to transform merely social into truly communal relationships. Hence a communal person, while maintaining a habit of withdrawal and solitude, must struggle for community— and for the spirituality at the center of community—in a setting of more or less anticommunal social relationships. Yet some social relationships are far more anticommunal than others. Where the established social order is supported by rigid prejudice or tyrannical force, for example, communality and spirituality have few opportunities. Thus the traditional concern of Christians for the social setting of spirituality is appropriate.

In granting this we immediately confront a noteworthy fact—that there is and always has been a consensus among Christians as to the requisite setting for spirituality. That setting is the Church. (The initial capital is used to recognize the Christian conviction that the churches are not merely diverse, humanly-authored organizations but in some way representative of a single, divinely-ordained community.) There have been Christians, such as Kierkegaard, who held the Church, or at least the churches of a particular time and place, in disdain. But not many. There is a two-thousand-year-old consensus that the Word of God requires a common response and that the required response, organized and sustained through time, is the Church. To be a Christian, this implies, depends on being a member of the Church, and Christian spirituality cannot properly be pursued apart from the Church.

The Church often fails so conspicuously to be what it ought to be that the image brought to many minds when they hear the word may be rather inglorious. Hence we should note that "Church," for Christians, is a way of saying "humankind"—in all of its global scope and divine depths. Secular discourse has perhaps come nearest to it in the idea of the human race united, not by a common faith, but by the moral integrity inherent in uncorrupted human nature. The vision here is of sheer humanity, unlimited in quality or range. From a Christian standpoint, such a vision is unrealistic, for there is no uncorrupted humanity. Yet it is clear that the concept of humanity as a single moral entity is meaningful for many people. Among these, as shown in the history of such organizations as the United Nations, are idealists of various races, nationalities, and religions. Among them also are figures of great moral and intellectual stature, such as Marcus Aurelius in ancient times and Kant in modern times. For such minds humankind is, or can be, a very real moral commonwealth. Their difference from Christians may be succinctly expressed by saying that they envision this commonwealth as lying within the scope of human powers. For Christians, however, since there is no uncorrupted human nature, the human commonwealth can be realized only through a divine act of redemption. Humanity in its purity is founded on grace and on faith. Eschatologically, it is the kingdom of God, historically the Church.

More precisely, the Church is the kingdom of God in the making. This, too, is a nearly universal tenet of faith among Christians. The Church is humanity undergoing purification through the ordeals of historical existence. It represents, within history, the end of history. Hence the Church is the natural realm of hope, the social and historical setting in which hope is most appropriately cultivated and lived. The spirituality of hope, and the solitude it inevitably entails, must be in some sense centered in the Church.

The communality implied by this definition deserves particular attention. If the Church measured up to the standard of its eschatological destiny, it would be a perfect community. This destiny of course is beyond earthly and historical fulfillment. Christian faith confers no immunity from sin or from the disorder and mutual estrangement effected by sin. The Church therefore has always been not a community but a society, or rather a cluster of societies, where, at best, communality has exceptional opportunities. For Christians the standard of community, emanating from the ordained end of life, the kingdom of God, carries powerful and unceasing authority. But a community is not merely a well-ordered collection of human beings; rather, it is that which comes into being when humans engage together in the difficult work of truth-seeking communication. Hence members of the Church must struggle continually to speak to one another, inquiringly, of the most serious matters, that is, of ultimate truth. For Christians, of course, that truth is God, and the Church, accordingly, is where human beings, brought together and guided by faith, engage together in a dialogical search for God.

The word "dialogue" is nearly worn-out through overuse. Nonetheless, with its intimations both of our highest concern—the Truth, or God—and of face-to-face relations, it is irreplaceable. Its value here is not to point out something new, but rather to bring to a focus themes discussed throughout this essay, such as community, communication, and the fusion of universality and particularity in the neighbor. The significance of the term in the present context is that it enables us to envision the Church as a living and personal association. In calling the Church "dialogical," I mean only to say that its essence is realized in that peculiarly difficult and significant task of bringing to life ultimate truth in a setting of face-to-face relationships—or, alternatively, realizing the plenitude of personal communion through common inquiry into ultimate truth. Often, of course, the Church is thought of, even by its own members, quite differently—most often, perhaps, as a dogmatic, rather than dialogic, association. I will try to show, further along in this section, why that is an oversimplification, if not a complete misconception.

In the light of this broad definition of the Church, we can see three imperatives bearing on it, each essential to the spirituality of hope, each therefore deserving brief comment.

(1) *Universality.* If the Church is a symbol of humanity as a single and perfect community, the imperative of universality is inescapable. There should be only one Church (just as there should be only one all-embracing human commonwealth) and all human beings should be within it; this, at least, is a standard which humans should strive, against their own limitations, to realize. The Church should reflect the universality of Christian truth (and of all truth) and the all-inclusiveness of Christian love (and of all love). Hence the diversity of Christian denominations is anything but a delightful reflection of the diversity of human personalities and types. From a Christian standpoint, it is a grievous failure, and the fragmentation of the Church brought about by the Reformation, and reaching its extremes in America, is an immense historical tragedy. This is not to imply that the Reformation should never have occurred and that ecclesiastical unity ought to override every other imperative. Human failures on the part of the Church have at times been so flagrant that the heterogeneity of the churches cannot be *a priori* condemned. There may be times when the ideal of universal community in the truth can be more nearly approached through disparate ecclesiastical groupings rather than through

one grouping alone. Nonetheless, ecclesiastical diversity is not a matter for celebration.

The ideal of a single, all-embracing Church is dictated ultimately, as Christians see it, by the oneness and sovereignty of God. God's address to the human race in Christ is single and undivided, and it claims the attention of all times and places. No one who hears it can legitimately claim that it commands multiple interpretations or that it can properly be ignored by those who find it uninteresting. Divine revelation calls for a single, inerrant human response. Yet the Christian doctrine of human fallenness tells us that such a response is unlikely to occur and, if it does, is a sign of divine grace rather than human wisdom. Hence the unity and sweep of the Church not only are commanded by God but, so far as they are realized, are called forth by God. The kingdom of God is so named because God, not man, is its creative source. Correspondingly, the Church, as an earthly analogue to the kingdom of God, is a divine, rather than merely human, order.

The concept of the Church would be completely misunderstood, however, were it forgotten that all love, hence all spiritually-significant truth-speaking, is face-to-face. This is implicit in Jesus' command that you must love, not the human race generally, but your neighbor. There is, of course, a likeness of universal love when someone lives with a readiness to recognize anyone he encounters as a neighbor; and there is a likeness of universal truth-speaking when someone writes a book or article which is published for all to read. But in both cases there is—until the neighbor is actually encountered—an insufficiency. Only when universality is fused with particularity, is love fully realized and truth not merely offered but grasped. The Church is real and alive, then, insofar as it consists of neighbors.

To say this is not to compromise the standard of universality. All-inclusiveness is vital to the Christian idea of the Church. And in the world at large, the technological acceleration of travel and communication has created a global consciousness unprecedented in history. This is surely not without value; there exists a new kind of human self-awareness. But what might be called the Athenian instinct, which led members of the Attic city twenty-five hundred years ago to fight stubbornly against Persian universality, and Plato to prefer face-to-face conversation to writing, retains a fundamental validity. The future of the Western world may depend on its ability to fuse its ever-expanding technological universality with the neighborliness so valued in ancient times. And the response of the Church to this issue may be more decisive, for the world as a whole, than that of any other grouping.

Universality, however, even when realized through particularity, does not suffice to define the ideal of community represented by the Church. All of us know that personal relationships founded on false understandings are worthless. In like fashion, universality without truth would be empty, a form without substance. This brings us to the second mark of the Church.

(2) *Truthfulness*. The Church is the one worldly organization concerned unreservedly with the supreme truth and the whole truth. All other organizations aim at lesser truths and at fragments of the truth—at truths defined in accordance with particular perspectives and particular functions. The academic disciplines all illustrate the search for parts of the whole truth. Granted, a university, by embracing all of the disciplines, concerns itself with a wide range of truths; but it has no way of unifying the diverse truths it reaches. The state has sometimes been viewed (for example, by Plato and Aristotle) as properly a servant of the highest and most comprehensive truth. But such a view is insufficiently attentive to the unavoidable distortions of insight that follow from the state's responsibility for order and its consequent involvement in the use of violence and deception. Every organization designed for a particular kind of action, such as manufacturing, or trade, or the acquirement of power, seeks truth; but it seeks only the truth which serves its practical interests. The Church is the one human grouping that seeks above all else to comprehend and voice, in its unity and depth, the one Truth that underlies and gives significance to all worldly truths.

This proposition needs one vital qualification, however. We have already noted Paul's claim that no human act, such as faith or self-sacrifice, has any value if unaccompanied by love. If Paul is right, then unless truth is spoken in love, it might as well not be spoken at all. It is love that renders truth-speaking a bond of community rather than the mere common objectivity which might be achieved, say, by a group of physical scientists, caring little for one another personally, but bound together by a particular methodology, along with the results of its application. If the truth needs to be spoken in love, however, let us remember the converse—that love needs to be expressed in the speaking of truth; otherwise, it is mere sentimentality. A love-relationship in which there is no effort to reach and share the truth necessarily reduces the stature of its participants, for they are not envisioned in relation to the absolute. If the Church is the one place on earth where the whole truth is sought, then it is also the one place where, within earthly limits, love can be fully realized and humans can reach their full stature.

The search for truth, among Christians, has traditionally entailed a concern for sound doctrine. Truthfulness, accordingly, has meant doctrinal responsibility. In our own time, concern for doctrine has seemingly declined; it is common for writers to insist on the relativity and inadequacy of doctrinal professions. Words, it is held, cannot capture reality. In some sense, this is certainly the case. Knowing the words that make up a true proposition is not the same thing in most circumstances as knowing the reality to which the proposition refers. And it can happen, even, that words—true words—obscure reality; hence Paul's declaration that the letter kills, while the spirit gives life. Still, only through the careful use of words can we search for the truth and give the truth, once found, some kind of permanent lodging in our minds. Moreover, the truth for which we search—beyond all human words—is still a word: the divine Word spoken, Christians believe, in Christ. The Christian concept of the Word points toward the power and dignity of words. It suggests that the inadequacy of human words is owing to our fallenness and that words will at last, in the kingdom of God, recover their pristine force—the force they had when God on the first six days named the light, the firmament, the sea, and the other things he created. It suggests also that even within the world, grace may allow some of our words to draw on the primal truth and power of the Word. Hence, to use words with care, and to formulate doctrines that can serve as repositories of truth, has an indispensable part in the human response to divine revelation.

Doctrinal responsibility obviously requires institutions vested with authority to define doctrine and ability to do so truly and persuasively. From this standpoint, the Catholic Church is unquestionably the most successful of the churches in the world today. Doctrinal responsibility requires something more than authority, however, and that is free and vital inquiry. In view of the inherent limitations of human words, as well as the fallibility of all human authority, discussing doctrine is of no less importance than defining and guarding it. This brings us back to the subject of dialogue.

To say that dialogue has a role in the life of the Church is not to thrust an alien, hellenic element into Christianity. The Greek ideal of dialogue, pioneered by Socrates and dramatized by Plato, affirms an activity deeply consonant with the religion of the Word. This is confirmed by the part that dialogue played, through questions and disputations, in so Christian a setting as the medieval university. The presence of God in Christ and, through Christ—through whom all things were made—in all creation, are mysteries which Christians must ponder again and again. The mystery of Christian truth imposes an obligation of ceaseless reconsideration. No doubt such reconsideration places truth in peril; dialogue is dangerous. It may be that here on earth, however, there is something almost as good as rejoicing in the truth—in the limited degree to which we can possess it—and that is poignantly missing and longing for the truth we do not possess. In the Bible this is called poverty of spirit. Here one is related to the truth in humility and readiness of mind rather than in mastery. Christian poverty of spirit is akin to the "ignorance" which Socrates confessed throughout a life of dialogue. Both mysteriously fuse knowing and not knowing the truth and in that way seemingly belong to our relations with transcendence—reality simultaneously calling for and eluding understanding.

Dialogue realizes the marriage of universality and particularity which is required by the concept of love for one's neighbor. The universality of dialogue lies in its orientation toward the truth as such. Dialogue aspires to truth that is true not merely for the interlocutors but for everyone. At the same time a dialogue is by definition an interpersonal exchange. By being dialogic, then, the Church cares for doctrine and at the same time resists dogma—meaning by this term abstractions which obliterate people's faces and give rise to coercion. Dialogue renders truth a medium of authentic communication and thus creates community.

Dialogue is the form not only of community, however, but also of solitude. This proposition will not surprise anyone bearing in mind the communality of solitude. Authentic solitude, as we have already seen, is a matter, not simply of being apart from others, but also of being attentive to others and ready to speak. The most important activity carried out in solitude is inquiry into the truth, and inquiry is carried on through inner conversations—through putting questions to oneself and trying to answer them. A dialogic Church, accordingly, is the most appropriate possible setting for solitude.

The ideal of the doctrinally-responsible and dialogical Church, translated into secular terms, is that of humankind united in the truth. For secular minds, the goal of bringing all human beings together through reason is no less meaningful than the goal of uniting them in their moral integrity. The progress of physical science in modern times has made all of us familiar with the notion of humanity as a truth-seeking entity. Even doctrinal responsibility is not an exclusively theological concept. Science seeks formulae which are acceptable to all nations and races, and in the science faculties of universities it raises up authorities responsible for the adequacy of these formulae. In short, secular minds can think of humanity as a noetic, as well as moral, entity, and derive from that concept a secular definition of hope. Seen from a Christian perspective, secular hope of this kind lacks adequate grounding, for truth that is altogether secular is bound to be incomplete and uncertain. The point I am making, however, is that when Christians speak to the world of the hope they attach to the truth inherent in the Word of God, they are not speaking in a wholly foreign tongue. Even those who reject Christ may be able to hear and in some degree to understand them.

Perhaps there will be neither doctrines nor dialogue in the kingdom of God. The truth may then be fully apprehended in an immediate vision of the Lord and Source of all reality. On earth, however, just as the universality of the Church is an eschatological characteristic, so defining and discussing doctrines is an eschatological activity. For this reason, doctrinal responsibility and dialogue—in a word, truthfulness—sustain hope and contribute to a setting in which the spirituality of hope can be advantageously pursued. Like the imperfect universality of the Church, the imperfect doctrines of the Church cast our minds ahead—to a time in which human words and God's Word will perfectly coincide. Within history, however, there is truth beyond doctrine, and therefore the Church must move beyond words. It does this by means of wordless pathways to ultimate reality, pathways which have been trodden since the earliest Christian ages. These are called sacraments.

(3) *Sacramentality.* John set forth the core of Christian faith when he declared that the Word was made flesh. God became incarnate in a man, Jesus of Nazareth. No proposition or set of propositions can fully convey this truth. The doctrines that try to do so—the Trinity and the dual nature of Christ—cannot be taken altogether literally, although their importance to Christian faith, and even to the entire human race, can hardly be overstated. Both are internally contradictory, one asserting that God is at once three and one, the other that Christ is at once God and man. Hence Christians must look beyond doctrines. The Church must be not purely and simply a doctrinal and dialogical association but also an incarnational association. What does this mean?

As thoroughly, even exclusively, Christian as the concept of the Incarnation sounds, the hope that arises from it is not incomprehensible to secular minds. During World War II it happened that one of the Japanese internment camps was placed in a high desert setting of great natural beauty. The photographer Ansel Adams visited and photographed the camp and its environs and later remarked that he believed that "the arid splendor of the desert, ringed by towering mountains," strengthened the spirit of prisoners in the camp. This remark expressed incarnational insight of a kind that is available to all of us entirely apart from explicit religious faith. No doctrinal commitments are necessary in order to sense in natural grandeur intimations of an unstated meaning pervading all of reality. Such insight may be gained not only from natural but also from artistic beauty; Georges Sand reportedly heard God in the music of Chopin. And there is incarnational insight in love for a human being and the consequent wonder of a particular human countenance. In all such instances we discern in a concrete, physical entity—a mountain, a work of art, a human face—a significance which seems limitless and, inexpressible. We perceive something sublime and immaterial in a material reality, and when this happens, our spirits are strengthened. This strengthening comes as a capacity for living into an unknown future, that is, as hope.

The Christian attitude toward Christ and the Incarnation is not entirely unlike Adams's attitude toward "the arid splendor of the desert, ringed by towering mountains." A meaning irreducible to words is seen in a visible, palpable reality—in a man. The Christian attitude is not adequately described, however, by saying that Christ is seen as an incarnational reality. Christ is the final and definitive incarnational reality, that is, the ultimate spiritual reality, God, fully and eternally present in an earthly reality. That this is so does not result from human initiative, nor that it is known from human insight. It is a work of God, made known by God. Christian revelation takes the form, not of secrets whispered in the human heart, but of a divine act of physical self-embodiment. Christian faith does not necessarily condemn the incarnational insight of non-Christians, such as Ansel Adams, but claims only that what has been glimpsed, perhaps in desert light or a piano sonata, is Christ, the Logos.

The sacraments, and preeminently the Eucharist, express the Christian understanding of Christ as the definitive incarnational being. They do this not only by pointing symbolically toward Christ but also by employing as their symbols immediate, sensual realities—water, bread, wine—which are also viewed as incarnational; Christ is in some way within them. When a baptism is performed, or the Eucharist celebrated, those taking part relate themselves, through things we can touch and taste, to the ultimate meaning of all life and history. Even to some Christians such an act seems unreasonable. To be unreasonable, however, may be said to be the point of the act. In celebrating the Eucharist, Christians acknowledge the encompassing mystery which human reason cannot reach. In other words, Christian practice implies that doctrine and dialogue are not enough. Once the teaching has been done and the sermons delivered, one thing more is needed: recognition that our words are earthen vessels and that ultimate truth is higher than the highest human truths.

The hope inherent in the sacraments is evident in the light that the Eucharist casts on the greatest threat to hope, that is, death. Ordained by Jesus on the eve of his crucifixion, the bread and wine are reminders of death. At the same time, however, since the Crucifixion was followed by the Resurrection, they are reminders of life. The bread and wine tell us that the full and glorious life of a person's eternal body, represented by the risen Christ, is gained only by giving up to God the deficient and inglorious life of the temporal body. The celebration of the Eucharist is in its own way for Christians what philosophical reflection is, according to Plato, for philosophers—preparation for dying. Hence the tie between sacramentality and hope. To be prepared for dying, as understood by Plato and by Christians as well, is to be fully cognizant of eternity and thus quickened, rather than intimidated, by the ultimate future.

We can legitimately imagine a sacramental life, a life animated by hope and carried on in a way that sustains and increases this hope. Such a life would be filled with concern for the sacramental realities surrounding us—for the glories of light and sky, desert and mountains, sea and forest; also for the splendors of art, science, and philosophy; and in particular (since love is "the greatest of these") for the incomprehensible sanctity of beloved faces. This would be a life that might, in some measure, be lived by people of secular persuasion. For Christians, however, it would be centered on the eating of bread and drinking of wine in accordance with ritual forms calculated to invest these acts with their full spiritual significance. A sacramental life would be physical in a far more complete and fundamental way than the life of the most dedicated hedonist but would, at the same time, be thoroughly spiritual. It would also be eschatological. Physical realities would be experienced as promises of eternity and thus as hopeful in every detail.

To summarize, by virtue of universality, truthfulness, and sacramentality the Church is an earthly analogue to the ultimate human destination, the perfect community called by Christians the kingdom of God. The Church stands on earth as the purpose of all history—a community all-inclusive, all-knowing, and in all aspects beautiful. It provides in this way the spiritual environment for hope. It is where human beings, in the measure of their faith, live into the future.

To understand a person's relations with the Church, however, it is vital to remember the difference between essence and actuality. Hope for the kingdom of heaven relativizes all institutions, and among these it relativizes the Church. It compels Christians to look on the churches critically and to support them only conditionally. Private judgment in religious matters is not merely a right which some, such as Martin Luther, have been bold enough to claim. It is a burdensome obligation, forced upon every Christian by the imperfection of the churches. Like every human being, a Christian is set apart from all others by a separate mind and a separate will. In contemporary social thought, as we have noted, "individualism" has become a pejorative term. It might be argued, however, that individualism originates in God. Not only did God refrain from giving us a common mind and will; he did not elect to save us in groups. Salvation depends always on a personal commitment, and this commitment can cause one to be not only isolated and scorned but even killed. Each one alone must decide what is true and false, and right and wrong. Granted, the surrounding social order helps one do this; but the social order offers nothing that can take the place of personal resolution and effort. One of the major strains inherent in the life of faith lies in the lack of any absolutely reliable intermediary between an individual and God. A Church which assumed such a role would be an idol. Idolatry can be avoided only by those who are capable of solitude.

The very grandeur of the Church, an eschatological rather than earthly attribute, is a temptation to idolatry. This is powerfully brought out in Dostoevsky's tale of the Grand Inquisitor. The Church is made into an earthly enclave where there is no insecurity, economic or spiritual. It is a source of unfailing bread, indubitable truth, and "miracles"—spectacles rendering faith virtually automatic. In short, the Church becomes a world—a detailed and self-contained order that is economic, spiritual, and political all at the same time—a goal the modern totalitarian state has come near to reaching. In the Biblical story of Jesus' rejection of the temptations in the wilderness (the scriptural source of the Legend of the Grand Inquisitor), however, it is implied that Christian destiny entails the physical and spiritual insecurity inherent in solitary responsibility. This destiny is lived only by being on guard against the worldliness of the churches—a worldliness manifest not only in the hedonism and material greed of prelates (although it has often enough been manifest in this form) but also in the pretense of providing an absolutely reliable order of life, where individuals need not trouble themselves with what they believe or how they should live but need only conform.

Solitude must in some sense have the last word. Inherent in the dialectic of hope is the necessity of accepting—even within the Church—the alienation inherent in our fallenness. When we do this in full awareness that alienation is not our final goal, but rather a part of the crucifixion we must undergo in order to be raised into the life of true community, we enter into the dialectic of human destiny. Within history, we live toward the end of history.

We can fittingly begin our consideration of the substance of the spirituality of hope by discussing the relationship of hope to the other two members of the traditional triad of Christian virtues—faith and love. That faith in some way underlies hope is immediately manifest, for faith is one's primary bond with God. But love too is in some way more basic than hope, as is indicated by Paul's declaration that love is the greatest of the three virtues. The cultivation of faith and love, it seems, must have a major part in the cultivation of hope.

Faith and Love

These two classical Christian virtues (the love we are concerned with here is primarily that for one's fellow humans) are not separate topics; they are two constituents of a single state of mind, and neither can be maintained apart from the other. This, at least, is true of Christian faith and Christian love. Love for human beings—others and self—is nothing other than recognizing that they have been created and redeemed by God. If you have no faith that this has happened, you have no capacity for love. Granted, people without explicit faith may in some measure love one another; but their love is incipient faith, and is necessarily frail and unstable until it is consciously grounded in faith. We testify to our faith, then, through care for our neighbors. On the other hand, if such care is lacking, we show forth the infirmity of our faith. Thus, while faith is presupposed in love, it is dependent on love: unexpressed in care for the neighbor it is bound to wither and die. It will be convenient, in the following pages, to discuss faith and love separately. But doing this will imperil true understanding unless we bear in mind their essential unity.

The question of how faith and love can be cultivated appears to be simple, yet it is somewhat disconcerting, for as soon as we begin to reflect on it we realize that while these virtues underlie hope and all the decencies of life, we cannot deliberately call them into being. Either they are given to us or we do not have them. When it comes to the ultimate grounds of our lives, it seems, we are not in control. Is there, then, nothing we can do? That does not quite follow, although we must recognize that no human efforts to approach God have sure results. Faith and love

are given by grace, and grace has no source but God. The very word implies gratu-
itousness. Nonetheless, it is a vital truth pertaining to both faith and love that even
though they are given by grace, human will has a role in their acquisition. Let us
begin by seeing how this applies to faith.

William James, as everyone knows, wrote of "the will to believe," thus seeming
to suggest that we can acquire faith deliberately. This sounds all wrong, for surely
faith that is willed is a mere human contrivance, without spiritual value. Yet Christian experience shows beyond serious question that the will to believe does play
a part in overcoming doubt and attaining faith. While Kierkegaard encouraged
an exaggerated emphasis on the spiritual power of will, when he gave currency to
the idea of a "leap of faith," he did not altogether falsify the realities. The key point
is that freedom and grace are not mutually exclusive. Rather, they mysteriously
coalesce. Hence the divine gift of belief and the human will to believe may fuse in
a single inward state. It scarcely needs to be said that the will to believe is not an act
of sheer choice, to be made at any moment personal caprice may light on; the possibility of willing to believe cannot itself be willed. Yet, when faith is beleaguered by
doubt, one may discover—*through grace*—one's own free engagement in the cause
of faith.

The nature of this engagement can be clarified by returning to a matter already
touched on—the relationship of faith in God and love for God. On the one hand,
that these are not quite the same is intuitively manifest even if it is hard to explain. On the other hand, they cannot be separated; love for God without faith in
God is inconceivable, while faith in God without love for God would be a poor affair, somehow lacking proper life and spirit. How, then, are they related? It is noteworthy that love for God is treated by Jesus, not as a passion which sweeps aside all
personal choices, thus engulfing human freedom, but as a command of God. The
"first and great commandment" is that you "love the Lord your God with all your
heart, and with all your soul, and with all your mind." (Matthew 22:37–38 RSV)
This is presumably the strongest possible claim on one particular personal choice:
that of God. I suggest that this claim is met through faith. If this hypothesis is valid,
then faith in God is obedience to Jesus' command. Although love for God is given
by grace, God's power and man's freedom come together in the faith in which love
for God is embraced.

The voluntary element in faith is plainly seen in a form of faith that is very
nearly the same as faith itself. That is fidelity. Having faith in God is in part a matter
of being faithful to God. Martin Buber sharply criticized Christianity for reducing
faith to "faith that—."[1] It is questionable, however, whether Christianity necessarily

---

[1] See Martin Buber, *Two Types of Faith*, trans. Norman P. Goldhawk (New York: Harper
& Row, 1961).

does this, although some Christians no doubt have. It is undeniable that adherence to particular doctrines ("faith that—") has an essential place in Christian life. But something more personal and less objective also has a place; fidelity is this personal and non-objective element. In holding to your faith, you not only affirm certain doctrines; you also remain faithful to God. A good example of the part fidelity plays in Christian life can be seen in the task of living one's destiny. The situational obedience through which this is done is a personal relationship with God, the author of destiny, and it has spiritual value only so far as it reflects fidelity to God. Thus a destiny may require someone to remain in a difficult and unvarying set of circumstances which bear no manifest relation to the merits or acts of the one who suffers from them. Only through fidelity to God can such a requirement be met without resentment or impatience.

Another form of faith, very much like faith in its essence, and showing forth the voluntary element in faith, is trust. Someone without faith in God could hardly trust in God. Trust is thus seemingly a manifestation of faith. Yet trust can in some measure be willed. You can *entrust* something to another person, and you can *entrust* yourself and your life to God. You can *place* your trust in God. Here, as always, freedom depends on grace; a capacity for trust must be given. But the capacity bears fruit in the ensuing act. As with fidelity and with faith itself, our dependence on grace does not entail sheer passivity. It is one of the paradoxes of divine-human relations that one can strive to do things which God alone can enable one—not only to do—but even to strive to do.

Faith can be cultivated simply by attending, in the right way, to the values we encounter in the world about us—truth, for example; or the good in any of its various forms, such as the moral law, and love among human beings; or beauty. All of these can awaken the religious consciousness that is consummated in faith. When, for example, we realize that truth must be sought and respected, regardless of whether it serves any human interest, we experience the presence in time of something eternal; when we find that a good act or a good person commands respect entirely apart from resulting benefits, we sense the appearance of the absolute in the realm of the conditional; and when we are moved by artistic or natural beauty we often, even normally, feel momentarily touched by a transcendent reality. It is easy, and not at all illogical, to conclude that each of these experiences arises from a single primal source of value, and this conclusion gives sustenance to faith.

The danger inherent in enjoying these values is that of idolatry. This would mean allowing the values to become ultimate, as though they were self-caused and self-contained, thus blocking, rather than opening up, the pathway to God. This danger is at its height with sensual values, such as eating and drinking. But it is present even in the cultivation of beauty (as shown in the existence of aesthetes) and in the search for truth (as manifest in atheistic scientists and philosophers). But we need not be ascetics to keep this danger at bay. Jesus was not an ascetic, and did not turn the wine into water. It is possible to love God's universe in a way that is tantamount to loving God.

Finally, we should note that faith can be sought through acts ordinarily seen as expressive of faith, such as liturgical participation, self-denial, and self-sacrificial service to those in need. These may seem basically different from acts such as entrusting oneself to God, since they entail bodily, hence fully voluntary, activities. They might be done without any faith whatever, whereas acts like trusting in God could not be willed without at least an iota of faith. That must be granted. Yet liturgical celebration and like acts would be meaningless if their performance involved no faith whatever; at the same time, they are essentially like acts of trust and fidelity in arising from deliberate choice, from will.

What does all of this tell us about cultivating faith, and through faith hope? Clearly, it specifies no reliable method for acquiring faith, for there can be no such method. Faith must be given to us. Our fundamental relationship to faith can only be one of receptivity. We can only live in readiness for faith and for the hope that arises from faith. And even to do that we are in need of grace and of the spark of faith which is given by grace. We now can see, however, that weakness of faith need not entail blank apathy. Faith is a rich and complex state of mind. It comprises fidelity to God, trust in God, and care for values. It entails activities, such as liturgical participation, which might open the way to deeper faith. In contemplating such acts we see that faith partakes of freedom, even though it cannot be chosen on a whim. Hence, even though faith depends on grace, preparing and waiting for faith-bearing grace—*through grace*—can be as rich and complex an attitude as faith itself.

Closely linked with the cultivation of faith is what is often called the problem of theodicy. A theodicy, of course, is a justification of God's ways, and the problem of theodicy is mainly that of explaining how, in view of the massive and numberless evils afflicting the human race, it is possible to believe in a benign and omnipotent God. How can faith be anything but defiance of reason? The problem is introduced here, not to propound or even suggest a solution, but to note that sound faith depends on handling the problem with discretion. The need for discretion arises from two closely-linked circumstances. One of these is that the problem of theodicy is humanly insoluble. If faith were conditional on an adequate theodicy, faith could not exist. It is not that an adequate theodicy cannot exist; presumably one exists in the mind of God. But human beings, in their finitude and moral fallenness, cannot comprehend God or justify his ways. Moreover, the claim to do so would dissolve God's mystery and transcendence. It would be the reduction of God to an object of human investigation and comprehension, and therefore blasphemous.

The other circumstance rendering discretion imperative is that the problem of theodicy is eminently worthy of attention in spite of its being an insidious temptation to intellectual pride and pretension. Theodicean reflections, *so long as they are unconcluded,* can illuminate our minds. They can furnish insights into matters they can never wholly explain. An example ready at hand lies in the glimpses of providence often afforded by the life of one attuned to the problem of theodicy. It is a common experience that evils we greatly fear sometimes turn out, when they come upon us, to mask a good we never anticipated. It is as though something governing the seemingly accidental course of daily affairs knows better than we do ourselves what we need and really want. Thus, while it would be impious to think we can fully understand the divine intent, it would also be impious to resign ourselves to total ignorance.

If there is one principle underlying both rules, and giving them proper balance, it is that God must be honored. On the one hand, God is not honored by those who set themselves up as judges of divine behavior. A human explanation of God is necessarily an exposition of the ways in which God serves established human purposes and ends; by no other standards can we understand him. The God of Christian faith, however, is the God whose definitive mark in history is the Cross. Established human purposes and ends are apt to be overturned. God is, to be sure, a God who brings us alive; but only after killing us—killing, that is, the selfish, dying creatures who falsely lay claim to our authentic humanity. God is duly honored, not when we see how he will solve all our problems, but only when we see that he is incomprehensibly greater even than problems which loom over us as too great to be solved.

On the other hand, God is not honored by those who ignore the power of God to enlighten us concerning matters we cannot on our own initiative decipher and who therefore ignore also the puzzles which faith puts before us. Such puzzles, making up the problem of theodicy, are not accidents that evaded divine providence, lying about like bits of refuse which God, busy with larger matters, never got around to cleaning up. They are divinely-authored invitations to think about ultimate matters and to open our minds to the light of grace. If the problem of theodicy is approached in the wrong way when faith is suspended pending a solution, it is approached in the right way when it is attacked *on the basis of faith.* This happens when one who sees no way of reconciling the scale of worldly evil with divine omnipotence and mercy, proceeds in spite of mountainous doubts to lay the problem before God and prayerfully reflect on it.

C. S. Lewis expressed skepticism regarding people who strike heroic poses and assert that only their own intellectual integrity keeps them from embracing a faith which deeply attracts them. He was surely right. It seems safe to say that few if any have allowed the problem of theodicy—except as a pretext—to block the road to faith. But those called to travel that road should beware of the way intellectual laziness can disguise itself as piety. Those who force themselves to think about things seemingly too big for the human mind may find their minds mysteriously enlarged. Enigmas of destiny, taken as providential instigations to reflection, may become sources of enrichment and strength for their faith.

Hope depends on our love for one another no less than it does on our faith in God. The link between love and hope, as we have already seen, is the perception of human beings, in their creation and redemption both, as God's handiwork. It is this perception that enables John to say that there is no fear in love and that perfect love casts out fear. (I John 4:18 RSV) John's statement may seem untrue, in that our worst fears are very often for those we love. Such fears, however, throw into question the quality of our love. The truth of the statement lies in the fact that authentic love means understanding the one who is loved as destined for the kingdom of God and thus, so to speak, placed by God beyond danger. Only through this understanding is the person loved seen in the context of divine mercy and redemption and thus seen fully and truly. In other words, loving someone means looking upon the one who is loved with hope—not with worldly hope, primarily, but with the hope implicit in the faith that human beings have been raised above the state of sin (that is, justified) by the crucifixion and resurrection of Christ. Love is an inkling of the eschaton. Hope is inscribed in its very essence. Love that is fearful and hopeless must in some way be love that fails to be love.

To understand how love can be cultivated, we must realize first of all that love is not, as so often indicated in romantic fiction and other forms of popular entertainment, mainly a spontaneous outpouring of emotion. Words like "obedience," "destiny," and "necessity," which have been prominent in our discussion and go far to define the context and character of love, carry strong connotations of constraint. Yet they are incongruous with the popular conception of love. Supposedly love is impassioned and wholly unconstrained. When we think in this way, however, we are not thinking of Christian love, which will be wholly unconstrained only in paradise. Here on earth real love, in more ways than one, is sober and disciplined.

This is partly because, as we have already seen, real love is not merely a connection with someone who attracts you strongly or inspires admiration. On the contrary, it may be with someone who is unappealing and less than admirable. Not that it has to be. The people most of us actually love will seem to us attractive and admirable, and that will not necessarily—*although it could*—detract from the value of our love. However, if love is for your *neighbor,* for anyone whom you happen to encounter, then whether someone is attractive or admirable is irrelevant. And if you love someone *because* the one loved is attractive and admirable, and for that reason alone, then your love falls short of the Biblical standard. This is not nearly so strained a view as it may seem to be at first glance. It is a common experience that love often begins with attraction (say, a man for a woman) or admiration (a friend for a friend) but readily survives the loss of beauty or the disclosure of moral defects. Love, ignited by the qualities of the one who is loved, often takes on in the normal course of development (more accurately, in the unfoldment of destiny) the universality of authentic love.

While love that is neighborly, and thus independent of the visible qualities of the person loved, is not an unfamiliar experience in everyday life, it is fully explicable only in terms of the divine act of justification accomplished on the Cross. As I argued earlier in this essay, justification, along with the sanctity implicit in justification, means exaltation and glorification: a finite and morally defective human being is tinted with the light of divine splendor. Love is seeing someone in this light. It is the esteem for human beings that necessarily follows from a recognition of the power and sweep of divine mercy. In the vision of the Cross, such esteem relativizes the natural qualities which repel or attract us. Repellent qualities thus are seen as forgiven and cast aside, attractive qualities as foreshadowings of sanctity. In sum, God through Christ makes us neighbors. Thus is authentic love made possible.

Once we realize that love is not primarily an inclination or a passion, we can begin to think of it in a way quite novel in a time so preoccupied as ours is with *feelings*. Love is a command. This is strongly emphasized in Kierkegaard's great *Works of Love*. We do not love certain people because our feelings compel us to or because we embrace the banal principle that love is necessary to our personal fulfillment. We love them because they are the people who happen to be in our lives—our neighbors—and we are commanded to love our neighbors as ourselves. In a word, love exemplifies situational obedience. Our neighbors are sharers in the circumstances in which destiny has placed us. This does not imply that love is without feeling but only that the feeling which characterizes our love has to be understood as a gift by which grace enables us to obey the divine command. Failure to love, then, is not, as we are so often told, neglecting the requirements of our own happiness; at least it is not that primarily. It is morally wrong. Real love has a stern and constraining aspect, and is not romantic.

Love, then, is for all the particular people—sometimes abrasive, sometimes dull, sometimes threatening, sometimes merely perplexing—whom we find around us, rather than for ideal people or for abstract qualities like goodness and wisdom which it is so easy (because of their abstract perfection and their freedom from the palpable and repellent imperfections of physically-present people) to think that we love. This is to say that just as love is not romantic neither is it erotic, in the sense of being a striving toward absolute beauty and goodness, as Plato conceived it to be. Christianity does not absolutely condemn *eros*, nor is it indifferent to the general qualities that call forth erotic love. All such qualities, however, must be understood as aspects of the sanctity which, through Christ, is inscribed in the destiny of every human being. *Eros,* accordingly, is subordinated to *agape,* to the universality of neighborly love. In other words, love is placed under the authority of faith and is not allowed to be the discriminating and exclusionary evaluation of human beings which it was in the philosophy of Plato. It is a relationship to which the adjective "obedient" can be readily applied.

If love in its very essence places us under moral necessities, in its daily re-alization it entangles us in practical necessities. Love enmeshes us in the web of circumstances which is the context of every human life. Again, we see love as ex-emplifying situational obedience. Entirely apart from love, practical circumstances such as having little money may severely limit the possibilities before us. But these possibilities would immediately multiply and expand if we were able suddenly to divest ourselves of all the obligations inherent in love. For most people it is love—for spouse, parent, or friends, and often for all of these—that fixes them within a certain situation and requires submission to the circumstances constituting the situation.

Now we can see more fully than we could at the outset why love is essential to hope. The principle that love is eschatological, that it envisions those loved as members of a divine commonwealth, was brought out in the preceding chapter. In the present chapter, we see that love engages us in the destiny leading us into that commonwealth. It is the necessities of a situation—necessities at once moral and practical—which place one in a destiny and determine what the living of that des-tiny requires. These necessities are reducible to the bonds of love. If one were free of these bonds, the constraints of destiny would be no more than the irresistibility of harsh facts. But merely submitting to harsh facts would not be a moral act; it would not be situational obedience but mere submission to fate. It would be an instance of the sort cited by Paul in his first letter to the Corinthians: that of a potentially noble act deprived of all spiritual worth by its separation from love. Just as giving one's body to be burned would be of no spiritual use without love, so following a destiny without love would be nothing more than bowing before the brute force of facts. It would be living without hope.

What does all of this tell us about the spirituality of hope? How can love—constraining and difficult, yet commanded by God and our destinies, and the indispensable ground of hope—be cultivated? As everyone knows, just as faith cannot be willed, so the emotions of love cannot be willed. If we find, for example, that a particular person is obnoxious to us we cannot change our feelings merely because we know that we should. How, then, can we attain to the love without which hope will inevitably give way to despair?

At this stage in our inquiry, the answer will be familiar. Love, like faith, de-pends on grace. The authority of love begins in the authority of God. But the love commanded by God, presupposing the justification accomplished by grace through faith, is heedless of the limits and imperfections inherent in human nature.

It is a vision of redemption, vivid in the countenance of one who is loved in his universal humanity. In contrast, the love which arises spontaneously in the heart of fallen man is faltering and weak, and where it is strong, it is ordinarily discriminatory and exclusive. Neighborly love, for us, is unnatural. It depends on grace. Even though love is so fundamental to our being that we can scarcely live without it, and certainly cannot in any proper sense of the word entertain hope without it, we are unable to acquire it deliberately. It must be given us.

We can be ready, however, for this to happen. As with faith, grace does not preclude human will. We can wait for love, even though we cannot summon it. We do this above all by adhering to the forms of love—treating others respectfully, helping them when possible, and always paying attention to them, bearing in mind that they are not things to be used, if useful, and otherwise ignored. In other words, we can obey the requirements of love whether we feel like it or not. Most of us, of course, do this as a matter of course. We maintain certain courtesies in our relations with others regardless of our inclinations. With serious people, I would argue, this is not mere conformity with habit or observance of an unspoken social contract. It expresses a consciousness of what human relations ought to be, and in doing this it constitutes a tacit openness to grace. Such openness to grace is itself dependent on grace to provide the iota of love on which observance of the fundamental courtesies depends. We must (through grace) see at least that others *ought* to be loved, even if they are not. To see that is to see what we often refer to as their "dignity." Hence, as with faith, were grace entirely lacking, there would be nothing we could do. But in that case, we would not care about doing anything. Our very concern with love, in spite of our unloving ways, testifies to grace and to the possibility of living in readiness for love, as we live in readiness for faith.

Adhering to the forms of love, in openness to grace, becomes increasingly important as human life becomes more-and-more global due to various forms of technological progress. As both Hebraic prophets and Stoic philosophers knew, humanity implies universality; this implies that humanity is inseparable from love that is neighborly or, at least, somehow independent of personal inclination. Few of us spontaneously think of those shaped by a strange culture as friends and comrades. This makes the forms of love exceptionally significant. It is not merely that the welfare of countless millions of people depends on them, but also that they express our openness to love. In this openness, which here and now means an unreserved communicative readiness, and which implicitly is eschatological, our humanity itself is at stake.

We should remind ourselves again and again, however, that love implies particularity. It is thus a commonplace of ecclesiology that the universal church is real only in the form of the local church; and innumerable social theorists have stressed that the state, without mediating groups such as families and neighborhoods, would be inhuman. Love is for singular and concrete people. True, the singular and concrete attains full recognition only in the universal; but the universal is real only in the singular and concrete. Love is lived in families, workplaces, clubs, and churches, and among relatives, fellow workers, neighbors, and friends. It is also in these places that love—and with it hope—is cultivated.

It follows that one's personal relationships have a good deal to do with whether the general cast of one's life is hopeful or despairing. Relations with daughter and son, wife and husband, professional colleague and next-door neighbor, enter vitally into the determination of whether one's existence on earth takes the form of destiny or merely of fate and accident. And how people treat those they encounter in their daily lives has decisive bearing on whether the churches make up the Church or are merely religious associations; and whether the state is a relatively humane organization or a world-historical monster. Although we cannot simply choose whether or not to be hopeful, there are ways of resisting despair and of facing in directions from which hope can reach us, and every personal relationship, as an opening for love, offers an arena in which the struggle against despair can be carried on.

To reflect on faith and love is to survey, as if from a mountaintop, the whole territory of the spirituality of hope. Since faith and love name our unity with God and all creation, there is little belonging to the spirituality of hope that is not in one way or another closely connected with those great virtues. Thus remembrance is a search for God and humanity in the past; suffering in accordance with the Cross is an effort to find God, and through God our fellow humans, in the trials and ordeals that come upon us; insofar as we die with Christ we die, to use a phrase of Martin Buber's, "into God" and into the kingdom of God. Finally, there are activities—to be discussed in the following section—by means of which humans have tried throughout history to speak to God and one another and to understand God and his ways with the human race.

Prayer, Thought, and Meditation

Prayer is a strange act, by worldly standards. It is talking to one who cannot be seen or heard—at least, not as the things around us are seen and heard; to one possessed of inconceivable qualities, such as omnipotence and omniscience; to one who may not, so far as natural intelligence can determine, even exist. Prayer is addressing a being whom we can neither objectively understand nor realistically picture. To a worldly mind, as typified by most intellectuals in our secularized times, this must appear as the very quintessence of irrationality. Yet prayer accords with the nature of both humanity and the universe, and even people uninterested in prayer should, if only to be realistic about human nature and the human state, see why this is so.

Aristotle defined man as a political animal. Man is also a praying animal. He is the one earthly creature able to conceive of—although not to apprehend as an object of knowledge—the world as a whole. Other animals perceive an array of things and these make up their more or less familiar surroundings. Only a human being can, and naturally does, think of the sum-total of such things, the "world" or "universe" (even though, as Kant demonstrated, such a concept may not correspond with any reality). This means that only a human being can, and naturally does, think of what lies beyond the world—that is, transcendence. Further, a human being is the one earthly creature fully aware of personality, as a mode of being distinct from the mode of being manifest in mere things. This awareness leads readily to the concept of transcendence as personal. These thoughts, so natural and so nearly inevitable, even in our fallenness, provide the setting for prayer, although accidents of tradition, circumstance, and temperament determine what kind of prayer, if any, actually occurs. Finally, the most powerful urge toward prayer probably comes from our weakness and fallibility. Anyone not utterly misled by youthful exuberance or by inordinate pride must sometimes be stricken by a consciousness of radical insufficiency, of having neither the physical strength nor the moral right to enter fully into life. What all of this together points to is that the act of prayer, however strange, is deeply natural.

The nature of the universe is no less favorable to prayer than is the nature of man. This is partly because it is unknowable in its origins and entirety. That it was created, and is governed, by a divine being cannot be proven, but it is strongly indicated by our sense of the absolute claims of truth and righteousness, and it is a reasonable possibility. Atheism is, if anything, more willful and arbitrary than religious faith because it is unsupported by the compelling and historically-recurrent experiences on which religious faith is based. Further, the hierarchical character of the universe is very suggestive. The three levels of reality, one made up of things that merely exist, another of things that exist and live, and yet another of things that exist and live and reason, constitute an arrangement that points upward. We readily conceive of reasoning beings free from the limitations of bodily existence, such as angels, and even of a reasoning being free of finitude altogether. The worst a skeptic can say about prayer, probably, is to call it a wager—one that human beings have a strong natural disposition to make.

It is arguable that those eschewing prayer (often the more learned and sophisticated) must find other ways of coming to terms with their own prayerful proclivities and with the ultimate mystery of being. They must find substitutes for prayer. Can the enjoyment of natural beauty be prayerful? Can the creation and contemplation of works of art and literature be prayers of a kind? Almost certainly so. Natural and artistic beauty can of course merely serve the sensual pleasure of aesthetes who lack serious spiritual concerns. And art can express hatred of reality, as evident in paintings that mock and distort the human image. Nonetheless, those who enjoy or bring forth beauty of any kind must sometimes find in themselves a longing for things ultimate, and a sense of dependence, that are analogous to the prayerful attitudes dramatically evident in monasteries and churches. The age-old alliance between worship and art is unsurprising.

Prayer is not just a search for results, a means toward ends other than itself. As a recognition of the absolute as absolute, prayer is an end in itself. As an expression of the awe called forth by the thought of ultimate reality, it is an act of obedience. When God called to Moses out of the burning bush and Moses answered, "Here am I," (Exodus 3:4 RSV) he exemplified the essence of prayer. To pray is to identify and locate oneself before transcendence. True, this normally is accompanied by an expression of one's needs and desires. This, however, is not just looking for results. It is confessing one's indigence and dependence. It is a way of saying, "Here am I." And when this is said in full earnestness, and in clear awareness of the unfathomable chasm between our own righteousness, and wisdom, and power, and the righteousness, and wisdom, and power of God, it is accompanied inevitably by a resignation of human thought and purpose before the majesty of God. One prays, with Jesus at the hour of the Crucifixion, "Not my will, but thine, be done." (Luke 22:42 RSV)

The most important point to be made about prayer in the context of this essay is that prayer is linked indissolubly with hope. Since hope is ultimately for God, and presupposes trust in God, by praying one assumes an ontological orientation, so to speak, in which hope can exist. And, given that orientation, it must exist. Prayer in which there is no hope is effectively nullified—shown to be destitute of faith and love. Dostoevsky asserted that prayer is educational; by praying we learn about God and ourselves. In pursuance of this idea, it might be said that through prayer we are schooled in hope. To pray thoughtfully is to settle on the things we hope for and in that way to clarify the character and order of our lives as we envision them in their present unfinished state. It is to do this, moreover, before God and thus to acknowledge that in the eyes of transcendental wisdom our plans may be foolish and that even if they are not foolish, they are fragile—beyond our own powers.

Prayer clearly has to do with living a destiny. It is an effort to bring one's whole situation, structured by conditions both global and personal, to the merciful attention of God. It is to say, "Here am I" by sketching out, for divine scrutiny, one's circumstances and purposes. Prayer is a way of gathering oneself together and calling to mind the environing realities that determine what one must do and suffer. And there is no other way of accomplishing these things. Attempting to envision one's self and situation without reference to God would not only be spurning the grace essential for self-understanding; it would also be leaving out of account the absolute, which relativizes and puts in proper order—the order of destiny—all finite realities and values. In the course of this essay I have tried to show that hope, very simply, is the spirit in which we carry on the life given us by God. Prayer is both a source and an expression of this spirit.

Prayer without hope, then, is spurious, and hope without prayer merely willful. In times of despondency, many will find prayer to be difficult or impossible. But the struggle for hope must involve the strange discipline of trying repeatedly to find counsel and strength in that incomprehensible and unimaginable being on whom our lives in every detail depend. Trusting in what we know of this being through Christ, we must believe that practicing the discipline of prayer will not be inconsequential. Even a solitary figure, harassed by feelings of futility, but striving to pray, is enlisted in the resistance against the despondency of our age.

Very different from the discipline of prayer, we are apt to assume, is the discipline of thought, particularly when thought is philosophical, that is, limitless in scope, and unconstrained by dogma or other prejudgments. The thinker is often envisioned as independent, if not irreverent—one who approaches transcendence with questions rather than expressions of awe. And there is truth in this view. Praying is quite a different activity from philosophical inquiry. The former is founded on faith, and in turn on revelation, the latter on uninhibited reason. Yet it is a theological commonplace that the two are closely linked: we believe in order to understand. Faith in God leads spontaneously to reflective efforts to understand God. Conversely, we seek understanding—whether consciously or not—in order to discover matters worthy of the unqualified commitment we often call faith. It is arguable that philosophy is fully successful only when it reaches something divine, that is, when it eventuates in prayer, or at least in prayerful attitudes.

What praying and thinking have in common is devotion to the ultimate; both are ways of seeking that reality beyond which there is no other reality to seek. It may be objected that faith affirms at the outset that the ultimate is divine. Philosophy, in contrast, makes no prior commitments and is guided purely by reason. Moreover, many thinkers never discover anything they are willing to call divine; many even conclude that nothing of the sort exists. All of this is quite true. But philosophy in essence is committed to advancing as deeply as possible into the ultimate ground of things, and that ground is assumed to be, if not divine, nonetheless worthy of a lifetime of inquiry. And to an extent insufficiently appreciated by unbelievers in our time, philosophy through the ages has been religious. Philosophers have again and again, in varying ways, found in the depths of reality something commanding unconditional allegiance. Thus it was that one of the few philosophers who refused such allegiance, Nietzsche, had to enter into combat with most of the major philosophers from the time of Plato to his own day.

Still, can faith settle down quite so comfortably in the same intellectual household with philosophy as all of this suggests? Nietzsche is not the only philosopher who has believed that clear and uncompromising thought was necessarily destructive of religious faith. More important, perhaps, in view of the religious premises of this essay, is that there have been great theologians, exemplified in our own day by Karl Barth, who have agreed. They have seen philosophy as entirely incongruous with, if not a deadly enemy, of faith. It is important to be clear about these matters because in talking about faith we are talking about hope as well. If we allow faith and philosophy to stand in a state of mutual hostility, we must ask whether faith is compatible with the normal attitudes and operations of the human mind. This is to ask, not merely whether hope depends on faith (as I have been arguing all along that it does) but whether it depends on faith of a kind that suppresses natural reason. If it does, then we are close to asking whether hope, except for a small minority (some, perhaps, not fully sane), is possible. I believe, accordingly, that it is important to see that there are reasons indicating that faith, far from being locked in everlasting conflict with philosophy, needs philosophy.

The religious role of philosophy is partly that of helping people who believe in God to think about God. A perfect example of a philosopher who did this is Thomas Aquinas. While maintaining explicitly that human beings on earth cannot achieve a rational understanding of God, he showed how earthly realities point toward God. They provide ideas about God, since it is God who has created them. Such ideas are not literally true but they nevertheless provide us with analogies which enable us to think about God. Thus the beauty and sublimity of a great mountain may tell us of the beauty and sublimity of God, even though God is quite different from a mountain, and different in a way we are unable altogether to understand. The things around us, not only individually but also in the common order which makes up the universe, are like directional signs on a highway. They do not provide an immediate experience of God, or even an unequivocal concept of God, but they tell the traveler who is looking for God which way to go. And they do this through concepts which, with proper care and reservations, can be instruments for thinking about God.

Barth deeply mistrusted assistance of this kind. He feared that humans would take their own philosophical conclusions for truths of a kind that we can know only if God reveals them to us. Philosophy might lure us into the worship of idols. Obviously, Barth's reservations about philosophy cannot be refuted in a paragraph. It is possible briefly to note, however, that these reservations rested, in Barth's mind, on a sense that man had fallen into depths that rendered him dependent totally on the light of revelation. Natural reason alone can only mislead us. But if that is so, how is it that there are great religious philosophies, like Plato's and Aristotle's? How is it that non-Christian philosophers like Kant have made important philosophical and theological discoveries? A strict Barthian would have to pronounce all such natural wisdom worthless. But even Barth himself was not a strict enough Barthian to do that. The truth surely is (a truth which here must be set down in perhaps too peremptory a fashion) that Christian faith puts itself in an impossible position by declaring war on natural reason and therefore on philosophy. It gratuitously makes an enemy of one whom it needs as a friend.

On the other side of the great divide, however, many philosophers have in effect taken the side of Barthian theologians. They have denied that philosophy can deal with God. And not all of these have been atheists. Even among believing philosophers, some have construed philosophy as purely an investigation of human experience and earthly life. The divine and heavenly are beyond the philosopher's reach. The question, then, is whether philosophy is wide enough in scope to be of assistance to religious believers.

Let us suppose, for the sake of the argument, that it is not, that philosophy cannot speak explicitly of God. It still can do something that is vital to faith. It can show that the universe, reasonably understood, does not preclude the existence of God—and in doing this show that the universe does not preclude hope. Not every person can be a philosopher, but every person has a vital interest in absorbing at least the rudiments of one philosophy which makes it possible to think that God exists. Most of us today inhabit a universe which makes nonsense of the concepts which typically structure the universe of faith—the Incarnation and Resurrection, for example, or "angels and archangels and all the company of heaven." Modern man flatters himself that his doubts about such things reflect a more advanced intelligence than earlier peoples possessed. But such doubts reflect if anything a narrower and less sensitive intelligence—a mind incapable of imagining that there are dimensions of reality other than those readily conceived of by everyday common sense. For such a mind, faith is almost impossible. One of the uses of philosophy is to broaden our minds. Let me offer one example of how this might be done.

One of the major causes of modern despondency is almost certainly the unthinking materialism of many people. Only material things are real, they assume, and only testimony of the senses is credible. It may be that most people, in most periods of history, have tended to make such assumptions. But the tendency almost certainly has been strengthened by the spectacular progress of science and technology in modern times. It is very easy for most of us to assume that a proposition which can be neither demonstrated empirically nor proven in practice has no strong claims to being true. As a result, the world we envision and inhabit forecloses faith. It renders God at best a questionable hypothesis—an option in the realm of private opinions and preferences, where a variety of dubious and bizarre beliefs are presumably to be found. Such a world, even while ostentatiously inviting material progress, precludes authentic hope. One of the most important philosophers who countered materialism is Kant.

Anyone who reads Kant more than casually is apt to experience, in spite of the demanding character of Kantian texts, a strange lifting of the spirit. This is not because he says very much about God, for he doesn't. Rather, it is because, with his massive argument that what we take to be material realities are in fact created by our faculties of perception and understanding, he breaks down the walls of the material prison in which many of us are confined. He makes it possible to believe in God without flying in the face of good sense, and in this way he creates the possibility of hope. It might be said that this, at least from a Christian standpoint, is the very function of philosophy.

In sum, philosophy can help faith in two ways: by showing how we can think about God, and by enabling us to think about the universe in ways that do not preclude the existence of God. Various philosophies, aside from Kant's, have fulfilled these functions. Ever since ancient times, Plato, with his poetic attunement to the absolute and his sense of the partial unreality of the visible world, has helped religious minds understand the metaphysical possibility of religious devotion. Augustine, a Neo-Platonist, illustrates in numerous ways how Plato's philosophy can be used by a Christian thinker. Plato's great student Aristotle framed a philosophy which, in spite of a general Platonic cast, was reflective of a far more empirical and practical temper than Plato's. Yet Aristotle's philosophy lent itself no less readily than Plato's to structuring a Christian vision, as was demonstrated by Thomas Aquinas. In modern times, the kind of idealism that envisioned reality as in essence conceptual, a view derived ultimately from Plato, often provided a philosophical structure for Christian principles. And the existentialism that had its origin primarily in Kierkegaard, gave rise to a variety of Christian and other religious philosophies in the twentieth century.

Having discussed prayer and thought, we can readily understand an activity which fuses the two, that is, meditation. In essence, meditation is thinking in a prayerful frame of mind about God, or about other realities, such as self and humanity, in relation to God. As *thinking*, meditation uses concepts and thus realizes a less immediate relationship with God than does prayer alone; God in some measure is depersonalized. As thinking about *God*, however, meditation is carried on in the consciousness that we can know about God only with the help of God and therefore is at least tacitly prayerful. For most of us, meditation accompanies prayer spontaneously and naturally. We cannot pray without thinking and, since thinking helps us attain the relationship with God which is sought through prayer, we should not try to. On the other hand, a Christian can argue that thinking cannot be fruitful without grace and that therefore we should not try to think without praying. Meditation and prayer, then, are natural allies.

A particularly fitting subject of meditation is the divinely-ordered constellation of existing circumstances that make up my own and the human situation at any particular time. Here I draw together in my mind the geographical place and historical period I inhabit, my own unique past and the past not only of my nation but of the human race, my daily activities and the role of these in the life of my people and of global humanity. I remember past failures and present perversities, on my own part and on the part of humans generally. As has often been said, a human being is microcosmic and microhistorical; to understand fully a single person would be to understand fully all time and being. The utter impossibility of doing this in any but a fragmentary way does not detract from the necessity of doing it as well as we can. Otherwise, the nature of the self, and the relationship of the self to the world and history, is altogether unrecognized. Carrying on a destiny becomes impossible. Of course, prayer and philosophical inquiry have a part in all of this. But prayer strives toward the purely personal relationship of the unique and particular "I" with the divine "Thou," a relationship into which meditation introduces the disturbing (if necessary) presence of concepts. Philosophy, on the other hand, tends toward the pure impersonality inherent in conceptualizing all of reality. Meditation is an activity intellectual enough to sort out personal and global circumstances that are apt to be forgotten in prayer, yet personal enough to consider particularities that philosophy may be inclined to leave out of account. Thus meditation becomes a kind of gathering together of the self and is vital to the task of being a self. It creates an inner ground for situational obedience. It is plain how intimately meditation is related to the hopeful conduct of a life.

Through meditation, however, one strives not only to understand and occupy a situation, but also to avoid captivity to a situation. A situation has spiritual significance only because there is something beyond it. As the immediate embodiment of a destiny, it opens up toward eternity. Hope, as an orientation toward eternity, presupposes a degree of detachment—the detachment inherent in the consciousness of belonging not only to an earthly city but to a heavenly city as well. Achieving the proper balance of involvement and detachment may be likened to playing a part in a play. Heedful of your responsibilities as an actor, you will strive not only to carry out every action, but even in some sense to experience, every emotion proper to your role. But you will be constantly aware that genuine life is carried on outside the theatre; distress simulated, and in some fashion felt, within the play will not destroy the aloofness inherent in knowing that the true drama of life transcends the drama enacted on the stage. Even the most intense involvement in a particular part will not eliminate an underlying and invulnerable detachment. Only in such a manner can one take part fully in the turmoil and troubles of life yet transcend them sufficiently to maintain hope.

In other words, a major function of meditation is that of comprehensive relativization, that is, of establishing the relativity—to eternal life—of all the things which look so absolute to the secular mind. It aims at liberation from the conditions that sometimes press so hard upon us that we forget the ultimate future and lose the power of hope. Properly relativized, earthly life is taken seriously, yet seen as unimportant in itself. If meditation is effective, we know that the life we are engaged in now is not life in its fullness (*it is life in its fullness which we hope for*), even though it is not to be neglected. Earthly existence is desolate because God is absent—or, more precisely, is present only as Christ, as one who is weak, scorned, and crucified. In consequence, man—the authentically human male and female—is not present either, since men and women achieve their authentic humanity only in communion with God. The world is inhabited by beings whose identity is more or less hidden and distorted. Life within the world is not life in the full sense of the word. This is why, as John declares, those who love their lives will lose them. The lives they love are illusory and have to be given up, sacrificed on the Cross, for real life to be gained.

Meditation is a struggle with our spontaneous worldliness. It is an effort (in need of support from prayer and thought) to see, within and beyond the realities around us, the infinite and immutable reality that is God. In the course of this struggle we may come to know, as Paul put it, that "the form of this world is passing away." (I Corinthians 7:31 RSV) And we may learn to live with a realistic regard for our circumstances yet with the detachment Paul spoke of when he wrote that those who have wives should live as though they had none, "those who mourn as though they were not mourning, and those who rejoice as though they were not rejoicing." (I Corinthians 7:29–31 RSV) Praying, philosophizing, and meditating all strike us as strange, and this in part is because the detachment they cultivate is contrary to our deeply rooted worldliness. They are necessary because that worldliness, however "natural," is in truth radically unnatural. It obscures and suppresses the power of transcendence in us—the power that prompts us to ask of every temporal hope, "Then what?" and through that question, stubbornly reiterated, to press toward the plenitude envisioned in eschatological hope.

The spirituality of hope is not concerned solely with the future, however. Confidence in the future is impossible if the past seems meaningless or malign. A god not evident in the events behind us cannot be counted on to be present in the events ahead of us. Hence cultivating hope involves looking back and trying to discern the contours of destiny in the things we have endured and done. We are often urged to forget the past and look exclusively toward the future. Humans have generally ignored such advice, however. This is shown by the outpouring, through the centuries, of histories and biographies, autobiographies and memoirs, and retrospective poetry and stories. Plainly humans are strongly inclined not only to face the future but also to face the past. And in this inclination they are wise.

Remembrance

The idea that we must learn to forget the past is plausible even if it is wrong. Common sense tells us that things happen which would weigh down our whole lives if we let them. So we must free ourselves from these things. And we can. The past, after all, is past, it is non-existent. Our responsibility now is to meet the demands facing us here and now. The past must not be allowed to deprive us of a future. In a nutshell: living with hope depends on putting the past behind us. In what way is such an attitude wrong?

It is wrong partly in ignoring the inseparability of past and present. A reasonable hope depends on an accurate understanding of existing circumstances, the circumstances we are responsible for dealing with now. We can understand these circumstances, however, only by understanding the past which created them; we can see where we are only by seeing where we have been. This may seem obvious, but a view diametrically opposed to it is presented in the best-known book on hope written in our time—Ernst Bloch's *The Principle of Hope*. According to Bloch, present circumstances must be construed mainly by looking ahead, not by looking back. They are revealed in the light of the possibilities delineated in utopias and dreams. In the course of three long volumes Bloch explores the stubborn efforts, made over the centuries by writers and visionaries of various kinds, to project their minds into the future. These efforts he sees as essential to our humanity and also to our lives in history. Only through the boldest acts of utopian imagination do we become fully aware of human potentialities and fully alert to the possibilities offered by our circumstances. But Bloch neglects the constraints inherent in our finitude. Flights of imagination cannot overcome our immanence in circumstances. Through reason we can gain a measure of transcendence—but only by studying those circumstances, and by studying the past which created them. One of the most revealing facts about revolutionaries, dramatically illustrated by both the Jacobins in France and the Bolsheviks in Russia, is the way they often unconsciously establish systems quite similar to the ones they are ostensibly dismantling. They are outwitted by a past they arrogantly and casually ignore. History as a series of temporal events has brought us to where we are; history as *memory*—as the recapitulation of these events—enables us to *understand* where we are. If memory is lacking, the past holds uncontested sway over us.

But memory plays a more vital and mysterious role than that of helping us understand and deal with practical contingencies. Readers will recall Kundera's paradoxical claim that we are far more interested in the past than in the future. Kundera is surely right at least in this: that the past in itself, and apart from all practical considerations, concerns us urgently. To understand this, we must go beyond common sense. We look to the past because in a variety of ways it unsettles and dismays and offends us. We do not look to the past simply in order to take advantage of the light it sheds on the present. We want to change it, or at least to change our understanding of it. Remembrance is a creative task, a struggle toward transformation of memories, perhaps even of past actualities. It is a commonplace that hope aspires to a better future. It also aspires to a better past. As puzzling as this may sound, it is not incomprehensible.

For one thing, it is not true that the past is non-existent or that it recedes further and further into oblivion if we simply allow it to do so. It hovers over the present moment and often casts a dark shadow—for example, of guilt—over the future. It is not only Christianity, and the principle that everything past remains fully real in the mind of God, that tells us this. Psychoanalysis does so as well; a past that is not recovered and understood becomes a dead weight, hampering every effort to move into the future. We should no doubt refrain, at least in this place, from trying to say just how the past endures. Not just by memory, certainly, as shown by the fact that one who has committed a wrong remains guilty even if all memory of the wrong disappears. Nor does the past endure just by affecting the present, for things have happened in remote places and distant times—indeed, civilizations have arisen and fallen—and have left no appreciable traces on the present; yet it remains everlastingly true that they happened. If we say that the past endures because it remains eternally present in the mind of God, we say something that all Christians will accept. Yet we do not thus provide anything that even Christians would regard as a metaphysical explanation. Lack of explanation, however, does not nullify manifest reality. It is clear that the past is in some sense ineradicable, and that those who ignore it, ignore reality.

For another thing, it is not true, as is often assumed, that the past is unchangeable. One well-known way in which the past can change is through future events that alter its meaning. If all is well that ends well, then past events will receive their definitive character only from things yet to come. Another familiar way in which the past can change is through forgiveness. If you have offended someone, the offended person can, by forgiving you, reshape the past. Again, we should no doubt refrain from trying to explain metaphysically how it comes about that the past is changed. Is it mainly, or only, memories that change? Or do realities that transcend memory change? However such questions might be answered, we can easily see that hope for a better past is not irrational. We can see also that hope in its full eschatological dimensions does not merely look ahead, to something so glorious that past evils might be forgotten. It also looks back—to an unexpectedly glorious past. Earthly life, filled as it is with terrible and incomprehensible occurrences, will not be allowed to congeal into an inalterable and irredeemable deposit of historical evil. The redemption of the human race will be the redemption of the human past.

Through remembering what we have done and suffered, we relate the past to the Lord of time, or at least to the mystery of temporal being. We pray that a past without manifest meaning become meaningful. This is to pray that we ourselves, unjustified by our past, be nevertheless justified. In a word, we ask that our lives may be destinies. Only in this way can we reach toward hope in the face of experiences and deeds which strike us as purely and irredeemably evil. An unaccepted and unacceptable past renders life meaningless. The ugliness and squalor disclosed by memory mock the faith that all things are governed by God. And they make it impossible to entrust ourselves to the future with hope. Memory seeks, through faith, a past capable of sustaining hope.

The redemption of the past was a matter of deep concern to Dostoevsky. The "furnace of doubt" through which he passed in reaching Christian faith was fueled at least partly by his fear that there had been deeds of human wickedness and depths of human misery that would for all eternity defy justification. That fear was at the center of the conversation between Ivan and Alyosha Karamazov to which I referred earlier. Ivan, it will be recalled, tells his brother of a particularly savage crime, that of a Russian landowner who had had a small boy among his serfs set upon and killed by his dogs, before the eyes of the boy's mother and all of the other serfs, in punishment for a slight injury the boy had done one of his dogs.[2] Ivan challenges Alyosha to explain how the final glory of the kingdom of heaven can render acceptable a universe—or the Creator of a universe—in which such a thing could happen. In short, Ivan sets himself against the eschatological vision on which true hope rests. Alyosha can only, in mute horror, invoke the all-encompassing mercy of Christ. What this meant for Dostoevsky can be gathered from an earlier work in which he had expressed an eschatological faith. In *Crime and Punishment,* the drunken and degraded Marmelodov, who has abandoned his family and forced his daughter into prostitution, imagines the second coming of Christ, who appears on earth as the Redeemer not simply of present persons but of all past crimes and miseries. "Come forth, ye drunkards, ye weaklings, ye infamous," Christ calls out to Marmelodov and all such refuse of the human race, "come forth!"[3] However, the gift Christ bestows on these people, weighed down as they are by past outrages, suffered and perpetrated, is not the gift we often feel we want—the shrouding of the past in a merciful oblivion. Rather, all that is terrible in the past—all crimes and failures, all anguish and suffering—are made understandable and acceptable. The end of the ages, according to Dostoevsky, comes as a final act of divine clarification.

Although the past calls urgently for attention, however, we often recoil from this summons. Even though we are sometimes impelled to search into the past, through reading and writing memoirs, biographies, and other such works, we are often shocked by the past. It is hard to look at it, we find, directly or for long. The whole theory and practice of Freudian psychology, with its emphasis on the power of repression and the difficulty of enabling people to recover and face their memo-

---

[2] Feodor Dostoevsky, *The Brothers Karamazov*, trans. Constance Garnett (New York: Modern Library), pp. 251–252.

[3] Dostoevsky, *Crime and Punishment*, p. 21.

ries, testifies to our fear of the past. This fear points to the fact that remembrance, from the Christian point of view, is an act of situational obedience—of obedience to God and destiny. The past is one of those great ineffaceable realities that structure every human life. It can be put behind us, not by being forgotten, but only by being remembered. We bow to one of the most imperious necessities involved in the human condition—necessities reflective not of mere harsh factuality but of divine intent—when we take on the task of remembrance. Let us now try to understand how this task is pursued.

The past threatens hope in two principal ways: through things done and through things suffered, through memories of wrongful deeds and through memories of intolerable experiences. The past also, of course, contains memories that are agreeable. This is shown in the experience of nostalgia. Hence the past seems a kind of eternal storehouse where there are many pretty and pleasant things but where there are also venomous serpents, so that a careless movement may expose one to a lethal bite. When memory thus becomes a repository of the intolerable, it gives time a malign appearance, undermining faith that time is meaningful or providential, and thus destroying hope. It follows that hope depends on transformation of the past. This in turn depends on the development of two attitudes. Through penitence—which must be distinguished from the despairing regret usually called remorse—one comes to grips with a past demanding censure. Through gratitude one gladly accepts a past containing things that once seemed foul and repellent. We shall consider penitence first.

Sorrow for deeds one has done may seem more like alienation from the past than like reconciliation. Since what is done cannot be undone, it smacks of despair. But as Paul declared, in relation to a person's past misdeeds there are two kinds of sorrow, one drawing the person toward death, the other toward life. (II Corinthians 7:9–10) The former may be called remorse, the latter penitence. Remorse is being helplessly afflicted, feeling doomed, by one's past deeds. Remorse is a deadly enemy of hope. Penitence is quite another matter. It is informed with a sense that guilt is not necessarily final, that life can somehow break free of the past. For Christians, this sense is founded in the life, death, and resurrection of Christ, and, as formulated in the doctrine of justification by faith, is the core of the Christian creed. In Christian penitence, the self is gathered together and entrusted to God in the confidence that it will be accepted even though, judged humanly, it is unacceptable. Penitence is instinct with hope.

One of the most noteworthy features of public life today is the rarity of penitence, or at least of expressions of penitence such as public acknowledgment of wrongdoing or candid apology (although politicians sometimes apologize for the misdeeds of predecessors, that is, people other than themselves). Almost never does a public figure admit, without exculpatory qualifications or evasive phrases, to personal misdeeds. This perhaps tells us something about the modern mind. It suggests that the spiritual grounds of penitence are lacking. Only the paradox of divine forgiveness—the mysterious acceptability of the unacceptable—can render genuine moral sorrow, and its expression before other people, bearable. Without faith in that paradox, people must either justify themselves, by obscuring and denying any wrongs they have done, or else face the lethal power of remorse. Penitence is impossible. And hope is impossible too, since, where there is guilt, penitence is essential to hope. It is easy to think that the reign of impenitence in present-day public life is a factor in modern despondency.

Let us turn to the second way in which the past threatens hope—through things suffered rather than through things done. Here, too, penitence has an important role to play, even though, as we shall shortly see, it cannot alone meet the challenge of past sufferings. What it can do is overcome the anger aroused by sufferings we attribute to the malice of others. To repent of one's own misdeeds puts one in a position to forgive the misdeeds of others. When forgiveness is genuine, anger is dissolved. This, of course, is not a small matter. It is a commonplace of modern psychology that unresolved anger has a disruptive effect on psychic health. And more broadly, much has been written in the last century on the poisonous consequences of an emotion closely related to anger, that of resentment. Anger and resentment both turn our minds toward the injury and destruction we would visit on others, hence away from community. In this way, since our deepest aspirations are for community, they subvert true hope. Forgiveness restores a communal spirit and thus revives hope. Forgiveness of others is ordinarily possible only among those who know that they themselves need forgiveness.

The objection might be made that where anger is warranted, what is needed is not so much forgiveness as justice. Those who have caused someone unfairly to suffer must themselves be made to suffer. Thus we often see victims of crime heatedly demanding that the perpetrators be apprehended and punished. Such demands cannot be casually dismissed. The God of the Old Testament is in some measure a God of vengeance, and Christians cannot simply reject this concept of the divine and insist that God always forgives. In the doctrine of Hell, orthodox Christianity grants that retribution has a part in the ultimate conquest of evil. It is doubtful, however, that anger and resentment can be altogether stilled through justice. It is too hard for us to know, through our common deliberations, what justice requires, and too hard for us also, through the halting machinery of our courts and bureaucracies, to do justice even when we know what it is. Human judicial and penal systems always are marred by malice and misjudgment. Hence the collective life of every people is entangled in perplexities and hostilities that defy resolution through justice. Forgiveness is essential if the spirit of community, and with that spirit hope, are to endure in any earthly society.

And even if perfect justice could always be done, would that suffice? Questions about the relations of punishment and forgiveness, such as whether a wrongdoer who has been punished still needs to be forgiven, are extremely difficult to answer with any finality. Nonetheless, Christianity seems to say that forgiving is a greater moral act than punishing. God's whole relationship with the human race through Christ might be described in terms of forgiveness; punishment, at the most, is subordinate. It is therefore questionable whether penal justice, even in principle, leaving aside the complexities and puzzles of practice, provides a way of overcoming the estrangement between the perpetrators and the victims of unfair suffering. Whatever healing is accomplished by punishment, it would seem, must be consummated in forgiveness.

Now, however, we must take into account the fact that even forgiveness, as difficult and noble an achievement as it is, cannot in all cases reconcile us with past suffering. The author of the suffering may be forgiven, but the fact of the suffering remains. And beyond this, there is a great deal of suffering that has no human author. When a child dies in agony from some illness, it is often no one's fault. Thus Albert Camus's memorable depiction of such an occurrence, in *The Plague,* is an indictment of the universe, not of any particular person. How can one be reconciled with a past which contains such an occurrence? The challenge here is almost dismaying. It is that of seeing the past, crowded as it is with horrifying events and personalities, as something which must—if it is not to stain and defile the future into all eternity—be gladly accepted. What is needed, in a word, is not penitence and forgiveness, but gratitude. How is that possible? Not just one fictional child, but countless multitudes of real people, have in the course of history undergone tormenting deaths. How can one be grateful for such a history? This question must have an answer, as Alyosha Karamazov realized when contemplating the killing of the little boy by the serfowner's dogs, or else faith in God—and true hope as well—is impossible. If things have happened which can never, in all eternity, be accepted, life is meaningless and hope is absurd.

Here, of course, we face again the problem of theodicy. Without returning to the fundamentals of this problem, it might be useful to look at possible solutions from a new perspective—from that of the great historical and collective evils undergone by the human race. Of these, the greatest and most notorious is probably one which occurred in our own time, the Holocaust. Let us probe into the possibility of gratitude by asking how one can view with gratitude a past—or the divine author of a past—that contains the Holocaust.

To try to justify the Holocaust in terms of unintended but beneficial consequences, such as the intensification of the Jewish sense of identity, or the moral ennoblement of the victims and their relatives, would obviously be an unwise and impertinent undertaking. Nevertheless, heated insistence that such an event can

never in all eternity be justified, which is very common in discussions of the Holocaust, often seems colored in some degree by the pleasure of proudly pronouncing
judgment on the universe. The first step that memory needs to take in its journey
toward reconciliation with the past is that of recognizing our finitude and temporality and our consequent inability to judge the universe as a whole. Even the
Holocaust does not provide a transcendental vantage point for grasping the entirety
of creation. The second step, where there is fidelity to the omnipotent and merciful Lord of history, is to acknowledge that the meaning of the past—assuming
that there is such a meaning—cannot be extracted by our own efforts but must
be disclosed to us. We must wait—attentively. Both steps depend on humility, and
it is a noteworthy fact that even so towering a human crime as the Holocaust—
something done by us human beings, and not by God—seems to have called forth
little humility. Even here, as exemplified in confident inferences that there is no
God, or that the universe is meaningless, human pride has found a foothold.

Waiting for the past to disclose its meaning is not sheer passivity, however. It
is watchfulness. And since an astute watchfulness requires an accurate sense of
the evil we are dealing with, it may help to note an optical illusion that we repeatedly fall victim to in contemplating an event like the Holocaust. The illusion consists in the assumption that the torment and death of six million people is six million times as terrible as the torment and death of one person. But as Graham Greene
comments, "Suffering is not increased by numbers; one body can contain all the
suffering the world can feel."[4] Writers who proclaim that Auschwitz has rendered
religious faith impossible seem to assume that we might excuse a god who occasionally erred to the extent of allowing a single innocent child to perish in a
paroxysm of fear and pain but that we can hardly overlook divine blundering on
such a scale as the Nazi death camps. But if one body can contain the whole sum of
the world's suffering, then the agony and death of a single innocent person presents
the problem of justifying God's ways and human history—and in this way sustaining hope—in its severest possible form. Thus the query with which the God-
denying Ivan Karamazov challenges Alyosha: "Imagine that you are creating a fabric
of human destiny with the object of making men happy in the end, giving them
peace and rest at last, but that it was essential and inevitable to torture to death only
one tiny creature . . . and to found that edifice on its unavenged tears, would you
consent to be the architect on those conditions?"[5] Alyosha, although fervently religious, feels compelled to say that he would not consent. No doubt the scale of the
Holocaust is relevant to any moral appraisal of its authors (even though it is not immediately manifest that killing a great many people is *necessarily* a worse crime than

---

4 Graham Greene, *The Quiet American* (New York: Bantam Books, 1956), p. 177.
5 Dostoevsky, *The Brothers Karamazov*, p. 254.

killing only one person). It is less clear, however, that the scale of the event is reflected in the scale of the challenge it presents to those striving to retain or revive hope in an age of despondency.

Another common illusion in assessing the Holocaust is that a general knowledge of the facts, knowledge of the sort derived from books, suffices for judging the moral and spiritual significance of Hitler's camps. It is noteworthy that those who unhesitatingly pronounce judgment in this matter are often wholly without firsthand knowledge—as distinguished from book-knowledge—of the facts on which they base their judgments. Vast metaphysical generalizations are founded on written accounts. This is not surprising, for it is easy to assume that those who experienced the Holocaust must have felt far more profoundly its horror—its absolute inaccessibility to any form of justification—than those who have merely read about it. Such an assumption no doubt has a degree of validity; yet it oversimplifies. Elie Wiesel is a well-known example of those who had intimate personal experiences of the camps without thereby losing their faith in the Lord of history. Another such witness, less well-known than Wiesel, but very impressive, was Etty Hillesum, a young Jewish woman who perished at Auschwitz. In the years and months leading up to her death, she knew what awaited her; and she did not look on her fate through the prism of any doctrinaire religious faith. Yet as she approached her doom, she declared that life was "beautiful." "How lovely and worth living," she exclaimed, "and just—yes, just—life really is."[6] Several such utterances are found in the diary which she kept during the time when, under Nazi authorities, she and her friends were being harassed, imprisoned, transported to the camps, and killed. Her experience suggests that paradoxically the injustice of the world—and with it, the problem of theodicy—sometimes appears more stark and irresolvable to spectators of terrible events than to victims.

In sum, it is not absolutely clear that even an event like the Holocaust, apparently a gross and irredeemable abomination in the human record, absolutely precludes any idea that history has meaning. We should guard against the supposition that the scale of the atrocity is necessarily matched by the scale of the challenge presented to theodicean reflection. Also we should guard against the plausible but apparently false assumption that dreadful happenings necessarily appear more irredeemable to victims than to literary spectators. In a word, we should bear in mind that we are finite. We need to do that particularly in the face of phenomena that tempt us to forget our finitude and pose as judges of all time and being. To remember that we are finite is an aspect of fidelity to the God who is infinite. Without such fidelity, in an age of despondency like ours, hope will forever elude us.

---

6 Etty Hillesum, *An Interrupted Life: The Diaries of Etty Hillesum* (New York: Washington Square Press, 1983), p. 220.

The wisdom of waiting for the past to disclose its meaning is suggested by the fact that, in some instances at least, the passage of time makes a great difference. The American Civil War may serve as an example. To read about the horrors of Shiloh, Antietam, or the Wilderness tempts one to say that these battles, like the Holocaust, were irredeemable occurrences. Such a judgment, however, would not accord with the vision of the Civil War which seems to be taking shape in the American mind. A conflict filled with personal experiences which in our battle histories sound unbearable has taken on an aura of tragic grandeur, and in discussions of the War there can be heard an unmistakable note of reconciliation. Any rational justification of this development would be apt to sound tasteless and crude. To venture a tentative comment, however, it seems that the American vision of the War is being shaped by a feeling that Americans would be a lesser people, and American history a less significant story, had that war not occurred. Today, the scenes of the most terrible battles evoke, not the disgust which would presumably be appropriate in the face of the ghastly and the senseless, but something like reverence. At the center of this reconciling vision one is perhaps justified in seeing the visage of Abraham Lincoln. Can events which raised up a witness of such profundity—and indefeasible hope—be meaningless? In Lincoln we glimpse, as in Christ we see fully delineated, the humanity that can only be forged in the fires of suffering and death.

The tendency for scenes of frightful happenings to become sacred ground is not confined to Civil War battlefields in America. Verdun, a site of unspeakable carnage in World War I, has become a hallowed setting; Hiroshima has become the goal of pilgrimages. Even scenes of the Holocaust, such as Auschwitz, are now as though consecrated by the atrocities they witnessed. Doesn't this tendency testify to the power of the human spirit (through the Holy Spirit) to find meaning in a past which ordinary reason tells us is meaningless? Doesn't it show (to ask the same question in a different way) that events which look at first like nothing better than bloody accidents can gradually, for discerning eyes, take on the form of destiny?

Not that the appearances of irremediable evil and ultimate horror, so abundantly provided by twentieth-century history, will ever, in the course of earthly existence, be wholly dissipated. The nature and significance of evil constitute, to use Gabriel Marcel's well-known distinction, a mystery rather than a problem, and cannot be confidently apprehended by the human mind. Hence not only is the problem of theodicy partially insoluble; even solutions may bear the look of enigmas. Insight such as Etty Hillesum's come from grace, not learning or intellectual brilliance, and insight like hers is not reducible to rational propositions. The vision of history as meaningful in its entirety and in every detail can only be eschatological; within history, such a vision can be a matter only of intimations and of faith. As I have already noted, however, the Christian attitude toward historical evil is implicit in the Crucifixion. That so dismaying an occurrence has not only taken on meaning but has come to be seen as the key to the meaning of all human life and history suggests that nothing whatever can break out of the destiny ordained for the human race and for every human being.

Bringing the catastrophes of our time within the scope of prayerful and meditative remembrance is essential to the recovery of hope in our time. It is therefore one of the most serious public undertakings anyone can enter upon. At stake is the morale of the human race. We cannot live with hope unless we can reduce the shocking events of our century, and indeed of all centuries, to forms and dimensions which allow us to feel that earthly events reflect divine wisdom, even if we cannot say just how. The trenches of World War I, the Holocaust, the Gulag, the war in Viet Nam, and like enormities must not be allowed indefinitely to stand athwart the road into the future, mocking the notion that human deeds and suffering have a logic and a purpose. Remembrance is a way of contesting the rule of historical absurdity. It might, then—as carried on among Christians with the prayer that God lead us in his truth and teach us, and among secular minds with openness to the mystery of being—play a vital part in the collective life of our age. It might, by reviving hope, restore the foundations of civility.

The spirituality of hope consists partly in the struggle against conditions mortally threatening to hope. As we have just seen, some of these arise from the past and lie in memories of personal failures and misdeeds or of shocking and inexplicable suffering. But suffering does not threaten hope merely as a memory; it threatens it also as present agony and as fear before the future. It pervades all of time and existence.

Sin, Suffering, and Sanctification

One of the singular characteristics of the present age, as I suggested earlier, lies in its aversion to suffering—an aversion which is not merely an innate impulse but a matter of principle. Of course suffering has never been welcome. But in past ages people have been more clearly aware than people in the Western world today that suffering is inseparable from our finitude, mortality, and moral imperfection. And at their best, they were aware that it is not always, in its ultimate consequences, a bad thing; it may cleanse and strengthen us. Hence they had some capacity for enduring suffering with hope. But new, powerful forces, like science, industrialism, and consumer capitalism, have intervened. Today, we assume that a life largely without suffering is technologically possible and spiritually unobjectionable. Suffering thus has become a sign of human failure, something abnormal and humiliating.

From this perspective, the prison camps of the Nazis and Communists stand out as strange and lurid departures from normality—from life as we think it ought to be and usually, more or less, is. Normality, we assume, must involve the material security and abundant pleasures and diversions available in present-day industrial democracies. Yet if we judge by the conditions of life we would expect to flow from our natural and moral limitations, and by the wisdom present in man's age-old acceptance of suffering, we might say that life in the prison camps reflects normality (whatever that might mean precisely) about as accurately as does life in the industrial democracies. The prison camps, as organized assaults on human dignity, are manifestly shocking and fearful. But the life cultivated in the democracies is also deeply incongruous with the needs and capacities of human beings, and it is scarcely going too far to characterize advertising and much of popular culture as an organized assault on human dignity and on a true understanding of human nature. No one would choose to be a camp inmate rather than a well-to-do American of our time. It is still possible to wonder whether the one is necessarily worse off, in the deepest sense of the word, than the other.

Whatever the verdict of "normality," the idea that earthly experience can and ought to be wholly agreeable is radically contrary to Christian principles. Christians have from the earliest times seen a close tie between suffering and faith; a faith centered in the Cross made this inevitable. They have also seen a close tie between suffering and hope. The reasons for this are easily seen. The main obstacle to hope is human worldliness, our stubborn desire to inhabit an absolutely closed and calculable order of existence, where everything can be pleasant and secure. Hope, in such circumstances, is redundant. Suffering, however, by making the world disagreeable tends to defeat our worldliness. To live without pleasure and security, but rather with pain and danger, is to find oneself on the periphery of the world, so to speak, and in a place accessible to God and thus favorable to hope. Suffering in itself, of course, contains no assurance of spiritual progress; sometimes it leads to despair. Nonetheless, for sinful creatures suffering provides an indispensable impulse. Feeling at ease in the world and at home in the body draws one into the present moment and renders serious hope nearly impossible. Suffering prompts one to look abroad, away from the present disagreeable moment, and it may impel one to cultivate hope.

Moreover, not only does suffering tend to call forth hope. Hope calls forth suffering. To entertain serious hope is to be conscious of lacking the good that one hopes for. To hope for any large worldly value, such as beauty in an urban environment or righteousness in a ruling group, is tantamount to realizing the spiritual and moral poverty of human life on earth. To hope for the kingdom of God is to be conscious of cosmic displacement, of having no fitting home and country. If someone reveling in all conceivable earthly blessings were suddenly seized with hope—hope in the full, eschatological sense of the word—the earthly blessings would immediately be seen as insubstantial and insignificant. Confinement to those blessings would become a kind of imprisonment.

At this point in our inquiry, however, we need to be more specific. What kind of hope is linked in these ways with suffering? The answer is very simple: hope for personal goodness, or sanctity. Unless humanity, in some way and at some time, can be sanctified, all true hope is in vain. The perfect community symbolized as the kingdom of God can be inhabited only by persons who are righteous. And only these persons can possess the truth we hope to know in the kingdom of God. It is the crucial role of sin in the fall of humanity away from all values that justifies us in putting sanctity thus at the center of hope. Human will turned against God and itself and that is why the peace and concord of creation was disrupted. Creation can be healed only with the healing of the human will. This, at any rate, is the Christian understanding of our fundamental situation.

The main argument of the present section is that sanctification comes about through suffering. This links up with my argument in the preceding chapter (in the section entitled "Sin, Suffering, and Forgiveness") that *justification* depends on suffering, that is, on participation in the passion through which man's primal guilt was erased. Setting aside a multitude of theological disputes, let us say that justification means being destined for righteousness; sanctification means actually achieving righteousness. The principle I am advancing here is that the latter, as well as the former, stage in conquest of sin depends on suffering.

The idea that suffering can be morally purifying is not simply a Christian fantasy. Mere common sense tells us that someone may become a stronger and better person as a result of personal trials and difficulties. And it is often said of a person whose character is less than admirable that "he's had it too easy" or that "that's what comes from having everything handed to you on a silver platter." There is an example of such common sense in our view of a particular chapter in American history. We look back in shame and horror on the degradation that blacks endured under slavery. Yet occasionally we realize that out of this degradation there sometimes emerged moral nobility and spiritual grandeur of a kind which would probably not have been attained by people enjoying comfort, honor, and material security. An insight of this sort testifies to a "wisdom of suffering" which is accessible to people of varying faiths or even of no faith at all.

According to the Christian understanding, suffering purifies us by destroying, or at least reducing, our worldliness. Through suffering, so to speak, the world is made uninhabitable. We are goaded into moving out of the world into the wider and deeper reality which is God's universe. As I have already shown, human sinfulness lies in the tenacious desire to live within a realm of realities which human beings can, all on their own, understand and control. We want to live in an exclusively human universe. That is why we rebel against God. Suffering checks our rebellion and renders its results intolerable. Thus, instead of saying that suffering purifies us—for many, today, an offensive statement—it might be said that suffering impels us to live amid God's realities rather than the amid illusions of our pride. More simply stated, suffering impels us to live.

We now can better understand the dialectical concept of ecstatic suffering. The Christian vision of community is a vision of common righteousness, for righteousness is realized in the love which binds all human beings together in the truth. The splendor of the paradisiacal consummation of all history is the splendor of goodness. It is a strange fact, however, that Christianity does not prize undeviating goodness as highly as it does goodness lost and regained. Thus two familiar parables: the woman who loses a coin, then lights a lamp and sweeps the house, seeking diligently until she finds it; and the shepherd with a hundred sheep who, losing one of them, leaves the remaining ninety-nine in the wilderness and goes off to find the one that is lost. There is more joy in heaven over one repentant sinner than over ninety-nine righteous people who have no reason to repent. (Luke 15:3–7) To live through the drama of sin and redemption, it seems, is in some sense better than lifelong virtue.

One of the signal lapses of the modern age has been its failure to understand the ecstatic character of suffering and, in consequence, its unwillingness to bear the dialectical strains of destiny. Suffering has been viewed as simply a horror and humiliation, goodness as a quality we might attain by psychological and sociological engineering. Thus communism repudiated the whole idea of sanctity as attained through suffering. It spurned the ancient Christian notion that righteousness has been lost beyond the possibility of human retrieval, and having done this it replaced suffering with action. Humanity was seen as capable of recreating itself in righteousness. This could be done by recasting the social environment— supposedly the single source of human wickedness. Thus, by doing away with the capitalist system, the primary source of man's selfish and competitive nature, and by creating a cooperative system, a new, communal human being could be brought into existence. Humans thus would be authors of their own redemption. Everyone now is well-acquainted with the disasters which ensued from these godly claims. The proud refusal to acquiesce in suffering is far from harmless.

It goes without saying that suffering is in all circumstances repellent and unacceptable; that is its very nature. Nonetheless, suffering can take on a welcome aspect by virtue of the role it plays in the rise of hope. Thus could Paul write that "we rejoice in our sufferings," in this way expressing perfectly the idea of ecstatic suffering. Paul went on to justify his statement on the grounds that suffering, by way of endurance and experience, calls forth hope—hope that is confirmed and partially fulfilled through "the love which is shed abroad in our hearts by the Holy Spirit." (Romans 5:3 RSV) Such love is presumably a foreshadowing of the ultimate end of hope, the kingdom of God. So long as we are enclosed in the world, in accordance with our desire to create and inhabit a sphere of being immune to interference from God or human persons, hence perfectly calculable and secure, the void which is of the essence of the world endures. No one confined to that void can truly rejoice. In suffering, however, the walls of the world begin to crumble, and spiritual possibilities are created. As Paul declares, where the walls of the world have been breached, there can flood in a love containing intimations of paradise. This is why suffering can prove acceptable. Knowing that we have to be forcibly separated from the delusory realities of the world in order to know the authentic realities transcending the world, we may, even while suffering, and in that sense not rejoicing, rejoice in our sufferings.

Doing this is obviously not easy. Indulging in despair is easier, for it is less paradoxical—less dialectical. As terrible as it is, despair brings relief from the ordeals inherent in the dialectical character of our destiny. But despair prevents suffering from being a spiritual discipline. The spiritual possibilities inherent in suffering have to be recognized by the one who is suffering. This recognition will not dispel the suffering, but it may bring hints of joy and will in any case increase the inner strength needed for resisting despair. There are times, Paul's words imply, when we must simply endure ("we rejoice in our sufferings, knowing that suffering produces endurance"). But they also imply that there is an inner dynamic in endurance, for "endurance produces character [which one may think of as an outward sign of eternal selfhood] and character produces hope"; hope in turn calls forth the love which is a partial fulfillment, and a confirmation, of hope in its anticipation of the kingdom of God. One may find hope in this very dynamic, and in this hope the strength to resist despair.

The possibility of rejoicing in suffering does not exist only where sufferings are light or only occasional. Paul's own life is illustrative. Paul's sufferings were anything but light, nor were they only occasional. They came from repeated beatings, a stoning, three experiences of shipwreck, frequent subjection to hunger and thirst and cold, and the constant dangers coming from both human and natural sources. Paul lived with the near-certain knowledge that sooner or later he would die by violence, as he did. Yet he was an exultant man of hope, not in spite of the the sufferings that flooded through his life but in some sense—if we take his words seriously—because of them. They enabled him to live the destiny which is discerned and embraced in hope.

Closely related to suffering as a spiritual task is the situational obedience which, I have argued, is at the center of the spirituality of hope. One can willingly consent to suffering only if it is seen as other than a mere worldly accident. One must see it as in some sense a transcendental necessity, as it is when inherent in a destiny. One can then submit obediently. "Obediently" of course is not the same as "gladly." Yet here again we can see the strange linkage of suffering and joy. The author of I Peter enjoins his readers (presumed to have been Christians threatened with martyrdom) not to be surprised by "the fiery ordeal which comes upon you to prove you, as though something strange were happening to you," but rather to "rejoice in so far as you share Christ's sufferings, that you may also rejoice and be glad when his glory is revealed." (I Peter 4:12–13 RSV) One of course does not enter gladly into any "fiery ordeal," even into a martyrdom which might be looked on as being, in some sense, a privilege. Still, one might do so with a certain tranquillity, with a consciousness of having a part in an eschatological drama. Sensing that the kingdom of God is at hand and that the end of all things comes somehow at the end of one's own life, and does not await the completion of a set span of earthly centuries, one might find that martyrdom does not entirely preclude joy.

How intimately suffering and obedience are allied with one another becomes apparent when we note that there is suffering in the bare act of obedience, regardless of what it requires. In all circumstances, it is more or less unpleasant to obey. True, obedience can in principle be coincident with freedom, for in obeying Christ the Logos I conform with the deepest demands of my own humanity. In the world, however, I am alienated from those demands and meet them only with a degree of reluctance. Hence the word obedience has connotations of constraint and even pain. This is to say nothing of the fact that situational obedience well may lead one from a state of earthly satisfaction into a state of earthly affliction. The sacrifice of comfort, personal advantage, or life itself, may be involved. Some of the supreme moments of human existence occur when a person does something exceedingly forbidding under the conviction that it absolutely must be done and that in doing it one is conforming with imperatives which were, so to speak, incorporated into God's original design of one's life. Jesus assented to his death on the Cross, according to the Gospel of John, with the words, "For this I was born, and for this I have come into the world, to bear witness to the truth." (John 18:37 RSV) The concept of suffering as an act of obedience to a destiny transcendentally ordained could hardly be more succinctly expressed.

There is a kind of suffering that differs from what we might call "tribulation," a name for suffering that has definite causes, known or unknown. It is experienced when we are conscious, not of particular troubles, but of exposure to troubles. It is, in other words, awareness of vulnerability, or insecurity. This awareness testifies to sin, for sin is worldliness, or affirmation of the world, and only in the world— separated by the walls of the world from God—can one incur the experience of insecurity. Such is an experience also of the *inadequacy* of the world, however, and in that way it testifies to transcendence. The world I inhabit—and persistently sustain, in my mistrust of God and my determination to comprehend and control all the things around me—is like a small boat on the high seas; I cling to it in fear, but I know that sooner or later it will break up and abandon me to the deep. As knowledge of the inadequacy of the world, insecurity places one in a state of accessibility—however reluctant—to God. Hence one may speak, using a phrase from Martin Buber, of "*holy* insecurity."[7] Anyone who is acutely aware of personal insecurity either resorts to God or gravitates toward despair. How all of this bears on the question of hope is easily seen. Human beings in their pride are unlikely to look beyond the world, perseveringly and with open hearts, unless they are forced to. Hence hope cannot be expected to spring up and flourish anywhere but in the soil of conscious insecurity. It is hope that hallows such soil, transforming it from the harrowing insecurity of worldly life into "holy insecurity."

Jesus was probably referring to the spiritually destructive character of worldly security, and of the consequent spiritual value of worldly insecurity, when he spoke of how hard it will be for the rich to enter the kingdom of heaven. Riches provide untold means for creating a seemingly impregnable world, a place of perfect security. Possessing riches, one can enjoy the illusion of dwelling behind unbreachable barriers against every danger. Only when this illusion is dispelled, either by poverty or by ills against which riches offer no protection, can one acquire spiritual possessions such as hope.

The state of holy insecurity arises from a realization of one's radical contingency. To be contingent means that it is not one's essence to exist, nor, consequently, is it one's essence to be beautiful, wise, compassionate, or in any other way admirable. One's entire being, and one's every virtue, might not have been and may, at any moment, cease to be. The experience of insecurity arises from various circumstances but where it is spiritually fruitful it consists fundamentally in a consciousness of being, in every natural and moral quality, contingent. All of one's reality and value is suddenly perceived as accidental. It is difficult to bear such a perception unless there is faith. From the standpoint of faith, however, radical contingency becomes an earthly sign of the non-contingent Lord, the "everlasting God, the creator of the ends of the earth," who "does not faint or grow weary," and "whose understanding is unsearchable." (Isaiah 40:28 RSV) Then hope is spontaneous and strong.

While various accidental circumstances can provide a sudden and disquieting glimpse of our radical contingency, none of them do this with as much force as the phenomenon referred to in the Book of Job as "the king of terrors."

Death

Whether death need be, or even is normally, terrifying can be questioned, there have apparently been many calm deaths. Characterizing death as the king of

---

[7] See Maurice S. Friedman, *Martin Buber: The Life of Dialogue* (New York: Harper & Row, 1955), pp. 135 ff.

terrors is a way of dramatizing the impact of death, not on our emotions, but on our sense of meaning. Death undercuts the notion that the lives of individuals and peoples have lasting significance, and in this way, with unique authority, it challenges hope. Death seems to say flatly to each one of us, and to all of us together, "You have no future." Seen from the standpoint of death, life comes to nothing. It may be enjoyable from time to time, but enduring accomplishments are precluded. Every act and event leads ultimately to absolute oblivion, and every natural reality, every human being, and every human achievement will be swallowed up in that oblivion. Such, at least, seems to be death's message.

The secular responses to this message are familiar. It is said, for example, that the prospect of complete and irrevocable extinction need not dim the joys of the present moment; indeed such joys may be heightened by our awareness of their ephemerality. This claim has an undeniable appeal, for it seems to banish the shadows of mortality which darken many of our experiences. It scarcely does justice, however, to our transcendental nature as manifest in our capacity to ask unendingly, "Then what?" As we have already seen, humans are marked off from animals by their power of transcending the present and asking about the past and future to their most distant reaches. Given that power, human experiences are essentially unlike animal experiences. Except in moments of intense pleasure or intense pain, they are never purely immediate; they have a manifest temporal context, and their character is determined by what has led up to them and what can be expected to flow out of them. Suppression of the context, through alcohol or sex, for example, can be seen as an effort—often tragically successful—to escape the human dimensions of experience. Moral advisers who urge us to "seize the day" treat suppression of the context as a moral right, or perhaps even a moral duty. They can be charged, however, with endangering something essential to our humanity. We cannot close our ears, except with intolerable spiritual risks, to the decree of nullification which death seems to pronounce upon our lives.

Another common secular rejoinder to death's message is the suggestion that death is surmounted when we live in a way that causes us to be affectionately and respectfully remembered by those we leave behind. Need it be said, however, that being remembered is not the same as living and is a pathetically inadequate substitute for living? And in any case, very few of us will be remembered for longer than a generation or two, or by more than a handful of people. Hence even if being remembered were a way of living after dying, death would still, in the form of the world's forgetfulness, sooner or later overtake and capture us.

Of course, my own death is not the death of the whole human race. History will go on after I have died. In that sense, it is not quite true to say, as I did above, that *everything*—every reality, person, and achievement—will be swallowed up by death. Every particular thing will finally perish, to be sure, but there will always be life remaining; the human venture will continue. From reflections such as these, some may draw consolation in the face of death; but, I suspect, not for long. The fact that the human venture probably will not continue forever, but that even the earth and its solar system will finally perish, is not the most serious weakness in such consolations. Their most serious weakness is that the life which continues after my friends and I all have died will be one enjoyed by utter strangers. I will have no part in it, nor will any of those I have known and loved. It can only be a very bleak reassurance which anyone draws from such a prospect.

A person may no doubt carry on a constructive life while believing that it will inevitably end in nothingness, for one must do something and one may be comfortable only in doing something others laud and reward. But there is no escaping the fact—if death be absolute extinction—that whether one lives constructively does not in the long run matter. Both success and failure will come to the same ultimate end; both will be entirely erased. Moreover, it is manifest that the prospect of complete erasure might undermine morality, for the most despicable deeds will finally be entombed, along with the most noble deeds, in a common oblivion. If most people who regard death as final do not commit despicable deeds, that may be because opportunities to gain greatly from such deeds do not present themselves, or because they lack the courage to confront dangers of legal retribution; or it may be simply because they are not coldly rational enough to draw out in their minds, and observe in their lives, the moral implications of their basic views. Thus they remain under the spell of customs and habits formed in more religious ages. If assurance of our unqualified mortality endures, however, those customs and habits will no doubt gradually crumble. As this happens, large numbers will come to share in the moral cynicism of the minorities always capable of despicable deeds.

Considerations like these bring us again to the idea that hope in essence is anticipation of eternal life. I argued earlier that hope, as thus defined, does not necessarily condemn our lives in time. Hope for eternal life to the exclusion of temporal life, with temporal life left to the depradations of despair, could not be true hope. So one-sided a hope, conceding worldly life and history altogether to the reign of evil, would mark a surrender of the principle of divine omnipotence. It would be tacitly Manichean. Nevertheless, hope in its depths is for eternity. Hope merely for things that pass away in time would, as I argued at the outset, be a form of resignation, rather than hope. If temporal values were not foreshadowings of eternity, they would be essentially insignificant and "hope," as in Marxism and other doctrines of worldly progress, would be a mask for despair.

Let us note again, however, how vital it is not to think of eternity as merely an endless afterlife (the very word "afterlife," by putting eternity in a temporal framework, is dubious). If eternal life is thought of as merely an interminable temporal life, then the concept of eternal life loses its numinous power; it merely signifies more of what we already have. So conceived, the idea of eternal life is implausible and not even very attractive. As Thomas Aquinas asserts, eternal life is simply God. Since God is the end of all human striving, and since we see who we truly are only in the light of what we love and strive toward, eternal life may be thought of as a state in which we all know God and hence know ourselves in our own authentic and irrevocable identities. Temporal life may be likened to a journey toward God in the course of which selfhood—my own and that of all my companions—is progressively defined and clarified. Eternal life correspondingly would be the end of the journey, a scene of light, where all is clear—every human identity and above all the identity of God. Here every countenance is fully illuminated. Such words provide us with no image of eternal life. They may, however, help us to think of that life, not as mere endless time, but as the culmination and the inner meaning of time.

Christianity accomplishes something like that which secularism supposedly accomplishes, according to many secular writers, yet cannot possibly accomplish: it incorporates death into the forward movement of life. When secularists commend such a principle what they mean, ordinarily, is that temporal life can be so potent and satisfying that death can be embraced along with every other stage of life. Christians mean very nearly the opposite. Our life on earth, ravaged by the ephemerality of all things and carried on in a state of estrangement from God and all creation, is not really life, not in the full sense of the word. It is a voyage toward life and is properly speaking life in itself only so far as it participates in its eternal end and goal. Death reveals the nullity of earthly life, in the Christian view, but it also reflects the ultimate purpose which renders it significant. It marks the arrival of earthly life at the boundaries of authentic life. Thus does death lose its sting.

Here we reach the key point concerning the place of death in the spirituality of hope. Because life is so infested with temptations to idolatry, and because we can never resist them entirely, yet in succumbing to them involve ourselves in a worldliness which stifles all true hope, dying has an essential role in what might be called God's pedagogy of hope. Death divests us of every finite source of security, that is, of every idol. It leaves us altogether without refuge or resources. In doing this it defeats pride definitively, for it strips us of the very powers by which resources are used. It is the last humiliation. Death thus creates a situation in which we must either trust in God or give up hope. The latter, despair, is not necessarily terrifying or otherwise intolerable; it may consist only in wordless acquiescence in the apparent senselessness of life. On the other hand, relying on God in the face of death—that is, the prospective loss not only of all worldly possessions but of worldly selfhood itself—is not apt to render the experience of dying painless. It will ensure, however, that hope survives. To have hope is to live, and to have hope that reaches beyond death is to live, through faith, beyond death. This is how Christianity incorporates death into life.

Death is a particularly forceful summons to trust in God. In dying with trust we rely on God not only to give us life but also to make us worthy of life, that is, to bestow justification. The latter is particularly stressed by Paul, as though once we are convinced that God considers us fit for eternity, we will not worry about his power to lead us thereto. According to Paul, the sting of death is sin. He presumably meant that our horror of death is rooted ultimately in our sense that death is what we deserve; it is rooted in our guilt. Sin, as rebellion against God, cuts us off from the righteousness that forgives and erases that guilt. As fundamental worldliness, sin is trusting altogether in oneself or in some other worldly entity, and no worldly entity can render us worthy of life. In brief, to be sinful is to be not only metaphysically defenseless (in being biologically mortal) but morally defenseless as well. Christianity of course maintains that, in the depths of being, this radical vulnerability has been overcome. In expiating human sin, Christ has overcome death. One may have only a faint spark of faith that this is so. But by fanning that spark into life—as the prospect of death may prompt one to do—hope may be recovered in the very act of confronting its most formidable enemy.

It needs to be remembered, however, that anticipating eternal life is, at least for the most part, a sober rather than a rapturous experience. As we have seen, it does not mean exulting in images of what life will be like in the kingdom of God but rather lucid and responsible habitation of one's present situation—in a word, situational obedience. Hope rests on the conviction that everything that happens, even death, is willed by God and is therefore meaningful. Where there is true hope, death is approached not as an occasion for dreaming of an afterlife but as a task given to me here and now by God: a claim on my obedience. I do not mean to suggest, as recalling earlier discussions will plainly show, that temporal life contains no intimations whatever of eternal life. Every value, such as truth or beauty, is an intimation of eternal life. And the Cross speaks so compellingly to many people of eternal life that temporal life is entirely relativized in their minds. Were it lacking altogether in signs of eternity, the earth would be a scene of utter desolation, temporal hope would be impossible, and even eternal hope would be rare and difficult. Nonetheless, living into death toward eternity is not accomplished mainly through mystical rapture but through doing and suffering the things God requires of us here on earth and in time.

Death shows us again the dialectical character of hope. Just as righteousness in its most exemplary form arises from sin and repentance, so life reaches its highest splendor in overcoming death. We do not simply live, if we follow Christ, but rather rise from the dead. Hope is patterned accordingly. We hope for life, not when we are lifted up by life, but when we are threatened with death. Through situational obedience we acknowledge our mortality. We place ourselves in temporal circumstances which impose various necessities on us, and among these, we know, will be the eventual necessity of dying. Situational obedience is participation in the Crucifixion. The core truth incorporated in the dialectical concept of hope is that the glory of God is fully displayed only in the conquest of evil. Death is perhaps the greatest of evils. If so, the glory of God is most radiant in the conquest of death. This hypothesis seems to be confirmed by the centrality, among Christian symbols of God, of the event of the Resurrection.

The prospect of death creates ideal circumstances for practicing the spirituality of hope. It is often said, when an older person dies suddenly and unexpectedly, "What a wonderful way to go!" This is surely questionable, for an unexpected death is apt to be one that is never incorporated into life through hope. A death suffered in full lucidity, with ample time for prayer and reflection, may reasonably be considered a more blessed end—however trying—than one that is sudden and unforeseen.

Of course, the prospect of death does not confront us just at the end of our lives. It confronts us every day, since we live with the consciousness that death is an ever-present possibility and an eventual certainty. Death is an essential element in the temporal context which gives a human life, in contrast with an animal life, a distinctive coloring. It must be granted that this coloring may be very different for a young person in good health than for an old person in ill health. It may happen, however, that someone young, and in no physical peril, is suddenly overwhelmed by a perception of the inevitability of death. An example of this is provided in the life of Leo Tolstoy, who, while still young, was driven to the brink of nervous collapse by the certainty of eventual death. Our bearing in the face of death can be a lifelong spiritual discipline.

The content and purpose of such a discipline, Christians believe, can be adequately represented only by the Cross of Christ. The crucifixion and resurrection of Jesus were divine acts rendering death a pathway to life, to God. They were in this way acts of mercy, in behalf of every person. But they were also claims on every person, for Jesus submitted to the Cross with profound reluctance and thus in pure obedience to God. Accepting the mercy means accepting also the claim. Through faith in Christ I am delivered from death but I am at the same time placed at God's disposal. I resolve to do willingly whatever I am called upon to do and thus to die willingly when that is asked of me. Through dying as an act of situational obedience, I may come to realize that by dying with Christ I live with Christ. In that way I gain the spiritual detachment which, as we have seen, is necessary for inhabiting time as we should. I am saved from trying to settle down comfortably within a world which it is horrifying to think of leaving.

A secular counterpart to the faith and trust which enable Christians to face death with hope may be found in courage, for it seems clear that men and women with courage, but little faith in a formal sense, have sometimes walked without despair into death. In some forms, courage no doubt manifests more pride, whether personal or collective, than Christianity could sanction. Suffering and dying in a purely Christian manner would manifest unalloyed humility; the will and interests of the self would be in every way subordinate to the will of God. Nonetheless, courage, even when entirely separate from explicit religious faith, can also manifest humility. It can mean submission to a code of honor or to necessities imposed by a goal like defense of a nation. One's life is subordinated to a transcendent value. There appears to be nearly universal, intuitive agreement that willingness to sacrifice one's life is, except in instances of fanaticism or despair, an authoritative sign of moral nobility, adding a redemptive note even to service in a bad cause, and that someone who will do anything to save his life is contemptible. This consensus suggests a widespread realization, independent of explicit theological principles, that there is something more important to every person than life itself.

Christians of course often disapprove of the military spirit and profession. Within limits, this is probably appropriate, considering the profound dissimilarity between the figure of Jesus and the figure of a soldier under arms. Still, Christians might be expected to regard the military ethos with a measure of respect, for it requires that one's worldly life in some circumstances be taken lightly. This requirement, moreover, is not a romantic sentiment but a discipline carefully inculcated and maintained. A well-trained military unit exemplifies the possibility of a kind of secular spirituality, a spirituality consisting in the principled and methodical subordination of one's life to more ultimate considerations. Is it unreasonable to think that such considerations amount to a glimmering, within the secular universe, of realities belonging to the universe of Christ?

There are, of course, examples of other kinds. Courage unconnected with explicit religious faith is occasionally exhibited in political activities, in public intellectual life, and in private relationships. It seems that in all such cases courage reflects a tacit sense of transcendental realities. People with courage, in any sphere of human effort, are willing to give up, if necessary, all temporal advantages, and even temporal life. That can only be because of their awareness of something more important than temporal advantages and more important than temporal life. That "something" may be spoken of simply as what is right, or as what is required by personal honor, or as a truth one is unconditionally obliged to acknowledge. But it is always, in one form or another, a manifestation of transcendence. And there may often be involved an intuition of personal immortality.

While the ideas of transcendence and of personal immortality are not precisely the same, they are not as different as one might think. The idea of personal immortality does not mean only that life can be set free from death. It also means that life can be glorious and pure—fit for immortality. When we use terms like "authenticity," "validity," and "dignity," as we often do to characterize people who have shown courage, we are apt to think of such qualities as in some sense marks of eternity. The consciousness of things more important than temporal life, which is present wherever there is courage, is apt to be consciousness of things that in calling forth self-sacrifice do not simply obliterate temporal life but raise it to a trancendental plane.

In a film on the American Air Force in World War II, a general exhorts his fliers, "Think of yourselves as dead!" Such an exhortation has a Christian ring and might appropriately be taken to heart not only in wartime but in the course of our daily lives. It directs our minds to the fact that sooner or later we will indeed be dead, biologically, and that our lives consequently might appropriately be spent in preparing for death. Thus Paul (or whoever wrote the book of Colossians) expressed the Christian truth underlying the general's exhortation when he declared to the Christians in Colossae, "You have died, and your life is hid with Christ in God." (Colossians 3:3 RSV) This suggests the paradoxical truth that to live with hope you must live as one dead to the world. It would be impossible to do this if you never suffered and never died. This is why suffering and dying can provide a discipline through which we learn to hope.

I do not mean to suggest that courage can take the place of faith. No natural virtue and no form of natural knowledge, in Christian eyes, can provide a normal means of redemption. It is important to recognize, however, that secular minds are not necessarily entirely impervious to the ultimate realities and values on which Christianity is centered. The Logos is centered in, but not confined to, Christ. This is why Christians can speak to non-Christians. And it is why Christ can be seen as the primary source of hope, not to Christians alone, but for all the world.

The Power of Hope

There is such a thing, clearly, as a struggle for hope. Indeed, it is reasonable to think that few if any, in our fallen state, can live without sometimes being threatened by despair. When this happens, a struggle for hope necessarily ensues. Our discussion of the spirituality of hope gives us some idea of what this struggle involves. It must, to begin with, be an effort to extend and strengthen the foundations of hope, which lie in faith and in love. It takes place in dialogue and in solitary trials. It involves prayer and meditation and remembrance. It comes about through suffering and through striving to come to terms with death. In its depths, it can be simply characterized; it is a struggle to live in the fullest sense—to live into an eternal future.

Throughout this essay I have offered a relatively pessimistic, or at least sober, version of hope. Hope is not exaltation but obedience. It is not the simple enjoyment of promising circumstances but is dialectical: it is the power of looking beyond unpromising circumstances. In the Christian vision, human life on earth is a drama of redemption rather than the kind of enduring good order often idealized by ancient political philosophers. And divine glory is wholly revealed only in the excruciating and graceful work of forgiving and raising up degraded humanity. It follows that hope is sustained amid distress, and there alone. To think of hope as normally looking merely for the improvement of imperfect but tolerable conditions is to see it in a truncated form. In its fullest and most needful form, hope is a virtue for crises.

It is vital, however, not to be excessively pessimistic—or even excessively sober. Hope without even a spark of exultancy would hardly be hope. Hope is not fear and turmoil. On the contrary, it is indefeasible and knows that it is. This is because it arises from grace, which is the kindness of God, and God's kindness will not fail. Thus the struggle for hope does not begin because grace has proved insufficient and human efforts must come into play. Without grace there could be no human efforts, and no struggle for hope could occur.

In the preceding pages I have argued that hope is both for and in God. This implies that struggling for hope is searching for God. It implies also, however, that searching for God is responding to the call of God and is underwritten by Jesus' words in the Gospel of Luke: "Ask, and it will be given you; seek, and you will find; knock, and it will be opened to you." (Luke 11:19 RSV) Since the very struggle for hope is a manifestation of grace, the outcome is not in doubt.

It is quite possible, then, to persevere in hope, and there is some reason for saying that this above all is what God asks of us. By persevering in hope we entrust ourselves to God and prove our fidelity to God. We live, through grace, in readiness for grace. If we live without hope, there is a sense in which grace is undeserved (even though it is often given to us anyway). We do not acknowledge the divine kindness and power in which grace has its source. Hope as obedience, as willingness to inhabit in moral earnestness and a practical frame of mind one's destined situation, is the definitive expression of persevering hope.

It is vital to remember, in struggling for hope, that hope is eschatological. It looks beyond mortal time and history and is therefore independent of temporal fulfillments. This is to reiterate a major theme of the present essay. Of course, hope is temporal, too; this is entailed by its grounding in faith in an omnipotent Lord. God reigns, and hope must be vested accordingly, in time as well as in eternity. And it is inherent in the weakness of human faith that temporal disappointments are usually discouraging. But they are not destructive of hope itself since hope is an orientation beyond all temporal events. Temporal disappointments destroy only the counterfeit

hope in which despair, through creeds like Marxism, and through the subtle idola-
tries that infest the daily lives of most of us, disguises itself as hope. Authentic hope
is anchored in grounds deeper than worldly life and history. It is manifest in the
mysterious and intransigent confidence expressed in Julian of Norwich's well-
known declaration that "all will be well, and all will be well, and every kind of thing
will be well."[8] It follows that nothing occurring in time, not even the most dismaying, need cause us to question the sovereignty of grace.

It can also help, in sustaining our receptivity to grace, to remember that in a
universe governed by the God who, as Father, Son, and Holy Spirit, is almighty
and merciful, there are no accidents. Hope is not vulnerable to chance occurrences,
and the struggle for hope never is occasioned by an outbreak of chaos. On the contrary, as we have already noted, "all things work together for good to them that love
God." (Romans 8:28 KJV) Hence, the ultimate end to which hope is attached is
not only independent of all temporal failures and disappointments; it is served and
advanced by them. All earthly tragedies will be finally transfigured. And all constructive earthly efforts, even those that fail most conspicuously, will bear fruit in
eternity. This is to speak again of destiny. It is true that both individual lives and
human history as a whole will be inconclusive. They are nevertheless meaningful.
They lead toward the kingdom of God, in every tiny occurrence as well as in every
great event, even though the kingdom of God will come upon us as an interruption
of, and a judgment upon, our earthly lives. Hence the ultimate outcome of temporal occurrences is not in doubt, and we never need to fear that God has withdrawn
the grace which ensures that every struggle for hope will finally succeed.

We might think of the power of hope as the power of the destiny that will
carry us into eternal life. We have already discussed Paul's dictum that we rejoice
in our sufferings, knowing that suffering produces endurance, and endurance
character, and character hope. (Romans 5:3–5) In place of "character," as in the Revised Standard Version, the King James version speaks of "experience." Experience
connotes a past absorbed and a future surmised. Combining the two translations
suggests the idea of character as a settled capacity for living in time with hope. Such
a capacity must rest on a sense of destiny as the essential order given to human life
in time by the One who has given to natural creation its own essential order. This
suggests that hope sustained in obedience to the requirements of destiny has behind it the whole power of the Creator of the heavens and the earth.

In the book of Isaiah the prophet addresses those who feel that their lives lack
all meaning. "Have you not known?" he asks, "Have you not heard? The Lord is the
everlasting God, the Creator of the ends of the earth. He does not faint or grow
weary, his understanding is unsearchable." (Isaiah 40:28–31 RSV) The prophet

---

8 Julian of Norwich, *op. cit.,* p. 225.

thus implies that a person's life is an affair not of mere chance but of providential order. Then he speaks of the life and strength God gives those who adhere to this order, that is, to their destinies. "He gives power to the faint, and to him who has no might he increases strength. Even youths shall faint and be weary, and young men shall fall exhausted; but they who wait for the Lord shall renew their strength, they shall mount up with wings like eagles, they shall run and not be weary, they shall walk and not faint." If I am right, those who live with hope only occasionally mount up with wings like eagles. Oftener they run without being weary, and oftener still they walk without fainting. But even in walking, they are borne up by "the everlasting God."

------⸙ chapter four ⸙------

THE POLITICS OF HOPE

Political Responsibility

Many people in the liberal democracies of the West feel that politics is somehow a secondary and dispensable activity. It is not so important as religion and art, for example, and probably not even so important as economics, the ways we work and accumulate wealth. In limits, this feeling is no doubt valid. Any idea we form of paradise is apt to be composed of images drawn from art, literature, and scripture. But politics is something we spontaneously expunge from our visions of perfect life. Politics has to do with power; perfect life is presumably formed throughout by love. Nonetheless, politics has an essential role in human efforts to live with hope and to cultivate hope. More precisely, it is not politics, not such activities as electioneering and voting, that has this role; rather, it is political responsibility, which might be expressed in electioneering and voting, but consists fundamentally in a certain attitude which the individual maintains toward the whole surrounding order of society. This attitude has two components.

Political responsibility involves first of all an attitude of attentiveness toward human beings everywhere. To be fully human is not, as with an animal, merely to exhibit spontaneously the natural characteristics of one's species. It is rather to be consciously present with one's fellow human beings, and this requires paying attention to them—to what they are doing, suffering, and saying—all over the earth. Poverty and oppression, even in distant lands, demand to be noticed. Famines and wars are not matters we can rightfully ignore. Political consciousness rests on a heedfulness, without boundaries, to all of the conditions and events in which human beings are involved. It may seem that such an attitude might be expressed in non-political ways, such as reading widely in world literature. But even in an apparently non-political activity of this sort one would be concerned much of the time with political realities, such as wars and tyrants, and would inevitably develop opinions about such matters; these would be political opinions.

For universal attentiveness to be fully political, however, it must be fused with a second attitude. Something tells us that attentiveness must, to be political, be particularly concerned with the present time. Just reading history, for example, would not suffice. Why is that? Mainly, I suggest, because present circumstances confront us with issues which are undecided and in doing this poses the possibility that we can, and in recognition of our common humanity must, help decide them. In other words, attentiveness toward the state of human beings at the present time opens the way beyond attentiveness into action. Possibilities of action in so vast an arena as that of the human race as a whole, however, are necessarily limited. Hence I shall refer to the second component of political responsibility in terms not just of acting but of readiness for acting. Attentiveness must be matched with what I shall call "availability."

Being available, in a political sense, means asking oneself in every political situation, "Is there anything I can do?" Very often there isn't. But to live as a human being is to live with a readiness to respond to the needs and troubles of other human beings. Such readiness is what I mean by "availability." It would not be real, however, if it consisted merely in ignorant and passive good will. It is real only in someone who takes the trouble to be well-informed and to judge carefully concerning the actions which might and ought to be pursued—by anyone in a position to act effectively—in problematic circumstances. Like attentiveness, availability is a rule of love. Unwillingness to act under any circumstances would mark a kind of deep disengagement from one's humanity. Such an attitude would rebound on attentiveness, stripping it altogether of moral worth. Attentiveness without availability would express mere curiosity rather than universal love.

Why accord these attitudes—attentiveness and availability—so central a role in the life of hope? The answer to this question can be given with a single word: universality. Hope, as we have already seen, is not just for oneself, nor is it even just for oneself and one's friends. It is all-encompassing. Such is prescribed by love. In Christian terms, hope is for the kingdom of God, a kingdom comprising—in the eyes of hope—all humanity and all creation. Such universality is political, for being alert to the circumstances of the human race at large, and to the possibilities of action such circumstances present, is maintaining a political stance. It is true that politics ordinarily has to do with a legal order which is less than globally comprehensive, such as a city-state or a nation. But the standard governing such an order is the kind of universality inherent in a way of life fitted for human beings in possession of their full humanity. Such might be called *moral* universality. Moreover, every legal order is bound to show its respect for global humanity—for *numerical* universality, so to speak—by seeking peace and justice in its relations with other such orders. In sum, when we seek or entertain hope, we must think of all human beings, in their full humanity, and not just of ourselves; and one of the ways in which we must do this is through the boundless attentiveness and availability which define political responsibility. Through politics I acknowledge the human solidarity, now ravaged by sin, which Christians believe will be brought to full reality at the end of time. If I fail to do this, if I fail in political responsibility, I close myself to the kingdom of God, the object of all true hope, and thus render hope illogical and impossible.

The fact that we are speaking of hope, however, implies that political responsibility is not an attitude merely toward the present time. Being fused with hope, it must be an attitude toward the future; and since the future is shaped by all that has gone before, it must be an attitude toward the past as well. And here we come again upon the concept of destiny—a concept in terms of which we have already defined hope and must also define political responsibility. My life is not just an accumulation of accidents but, potentially at least, is a story, with a beginning, an order of unfoldment, and a purpose. Beyond that, and crucial for understanding the politics of hope, is that my own story mirrors my involvement in the story of my people and, through my people, in humanity as a whole. My personal destiny, in other words, is not exclusively mine but a manner of participating in the destiny of all human beings. If I do not become engaged in universal human destiny, to the extent and in the way my own circumstances allow, neither can I lay hold of my personal destiny. This means that I must try to make sense out of the sufferings and actions of the whole human race, in the past and future as well as in the present; only thus can I make sense out of my own life. This may sound like too much to ask of human imagination and intelligence. But ordinary human beings do it continuously and spontaneously, if only through such relatively crude concepts as "the free world" and "the working class." And in reading newspapers and in watching television programs about history, people with no claims to learning or philosophical sophistication look for meaning in the events of their time. Sometimes they find such meaning by hearing and following a great leader. What is needed on the part of the individual is not philosophical profundity but the moral sensitivity to feel that one's life has meaning, and that its meaning is connected with the part one plays in the life of humanity. Such suffices for politics to be practiced and hope to be possible.

Political responsibility, then, is historical. Attentiveness comprises all human events, whether remembered, experienced, or anticipated, and availability is a readiness for participation in all the events one can affect. As human, I am concerned with everything that humanity has undergone and accomplished on earth and with everything it may undergo and accomplish in times to come. The universality which renders political responsibility essential to hope encompasses the entire human story. We would have to be infinite, someone may object, to meet the demands of universality. Yet, even though we are not infinite, infinite demands press upon us—as seen in the irrepressible question "Then what?" in contemplating a prospective achievement and in our natural and ineradicable concern with an infinite being, God. Our concerns are infinite even though our nature is finite. Hence the human ability and desire to reach out toward the remote past and the remote future should not be underestimated; witness the seemingly inexhaustible interest in such genres as historical and science fiction.

Politics is thus the activity through which men and women survey, and within the limits decreed by their finitude shape, the historical conditions they inhabit. So sweeping a conception of political responsibility is far from new. Since the time of Aristotle, it has been recognized that politics is the sovereign human activity in the sense that it oversees and harmonizes all segments of human life. This is not to say that government should try to control all of life. But the question as to what it should and should not try to control is itself a political question, to be decided by political deliberation. Thus the principle that through politics we accept responsibility for our lives in common goes back to the era of the Greek city-states. Christianity, however, has recast this principle by envisioning our lives as historical. Political responsibility becomes historical responsibility—which might be called an Augustinian reformulation of Aristotle.

The idea of attentiveness to the past seems to imply, however, that knowledge of history is a moral and spiritual obligation, and this may seem quite ridiculous. It is easy to sympathize with Kierkegaard's scorn for Hegel's apparent conviction that deep spiritual insight is heavily dependent on broad historical knowledge. Surely these are quite disparate achievements. And not only that: the limits on our historical knowledge are severe. These are limits partly on what anyone can know about so mysterious a process as the passage of human generations, and they are limits partly on what the average person, taken up with the multitudinous tasks and distractions of daily life, has time to study. Nevertheless, we are no more free to ignore fellow human beings now dead than we are to ignore those now living. How, for example, could we avoid reprehending someone who was simply uninterested in the Holocaust? And there is not only the standard of universal attentiveness but also the need to make sense of our lives. This we cannot do without looking back on apparently senseless events in the past and in some way coming to terms with them. In sum, the people of the past cry out for attention, the tragic events of the past for reconciliation. Concerning the spiritual significance of history, Hegel was more nearly right than was Kierkegaard.

It may be objected that people whom we only read about are not neighbors, in the biblical sense, and that so sweeping a concept of responsibility as I have suggested therefore involves a departure from the biblical understanding of love. If this objection were valid, the very ideal of universal attentiveness would be jeopardized. It is true that the concept of neighborly love gives priority to concrete and immediate relationships. It implies, however, that any human being, of any time or place, is a possible neighbor. The particular person who is one's neighbor is a representative of universal humanity. Thus the line between neighbors and non-neighbors is not as sharp as we might like it to be. We realize this, too, when we note that modern media of communication bring the deeds and sufferings of distant people vividly before us. Is someone whose anguish we behold in a dramatic photograph (for example, the little Vietnamese girl fleeing in terror before napalm bombs) a neighbor? Are people long dead, whose sufferings are vividly recounted in historical records, neighbors? Are the early Christian martyrs neighbors to Christians who read about them? There are no clear answers to such questions. The standard of universal attentiveness does not deny that love is first of all for the particular person immediately before you. It implies, however, that neighborly love is authentic only when you are ready to find in anyone whatever the visage of the neighbor.

Moreover, we see the link between historical knowledge and neighborly love in this, that even the concrete person in my immediate presence is not abstracted from history. A human being, fully understood, is not only a product of timeless nature but is also a unique embodiment of history—of the past that has given the human race its present beliefs and forms of life. Suppose that the person I face here and now is a late twentieth-century American. To know and love that person in all of his concrete reality I must know something about American history—about America's revolutionary break with Europe, about the Civil War, and about the development of industrialism and its impact on American society and attitudes. If my neighbor is an African-American, I achieve a neighborly relationship only so far as I am conscious of the blight of slavery and the long agony of racial discimination that followed the end of slavery. In a word, my neighbor is microhistorical—a concrete embodiment of human destiny. If I am inattentive to the historical past I am severely handicapped when it comes to being attentive to the neighbor whom I confront here and now. This is not to say that love for one's neighbor depends on a scholar's knowledge of history. But it does depend on a certain breadth of mind—on an interest in, and an intuitive sense of, what human beings have done and suffered throughout the ages.

Once the principle of universality in its full historical scope is established, however, it becomes vital to recognize our finitude and moral fallibility and the implications these have for our relations with history. Such relations are distorted not only when we fail to recognize how all-encompassing they are; they are distorted also when we forget how weak and faltering the human mind is even at its best. In other words, there are two illusions to be on guard against. The first is the one we have just discussed: that of immediacy, consisting in the notion that people distant in space and time do not concern us. The second illusion, which needs brief attention, is that of grandiosity—of allowing ourselves to think of the mind of a human being as though it were the mind of God. Here again the example of Hegel is instructive.

One of the most seductive forms of the illusion of grandiosity is its noetic form; this is the illusion of supposing ourselves able to know history objectively, thoroughly, and in its entirety. Hegel, while overcoming the illusion of immediacy— that only what is immediately at hand need concern us—with all the power of genius, succumbed to the illusion of grandiosity in its noetic form. For Hegel, it might be said, our responsibility for history is above all that of comprehending it, in all of its major patterns, from the earliest to the final ages. Such knowledge is not merely for the sake of action; it is an end in itself. Our involvement in history is at its highest contemplative. All events, societies, and great personalities are defined by their roles in a vast historical drama, and the drama is not completed simply by happening; it has to be known. We reach the summit of human development as we become (borrowing Plato's famous words) spectators of all time and existence. Contemplating the human adventure in its full extent and glory, the minds of men and women become like the mind of God.

Seen from a Christian perspective, Hegel was profoundly in error. His error consisted in the supposition, not that human life can be construed as an all-encompassing story, but that the story can be reconstructed and told by human beings on earth and in time. This supposition did have roots in Christianity. In Christian faith, the life of Jesus is a revelation of the very meaning and essential order of human existence. It is the Logos and, if fully understood, would disclose the order and significance of all historical events. Jesus' life is in the nature of a mystery, however, rather than a compendium of knowledge, and it does not permit us to frame a story comprising all past empirical occurrences. At best, it enables us to sketch a few lines of meaning, these concerned mainly with sacred history—the history of revelation and the Church. Christians have not normally claimed an understanding of the overall pattern of history, even though they have asserted that such a pattern exists and is known to God. Thus Augustine, in *The City of God*, powerfully conveyed his faith that the course of history was not a mere tale, full of sound and fury, signifying nothing; as befitted the great enemy of Manicheism, he held that a divinely-authored story was implicit throughout. But he never attempted to recount the story beyond commenting, in a mainly cautionary manner, on the character and fall of the Roman Empire, and summarizing the essentials of sacred history. Hence, even though Augustine was an intellectual ancestor of Hegel,

The City of God was fundamentally a different kind of book from *The Phenomenology of Mind.*

It is not hard to see why Christians have normally refrained from undertakings like Hegel's. So far as they are true to their faith, Christians are acutely conscious of human finitude and, correspondingly, of the fact that humans are immanent in the historical process and lack the transcendental vantage point which would be necessary for history in its entirety to be surveyed and known. Christians believe that history is known perfectly by God but very imperfectly by its human participants. Albert Camus, although not a Christian, expressed a Christian attitude when he said that history as a totality does not exist for the human mind.[1] Hegel's effort to comprehend history as a totality was based on a spectacular neglect of human limitations. It is not surprising that when this neglect found a place, not merely among intellectuals whose primary interest was theoretical, but among revolutionaries for whom the point was not to understand the world but to change it, there were tragic consequences for the whole human race.

Entering into fitting relations with history must therefore be understood as primarily a participatory, rather than noetic, undertaking. As a finite and morally fallible creature, one can only be a *part* of history—a part that is conscious and responsible, hence a *participant*. Participation presupposes knowledge, but the presupposed knowledge is limited and relativized by one's historical role. Properly speaking, Marx and Lenin tried not so much to be participants in history as commanders of history. But command precludes participation. The former aspires to the divine, to total mastery. The latter, unaffectedly human, is achieved only within historical situations—those that come to light among people who recognize that they are responsible for one another, yet possess only limited capacities for knowing and controlling the circumstances they inhabit.

Again we encounter the concept of situational obedience. Clarifying the existing situation is fundamental for construing rightly our relations with history and human destiny. Although history is fragmentarily present to us as an object of study and understanding, it is adequately present to us in our human finitude and responsibility only when it takes shape as a situation—a set of circumstances which is a source both of noetic limits and of moral demands. Human destiny can be lived to the limits fixed by our finitude and fallenness only when it becomes present in a set of conditions which I apprehend as the mold in which my life must be cast in order to be human. As we have seen, living with hope does not consist in imagining an exhilarating, or even pleasant, earthly future. Hope is eschatological, and the future we hope for is beyond the scope of earthly conditions or human imagi-

---

1 See Albert Camus, *The Rebel,* trans. Anthony Bower (New York: Alfred A. Knopf, 1954).

nation. Our primary duty is that of dwelling responsibly within the situations in which we find ourselves. Our aim, then, should not be to escape our common entrapment in circumstances—a condition reflective of our finitude and fallenness—but through mutual responsibility and resolute humility, to transform that entrapment from a purely accidental into a moral and spiritual condition.

It can now be more clearly seen why political responsibility enters necessarily into the life of hope. Circumstances which are important to me are rarely if ever purely my own circumstances and no one else's. My situation is shaped decisively by national and global conditions, and the sufferings and duties that bear on me are like, or even substantially the same as, those bearing on many others. Failure to understand this and to structure my attentiveness and availability in accordance with global circumstances is a failure, so to speak, in elementary humanity. And it is disruptive alike of true political consciousness and of hope. When I inquire into our common situation, that of my country and the human race, and ask what we—and I personally—must do, I am thinking politically. Living with hope is thus in part a political undertaking. It is a matter of entrusting oneself, as lucidly and responsibly as possible, to the life which all of us together are living. The life which carries us to the shore is the life not just of particular persons but of humanity, and navigating and remaining afloat among the currents of that life is a political art.

We began this chapter by considering the nature of political responsibility, in particular its universal and therefore historical scope; then we explored the implications of recognizing that in spite of the infinite reach of human concern, humans are finite and morally fallible beings. We are now in a position to note one of the signal characteristics of political responsibility—signal because of its bearing on the spirit of politics and on the way that spirit has been vitiated in the twentieth century. Political responsibility should rest on hope, not as exaltation, but as obedience.

This is because politics is a sphere of limited possibilities, these rooted not simply in the moral fallenness of human beings but in the way in which society confirms, and tends even to strengthen, the immorality of individuals. Rulers and ruling groups experience particularly powerful temptations to pride. Hence, there have been saintly individuals but no saintly societies. Perfection is a suitable standard for persons but a rash and dangerous one for states. Even utopias explicitly offered merely as critical vantage points, and not as practical projects, are risky; they obscure the fact that state and society in their very essence—the state, for example, being essentially an agent of coercion—are antithetical to the perfect community sought by hope. All of this is acknowledged by most people in the West today, as shown by the widespread acceptance of "checks and balances"—organizational devices dividing major power centers and inviting tension among them. Such devices are assumed to be essential for governments although having no application to private individuals. Illustrative is the separation of church and state. For societies, this is a maxim of elementary decency; ignoring it has played a primary role in the totalitarianism which has defaced the twentieth century. But for individuals, it would be a sign of moral depravity if spiritual and practical life were not intimately fused.

If politics is a sphere of limited possibilities, it is a sphere also of limited hope. This is why the politics of hope must be construed in terms of obedience rather than exaltation. Some of the most tragic political illusions of our time have been entertained by men and women whose hearts were lifted up by exalted hopes. Communist revolutionaries in Russia, China, and elsewhere have been captivated by the mirage of perfect justice and induced thereby to engage in political conduct that visited incalculable suffering on millions of their fellow human beings. The myth of revolution and the myth of total power have alike been born of boundless hope.

This is to say that political hope, insofar as it is hope for the polity, is less sharply dialectical than is personal hope. It is dialectical to a degree. A polity can become morally degraded, and those within it can hope for its regeneration; it can behave unwisely, and there is properly hope for wiser leadership; it can be threatened with extinction, and those who care for it will hope for a renewal of its life. But only in a fashion are such hopes parallel to personal hopes. A polity cannot attain sanctity, or reliable wisdom, or eternal life. A polity cannot achieve redemption. And while human destiny is enacted in history, and polities participate in this history, it is questionable whether one can say that a polity has a destiny. Some of the most egregious political errors of our time have come from attributing to humans collectively the same dialectical destiny that pertains to individuals. The tragedy of Communism was owing basically to the notion that there could be such a thing as collective redemption. And savage forms of nationalism have come from the idea that a destiny belongs mainly, not to an individual or to humankind, but to a state or a nation.

It may have seemed, in the course of this essay, that the concept of hope as dialectical has a pessimistic edge. And so it does: hope is inseparable from distress. But that concept also has an optimistic edge, in that hope can be for resplendent ends—for righteousness, and wisdom, and eternal life—ends attainable by individuals but not by polities. Such a perspective accentuates the eschatological horizon of human existence. Not that polities enter into the final consummation of history, but rather that they do not: their presence in historical life makes it continually obvious that there must be an eschatological break. The life that has been lived in history must finally be judged and transfigured.

In short, polities are not crucified and are not raised from the dead. They do not enter into the glory of the Resurrection. This is why any effort to establish a

Christian polity is so inappropriate. Such an effort can lead only to an hierocratic order which suppresses and obscures the drama of sin and redemption. Such an order, losing sight of the dialectic of human destiny, is necessarily hopeless. From this vantage point we can see why the liberty which authorizes and safeguards a life apart from the polity is so vital to the task of understanding and sustaining hope. We shall pursue this matter in the following section.

Here we need only note that one of the first rules of statesmanship, following from preceding comments, is that of *bounded* hope. The main question for rulers should never be, "What exciting possibilities can we envision?" but rather, "In view of the moral law and existing circumstances, what must we do?" It follows that political responsibility belongs, with such activities as meditation and remembrance, to the spirituality of hope. Politics is as much a search for hope as an outflow of hope. We engage in politics because our situation, construed as the face of human destiny, requires us to. Politics is a hard and not entirely welcome obligation. For the revolutionaries and tyrants of our time, however, politics is exaltation and glory. They have been impelled by hope of a kind that has made them reckless and exultant, rather than sober and obedient. The realities of the political world show which side the truth is on. Anyone who pays heed to the daily life of the political order knows that circumstances are often discouraging. Political practitioners who are clear-sighted, and looking for public rather than merely private advantages, are often reduced to hoping for hope. For them, politics means striving to discern and conform with a logic of personal and historical life which is oftener obscure and onerous than exciting and uplifting. In a word, the proper mood of politics is sobriety.

Very different was the mood of ancient city-state politics, as classically expressed by Aristotle. For Aristotle, as everyone knows, humans are essentially political, since they are by nature both social and rational, and accordingly (leaving to one side Aristotle's concern with theoretical reason and meditation) find in political life and activity complete personal fulfillment. The exercise of political responsibility is therefore spontaneous and joyful.

The viewpoint of this essay is far more guarded. Complete personal fulfillment cannot be found in any earthly association or activity, and so far as there is partial fulfillment, it is apt to be found in greater degree in the Church than in the state. Political responsibility consequently comes to be marked more by obligation and constraint—by sobriety—than by spontaneity and joy.

The grounds of sobriety lie in our finitude and moral unreliability. A politics of exalted hope, like that of modern revolutionaries, from the time of the French Revolution to that of the Communist Revolution in China and even to the present day, is false to human nature. We have neither the intellectual comprehension nor the moral discipline called for by large-scale projects of social reconstruction. This has been amply demonstrated by the results of modern revolutionary efforts. Those who close their eyes to human limits debase hope by deflecting it from eternal goals and subordinating it to willful earthly fantasies. The ideal of historical mastery is a delusion of modern pride. Merely to discern, and to carry on a common life in response to, the claims of destiny as reflected in a set of historical circumstances, is a difficult and noble task, and that is the task—rather than historical mastery— to which we are called by hope that is undistorted by pride. Such hope gives rise to a political spirit nearer to that of the later Stoics, such as Marcus Aurelius, than to Aristotle; it is a spirit colored by attunement to duties inherent in the basic order of things—in the Logos. Sobriety is inhospitable to stirring political images and slogans, hence perhaps lacking in allure for some. Still, it cannot be wholly unappealing to people who have lived in a century so disastrously deficient in sobriety as our own.

A politics of sobriety would take the form sometimes of a stance seldom adopted in so impatient and restless a society as America. The stance is that of waiting. As we have seen, the idea of waiting for God is strongly emphasized both in the Old Testament and in the words of Jesus ("Watch and pray"). There is such a thing as waiting for God in a political situation. It comes about when the demands of a situation are contradictory or obscure. Hence we hesitate, hoping for clarity of mind and conscience. We wait for the leadership of God. In such circumstances, the waiting is itself a form of obedience—an act taken, so to speak, in anticipation of further instructions. In an age beguiled by unrealistic hope, waiting is a repellent notion, darkened by a consciousness of human limitations. But neglect of those limitations, in our time, has been calamitous. A realization of their inescapable reality would be one of the benefits of a true understanding of hope.

A sober politics of hope would bring a willingness not only to wait but also to suffer; it would match the idea of political action with the idea of political suffering. The perplexity the idea of political suffering is apt to cause us, in contrast with our ready understanding of the idea of political action, suggests the extent to which our minds have been captivated by the ethos of mastery. We gladly think of acting on, and resolving, problematic situations; but suffering from them strikes us as useless and humiliating, something that greater vigilance and wider knowledge might enable us to avoid. Yet isn't it manifest that political suffering often occurs and that not always is it inconsequential?

Consider one figure who suffered politically in our time—Dietrich Bonhoeffer. In a sense, Bonhoeffer accomplished nothing; he was arrested and executed before the fall of the Nazi regime, and that fall was brought about by the Allied armies and perhaps not furthered even in the slightest degree by the German Resistance. Yet surely Bonhoeffer's suffering, which upheld the honor of the human race, was as vital to the ultimate cause fought for by the Allied armies as any action taken by anyone with political power.[2] A similar point could be made in reference to numerous dissidents in present and past times.

Practicing the politics of hope, with hope construed as situational obedience, is an unexciting discipline. It does not kindle dreams of earthly triumphs and perfections. But it is very far from despair. The hope it rests on and searches for inheres in the faith that there is sense even in apparently senseless events and that, by standing fast in that faith and by acting on it in the ways prevailing circumstances require, the meaning of events will be shown to us, wholly at the end of time and perhaps partially during our lives here on earth. The twentieth century has been badly served by a politics of impatience. It is time, perhaps, to open our minds to politics of a different kind.

To understand more fully the nature of political responsibility, and its role in calling forth and sustaining hope, we must consider the institution on which politics is centered.

Liberty, State, Dialogue

The state has gained an evil reputation in the twentieth century. The reason is obvious; it has played a central part in some of the worst crimes of our era. The state is not evil in essence, however. It has an indispensable role in historical life, and insofar as it fills that role it is second only to the Church as a vehicle of eternal and temporal hope. That the state has been idealized by some political philosophers is not accidental; the state does have an ideal aspect. It is particularly important that this aspect be brought out in a time like the present, when the state is so widely—and with so much justification—denigrated. We shall begin, then, by noting the ideal which the state ought, and in some measure is able, to realize. Then we shall take cognizance of the evil aspects of the state. This will enable us to see that even though the state is not in essence wholly evil, its operations are inevitably attended with evil—a fact which leads to the imperative of liberty. The state and liberty are polar opposites in that the one entails coercion, the other personal spontaneity. Nevertheless, they define the framework of human destiny on earth and, in that way, the framework of earthly hope.

The state in essence is universal. It exists to integrate all human activities in a single order of life, and even in its worst moments it cannot evade this definition; it must provide some sort of order for all of life. This is to speak of "moral universality." But "numerical universality" is implied: an order designed for humanity in

---

2 See Eberhard Bethge, *Dietrich Bonhoeffer, Man of Vision, Man of Courage,* trans. Eric Mosbacker, Peter and Betty Ross, Frank Clarke, and William Glen-Doepel (New York: Harper & Row, 1970).

its essence must, in some sense, be open to all human beings. Thus, as instanced by Nazi Germany, the worst states—those furthest from moral universality—are apt to be the most violent and categorical of states in their repudiation of numerical universality. This essential universality—the ideal aspect of the state—is what links the state with hope, which is, as we have seen, for all persons, in their full humanity, and not for the self alone. Its essential universality also links the state with the uncircumscribed attentiveness and availability which constitute political responsibility. Arising from the concern—inherent in hope—with universal humanity, political responsibility necessarily brings involvement in the forming and sustaining of states. It is not just happenstance that the Enlightenment, in all of its conscious and aggressive (as well as naive) universalism, brought forth numerous modern states, such as France and the United States.

It is vital to grasp the two kinds of universality characterizing the state—that of adequacy to universal human nature, and that of global inclusiveness. The former has a certain primacy, even though the latter has great moral weight. Strictly speaking, a global state would not be universal if it were based on radically false or inadequate views of human nature; Nazism could never have become universal, even if it had conquered the world. On the other hand, a tiny state, providing an ideal environment for human beings at their best, would possess a kind of universality. For Aristotle, as we all know, a state no larger than a relatively small modern city might provide for the full realization of human nature and in that sense be universal. Indeed, a larger state, even a global state, could not realize a good life to the degree a polis could and thus could not be truly universal—a conviction widespread in the age of the polis and a major factor in the fierce resistance of the Greeks to the Persian invaders in the early part of the fifth century before Christ.

Every state possesses a kind of universality in the moral sense; a state, as I said above, cannot evade its own universalist definition. Not that every state is adequate to the full range of human potentialities; indeed, we may safely say that none of them are. But every state is responsible for organizing a single and all-inclusive order of life. The mark of the state is comprehensiveness, and the term state is simply not applied to any organization which fails to acknowledge this standard. The state is the one group, aside from the Church, that is responsible for the whole order of life. This does not mean, of course, that the state has a right to regulate the whole of life. Indeed, it is arguable that the state should regulate very little. It is the state, however, as even libertarians would acknowledge, that must define and safeguard those areas of life that are properly exempt from regulation. It is easy to see why politics, as the activity in which we take cognizance of and responsibility for the common situation of the human race, is connected with the state in a way it is not with any other group. To reflect on our common life, and on what we can and should do to shape it, necessarily calls forth the concept of an organization responsible not for one particular interest or another but for the common life in general.

It seems, then, that the so-called "nation-state system," a world of diverse and competing states, is hard to justify. A state adequate to human nature as such is in some sense properly the home country of all human beings, and if a state proclaimed that by its very essence it could not accomodate a particular race or other genetic type—as has, of course, happened, even in recent times—it would thereby in large measure renounce statehood itself. Shouldn't the entire human race, then, be in one state? Isn't the present multiplicity of states in contradiction with our every humanity? Insofar as we are able to form states adequate to human nature, the answer to both questions must be Yes. The ancient ideal of humankind as a great cosmic city—an ideal based both on Stoic philosophy and on Christian theology, and realized in a fashion by the Roman Empire and later on by the medieval Catholic Church—possesses nearly irresistible moral authority and enters accordingly into any definition of ultimate human hope. The multiplicity of states is as stark a sign of human failure as is the multiplicity of churches.

The one argument in favor of a multiplicity of states—a conclusive argument, I believe—is similar to the argument I advanced in favor of a multiplicity of churches. Human beings in their fallenness are incapable of creating a state adequate to their potentialities; moral universality is beyond them. Numerical universality therefore is not imperative, and may even be undesirable. By relativizing one another, diverse states testify more clearly to our imperfections, and may represent more fully our perfections, than a single state could. Also, diverse states serve the realization of human potentialities by offering individuals an opportunity that would be unavailable in a global state—that of emigration. Thus Gibbon noted that the very vastness of the Roman Empire made it peculiarly oppressive: it was virtually impossible for anyone to leave it. None of these considerations imply that the nation-state system is ideal. On the contrary, they bring sharply into focus the difference between eschatological and historical hope. The former envisions a cosmic city, inhabited by all human beings in their full humanity. The latter, restricted by earthly conditions, is perforce confined to a multiplicity of parochial and imperfect states, all inhabited by fragmentary and imperfect human beings.

The value underlying universality has already been discussed in this essay: it is truth, sought out and known in common—a condition we have called community. A good state, that is, a morally universal state, is one in which truth is to a high degree prized and known. Thus, if we ask what makes ancient Athens admirable our answer is apt to center on the tragic drama, history, philosophy, and other ways in which truth was in some degree seen and shared. Common pursuit and knowledge of the truth expresses the two primary human virtues—the wisdom, or faith, which enables us to lay hold of the truth, and the love which impels us to share the truth. If there could be a state in which all truth was perfectly known, it would necessarily reach out to encompass the human race. There is universality (and hope is fulfilled) wherever there is truth; even a solitary person— Saint Paul in prison, Kant in his study—can, in knowing the truth, be a kind of universal city. But unqualified universality is found only where all truth is known by all persons.

Defining universality in terms of truth brings us back to familiar themes—first of all to the theme that humans are by nature communal beings. We hunger as naturally for the truth as we do for food, and when we know, or think that we know, the truth, we feel an irresistible desire to share it. If community is that which arises from the communication of truth, or from the common search for truth, then community is an imperious need and an ultimate hope. And, as there are no limits either on the degree of truth we would know, or on the extent to which we would share the truth known, we are oriented in our primal, created being toward universality. And another theme that again comes before us is that hope is for God, since God is truth—a common principle among theologians. This is not merely a way of saying that the highest truth is *about* God. Rather, the truth—*all* truth—*is* God. God knows all things and in this way is wise infinitely beyond the way in which any human being is wise. It is not accurate to say that God *possesses* wisdom, however, even though we spontaneously speak in that way. If God merely possessed wisdom we might think of God as not having wisdom, that is, as foolish; and to think of God as foolish would be not to think of God. As infinite and perfect, God must be not simply wise but identical with wisdom. That is, God must be truth itself.[3] In seeking truth, we are seeking God. The basic principle here is expressed in classical theology by saying that God is utterly simple.

Another familiar theme that comes to mind when we speak of the state in terms of a universality that is realized through searching for and possessing the truth is dialogue. If humans are impelled by an ineluctable law of their being—by love for the God who is truth and by love for their neighbors—toward a state of shared truth, then they are by nature dialogical. They are fully themselves, and face in the direction of the community they hope for above all else, only through truth-seeking speech. Human destiny is lived through dialogue. It must be granted that successful dialogue is a rare achievement. Nonetheless, a society in which people do not strive to speak seriously with one another is deeply degraded. This standard helps explain the horror of totalitarianism, which one might roughly define as an order replacing dialogue with propaganda, mass hysteria, and terror. It also helps explain the profound dangers inherent in rampant commercialism, filling public space as it does with advertising and slogans. It is fitting that freedom of speech,

---

3 See Thomas Aquinas, *Summa Theologica*, I, Q. 16, Art. 5.

providing, as it were, a fortress for dialogue, holds a place of particular honor among American rights.

It is not surprising, then, that in defining the two public arenas in which hope is practiced—Church and state—we have in both cases necessarily discussed dialogue. The section on the Church in the preceding chapter was entitled "Solitude, Church, Dialogue." The title of the present section is "Liberty, State, Dialogue." These titles are intended to mark the fact that where humans come to grips with their ultimate purposes, where they live with hope, they search together, through speech, for the truth. In some cases the truth is explicitly spiritual, concerned with God; in other cases it is concerned with the wellbeing of the state, it is political. What is crucial about dialogue, however, does not lie in its accomplishments. These are often meagre; even the ideal dialogues delineated by Plato typically end inconclusively. The crucial characteristic of dialogue lies in its essential orientation: toward perfect community. That, of course, is the object of hope. Hence anyone indifferent to dialogue faces away from the human goal, so to speak, and is necessarily hopeless.

Church and state both owe their moral authority to the standard of universality, a standard they observe in different ways. The concept of universality, however, suggests to our minds something abstract and impersonal. This makes it particularly important to link the standard with dialogue, which is ordinarily envisioned as concrete and personal. In connection with the Church I spoke of the necessity of its being embodied in churches, where people meet face-to-face. At various points we will see this necessity in connection with the state. The linkage of the universal and the dialogical is vital in both cases because it manifests the fusion of the all-embracing and the immediate which, as we have seen, belongs to the essence of love. Christian love is paradoxical; it is all-inclusive, since it is for your "neighbor"—anyone on earth whom you happen to encounter; yet it is also stringently exclusive—since it is for your neighbor, the one you here and now have actually encountered. Dialogue realizes, in the most serious possible way, both the universality of this relationship—in the striving toward absolute truth—and its concreteness, since the striving is carried on in the company of particular people.

The concept of universality, when understood in a dialogic fashion, sets a standard by which actual states can be judged and the conduct of state affairs carried on. It establishes a purpose, or rather a dual purpose: first, to render processes of inquiry into truth as effective as possible, by such means as rigorous education, vital cultural practices, and articulate political leadership; and further, breaking through class, racial, and other boundaries, to draw into these processes as many people as possible. The worst states will be those based on propaganda and violence, and also—a point imperfectly understood in the Western democracies—those continually diverted by advertising and entertainment. But even the best states will not be very good. They will comprise only a small portion of the human race, and the truth actually known will be no more than a fragment of the whole truth and will be very unevenly shared. Numerical and moral universality will ordinarily be in tension, the one inclining toward democracy, the other toward aristocracy. And every state will be weighed down by great numbers of people, some of them wealthy, famous, and influential, who care nothing for either truth or communication. Nonetheless, the universality of the state is not irrelevant to the realities of the world. It represents hope, and hope will draw people continually in the direction of deeper truths, more amply shared.

Although the state cannot be the same as the Church, clearly it is only by means of the Church (and of the culture which, in its dedication to beauty and truth, is the secular counterpart of the Church) that the state can fulfill its essential ends. The Church, in its responsibility for the ultimate truth incarnate in Christ, is more immediately involved than any other agency with the universality which is the final goal of history and the state. If the state is the earthly form of community, the Church is the earthly substance of community. A state without the Church cannot sustain politics as participation in history or provide liberty that ministers to ultimate aspirations.

In short, a state secular through and through could not provide a setting where people could live with hope. It is true that culture, that is, the realm of art, literature, science, and philosophy, can be secular in the sense of being outside the bounds and authority of the Church, yet at the same time transcendental, in seeking absolute truth. A vital culture can play an important part in the fulfillment of a state's purposes, as is dramatically illustrated by ancient Athens or Renaissance Florence. Christians will be interested in and supportive of such a culture. Seen from the Christian standpoint, however, culture does not suffice. It lacks the faith and the explicit commitments which bind the Church to the eschatological goal of truth absolute and universally known. We should not let the familiar phrase "separation of state and Church" hide from our eyes the deep interdependence of these two institutions.

Up to this point, however, we have discussed only one aspect of the state—the ideal. I have been concerned to bring out characteristics of the state emphasized by philosophers such as Aristotle in ancient times and Hegel in modern times. But the state is radically ambiguous—not only genuinely spiritual but also harshly temporal. Although shaped by the universality inherent in its function of ordering the whole of life, it must make its way across the seas of violence and heartlessness that pervade a fallen world. The temporal—or "realistic"—aspect of the state has been emphasized by writers such as Thucydides and Machiavelli. Why theorists of the state have tended so stubbornly toward one-sidedness is an interesting question but outside the bounds of our present concerns. For whatever reasons, the philosophy of the state is characterized from the beginning by extremes of ide-alism and realism. The latter, which we must now discuss, is no less necessary to an adequate view of the state than is the former.

The harsh realities that necessarily enter into the life of the state and consti-tute the radical difference between state and Church, have their source in a right the state shares with no other group—that of using violence. This right is of course rooted in the responsibility of the state for the whole of life; it must have the tools to see that life remains a whole and is not broken apart by contending factions. In peaceful and stable times, the tools of violence will oftener be held in readiness than actually used. But possession of weapons, and command of organizations skilled in using them, are conspicuous and essential characteristics of the state. In conse-quence, the state is very different from the Church even though both of them aim at spiritual and global universality. On the one hand, the right to use violence renders the state organizationally superior to the Church. It is the state, not the Church, that determines the form of the social order and the role of the Church within it. On the other hand, the use of violence renders the state morally and spiritually inferior to the Church. The ancient conviction that Church and state should be distinct and in some manner separate may mirror a realization that the hands of the state inevitably become stained with blood and that the Church ought to play a less compromising role in the drama of history.

It should be noted that not only the use of violence, but of power in general, lies at the source of the state's morally problematic nature. Power is a broader cate-gory than violence, including every means of inducing others to serve one's own purposes (which are not necessarily selfish). Some kinds of power, such as verbal persuasion, are relatively innocuous. But power in essence involves the use and consequent objectification of human beings and is therefore a degraded rela-tionship if judged by the standard of love. Power of course is found in all earthly groups, even in intimate ones such as the family. The Church, as everyone knows, is laden with power relationships and has often been one of the chief powers in the world. But the state not only is the sovereign power among the power-centers of so-ciety; it has to sustain existence in a world of competing states. Hence, to a degree unique among groups, it is structured by power-relationships and related to the human race at large through power.

Steeped in violence and power, the state is morally impure even at its best. And it is never at its best. State power is rarely in the hands of people who are morally very good. This is partly because few such people exist. And it is partly because high positions in the state are nearly irresistible incitements to pride. The leaders of states enjoy privileges, pleasures, and adulation to a degree that can leave only the most extraordinary personalities undefiled. Abraham Lincoln achieved moral and spiritual grandeur in a position of high political power, but he is perhaps the only

American President of whom this can be said, and it can be said of Lincoln partly because the Civil War made the presidency a scene of torment and humiliation—and, for Lincoln, a scene of moral and spiritual purification.

The state, then, in part necessarily, in part gratuitously, is complicit in evil. This cannot but affect decisively the way in which it pursues its ultimate aims. Universality cannot usually be attained through imperialistic unification or coercive support for truth. A genuine global community cannot be created by conquering armies, and recognition and communication of truth cannot be effected by the police. Hence the state is largely restricted to protecting those agencies that can undertake a direct responsibility for communication and truth. These include both the Church and all manner of other cultural and educational institutions. Since separate individuals, as well as institutions, can be spiritual agencies, as shown in earlier reflections on solitude, they too must also be protected. The state of course can affect the minds of citizens through leadership, example, and morally-motivated legislation. But its direct responsibility is for order, and the means that end requires bar it normally from playing a very creative role in a people's spiritual life. It must concentrate on protecting those better fitted for playing such a role.

This implies that the immediate end of the state is liberty. Not that universal communication is always advanced by liberty. It is sometimes set back, for liberty gives humans in all of their perverse and erring ways power to delay and obstruct the fulfillment of true hope. The liberty intended primarily for aristocrats of the spirit is seized by every manner of opportunist and profit-seeker, and there is no practical way in which this can be prevented. Hence those who represented the most exultant and intransigent hope of our time, that of Communism, invariably rejected liberty and idolized the state. But liberty is indispensable to universality. There can be no common search for truth, and no sharing of truth attained, unless people are free to think and speak as their consciences command. This too is illustrated in the Communist world. Wherever liberty was crushed by the totalitarian state, gross falsehoods and oversimplifications—concerning history, human nature, and even the physical world—gained uncontested control of public intellectual life. Hope is therefore compelled to submit to the hazards of liberty. If inquiry, understanding, and faith are to flourish, tolerance is not so much a manifest benefit as an imperious necessity, hence an unavoidable risk.

The liberty that serves community cannot be understood as bare absence of legal restraint. It is that in part, to be sure. The greatest threat to liberty comes from government, and the prime requirement for liberty is consequently the establishment of effective restraints on government. Liberty demands constitutionalism. But it demands more than this. Liberty depends on conditions such as leisure and literacy, which the state can do much to define and protect. To specify liberty as the end of the state is not to idealize the negative state. It is rather to bring into view a broad range of social circumstances restrictive of liberty and thus to make us aware that state action may, by restricting the sway of restrictive circumstances, magnify the total area of liberty. Not that this is easily done. Bureaucratic ineptitude is a far more stubborn and destructive facet of state activity than was realized when the New Deal was flourishing. Almost all parties and shades of opinion, nevertheless, now recognize that the liberal state has far more to do than merely to keep the peace.

This point has particular importance in relation to the poor and underprivileged. A state has little claim to universality unless liberty is available to all who live within it. This will rarely, if ever, be the case without state action in protection of the weak. This was first realized early in the industrial revolution, when it became apparent that, in the absence of state intervention, workers were inevitably victims of corporate despotism. Liberty depended not only on constitutional states but also, in a manner of speaking, on constitutional corporations. In the century that has passed since Western states began widening the liberty of oppressed laborers by narrowing the liberty of their corporate oppressors, numerous groups have laid claim to state protection. Even the most conservative parties do not now contest the need for a measure of such protection. To think of all this in terms of compassion for the disinherited and the downtrodden, however, is risky. It tends to obscure the ultimate aim, which is not that of doing away with suffering, but is rather the involvement of as many people as possible in the kind of public and private truth-seeking discourse which constitutes the universality of a state. We show little respect for people merely by admitting them to the distractions of a debased popular culture. As Plato and other Athenians realized two-and-a-half millenia ago, the supreme mark of respect is to speak with someone about the truth.

The ultimate end, however, remains simple: liberty, under conditions enhancing the probability of its bearing fruit in community. Among the immediate purposes of the state, liberty is prior in importance even to the advancement of communication and truth. As already noted, the state is not entirely without spiritual responsibilities. Governments can in various ways elevate or debase the minds of citizens, and obviously they must consider which it is they are doing. But spiritual aims must be absolutely subordinate to liberty, and state activities in support of community, such as funding for the arts, must be curtailed whenever they threaten to infringe on liberty. And it is probably better, in being more expressive of the essential antithesis of the spiritual and the political, for private agencies to fulfill spiritual functions even when the state might fulfill them without appreciable harm. Insofar as this happens, the immediate spiritual responsibilities of the state are diminished. But the state can never allow its responsibility for liberty to be diminished. It must see that this primary condition of community is never abridged, more than the necessities of historical life require, by its own agents, by the Church, or by any other private group.

The priority of liberty can be seen by setting liberty alongside other public aims, such as material prosperity and justice, and comparing them in value. Consider, for example, a public good often treated as elemental, that of order. Imagine a society in which perfect order prevails, a society in which a person's life is never in any way subject to disruption by capricious, unforeseeable acts on the part of others. If the reigning order were not a framework for liberty, or at least a basis for eventually achieving liberty, one might reasonably prefer anarchy. Indeed, were we to look deeply into our desire for order we might find it to be a desire, not for any kind of regularity whatever, but for the regularity that allows us to plan and carry on our lives without fear of arbitrary interference from others. That is, we might find that our interest in order is fundamentally an interest in liberty. What we often forget is that order does not necessarily provide liberty. Numerous examples, such as ancient Sparta or Fascist Italy, make this obvious. Order can be totalitarian and oppressive. Forgetting this, we mistake order for a value having claims on our allegiance as strong as those of liberty.

A similar test can be carried out by imagining a society realizing a high degree of economic efficiency. If the resulting material abundance served a life without liberty, as in Dostoevsky's fantasy of life under the Grand Inquisitor, one might feel that poverty, with liberty, would provide a better environment for the human spirit. What is the strongest argument in favor of material prosperity? Not, surely, that it brings a multitude of pleasures to daily life, but rather that it releases people from oppressive economic constraints. In short, it enhances liberty and frees people for inquiry and communication; activities such as science, art, and philosophy become possible. Conversely, the truest critique of prosperity is that it softens people, and spoils them, rendering them unfit for liberty and insensitive to the truth.

In many cases the priority of liberty to other public aims comes, as with truth and communication, from the radical dependence on liberty of the public aim in question. Consider justice, for example—one of the oldest ideals in political philosophy, and in the minds of many a standard transcending all others in importance. To subordinate justice to liberty looks almost frivolous. But imagine a perfectly just society which is maintained altogether by force and propaganda. The absence of liberty would deprive it largely, if not wholly, of worth. The people making up such a society would not be just in themselves, for they would not be freely just. Values are realized by being deliberately chosen, and in that way alone. The notion of their being imposed is a contradiction in terms. Where it seems that a society has imposed values by force, as in modern totalitarian states, close examination will show in every case, I think, either that the values have mysteriously evaporated in the very act of imposition (for example, truth) or that the values imposed have in fact been meretricious—not real values (for example, uniformity). Hence a society which gives up liberty for the sake of justice loses both. Justice as a true value can be affirmed only by subordinating it to liberty. It is true, of course, that people are occasionally forced into acting justly, and in these cases the relationship is reversed: liberty is subordinated to justice. But to make the reversed relationship a permanent principle of the social order would banish liberty and justice alike.

The priority of liberty to values such as truth, community, and justice, is paradoxical. It is not that liberty has great intrinsic value; indeed, it has no intrinsic value at all, since there is no value in choosing freely if one does not choose authentic values. The value of liberty is relative: things that do have intrinsic value depend for their value on being freely incorporated in human lives. They must be chosen by people who are free not to choose them. This means, very simply, that the fulfillment of hope—for truth, community, justice—requires that individuals and peoples be in a position to frustrate such fulfillment. It is an ineluctable necessity that hope be rendered vulnerable to human fallibility and wickedness.

Liberty plainly calls for a life of obedience rather than exaltation. This is because liberty itself is an obligation, the meeting of which may be onerous, since liberty entails responsibility. It might be said with little exaggeration that today in the industrial democracies, liberty is valued mainly because it is thought to be fun. It enables you to do what you feel like doing, and that, presumably, is to live a pleasurable life. But if that is all it is, liberty is paltry. It may be something you would like to have but it is scarcely something for which you would risk your life. On the other hand, if liberty is not paltry—if it is intrinsic to our full humanity and thus to the life of hope—then it is not fun. Rather, it involves difficult tasks such as deciding what is true and trying to be good. It engages one in the travail of trying to find and communicate the truth, and of trying to live in accordance with the truth. As writers such as Erich Fromm have argued in connection with Nazism, liberty may in some circumstances, far from being pleasurable, be a thing from which people flee.[4] In other words, if liberty is serious, it is prized because it is essential to the conduct of a destiny. To be free is not, ordinarily, to be exalted but to heed the deepest necessities of one's life.

Liberty is imposed by the elemental circumstances of human existence. There is truth and righteousness, and there is error and evil; these are ordinarily mixed together in the most confusing ways, and we must choose between them. Such are the primal conditions facing every person. To ignore them, as is often done—for example, by relativists, who deny that we face moral alternatives, and by determinists, who deny that we have the power to choose between them—is to forsake our humanity. According to Christianity, the burden of liberty is placed on human shoulders in the divine act of creation. One who would live faithfully to God must

---

4 See Erich Fromm, *Escape from Freedom* (New York: Rinehart, 1941).

accept the burden and bear it in conformity with divine commands. Indeed, obedience is not simply entailed by liberty; obedience is the very purpose of liberty. This is why the life of liberty partakes of the sobriety identified above as the spirit of political responsibility. Rather than being fun, this life can scarcely be carried on without suffering—the suffering inherent in being intellectually fallible and morally impaired, yet, in Sartre's famous phrase, "condemned to be free."[5]

It is not surprising that most people, in most periods of history, have rallied to one or another standard of absolute authority. The standard of liberty requires society to give flawed humanity a chance, within broad limits, to do its worst. If the spirit of obedience is entirely lacking, liberty will bring disorder and degradation inevitably. This is not a mere theory or conjecture: witness American life today. Not all Americans misuse their liberty, of course, but a great many do. This is evident in the baseness of popular culture and the sexual disorder manifest in current divorce and abortion rates—to say nothing of drug use, financial corruption, and other signs of social disintegration. To be tolerant, or supportive of liberty, depends on having the patience and strength to put up with the failures and misdeeds which are sure to be conspicuous on all sides, as well as painfully present in one's own mind and conduct, in a liberal society.

Liberty depends radically on hope—not on the mere hope that free people will behave in ways that are harmless, but on a far higher hope: that they will be good. Liberty cannot be justified unless a real possibility exists that those liberated will live as humans ought to live. Only those capable of righteousness and wisdom have a valid claim to liberty. When the love of liberty expresses merely the will to indulge personal impulses without interference, it is frivolous. Liberty can no doubt exist, at least for a time, on the basis of a hedonistic calculus. But then it is worthless. And since liberty will not in all circumstances prove pleasurable, it will eventually be cast aside. To live with hope is to live in conformity, as far as possible, with destiny; and that, in turn, is to heed the moral necessities intrinsic to a personal and historical situation. In other words, hope not only anticipates the righteousness and wisdom which are the best fruits of liberty; it begets the spirit of obedience which is essential to serious, rather than frivolous, liberty. In both of these ways, hope is the fountainhead of liberty.

This proposition cannot quite be reversed; we cannot say that liberty is the fountainhead of hope. Yet a regime of liberty recognizes the nature of hope, and provides room for hope, more fully than does any other regime. In this sense, and to this degree, hope depends on liberty. The point can be expressed most adequately, perhaps, by saying that liberty allows for the full unfolding of the dialectical

---

5 Jean-Paul Sartre, *Being and Nothingness: An Essay on Phenomenological Ontology*, trans. Hazel E. Barnes (New York: Philosophical Library, 1956), p. 439.

antitheses involved in every destiny. As we have seen, the concept of destiny pertains to individual persons and to universal humanity in a way that it does not pertain to polities. Hence where the individual is submerged in the polity, and humanity is wholly defined by the polity, destiny is suppressed. But this is to say also that hope is suppressed, since hope arises from a sense of destiny. We have seen how this happens in an earlier discussion where it was noted how the effort to establish a Christian polity comes into conflict with the drama of sin and redemption. The result is a more or less fixed, and undialectical, hierocracy.

The purpose of liberty, then, is the life of hope. Hope is for the common righteousness and wisdom centered in the vision of God—in a word, eternal life. But this vision can only be a dialectical achievement—that of attaining righteousness through the forgiveness of sin, of gaining wisdom by overcoming folly, and of entering into eternal life by following the dark pathway of mortality. This is the shape of destiny, hence the form of authentic hope. When hope takes this form, it enables us to live as we should—but could not if our lives were formed wholly by the state. In other words, the purpose of liberty is that we lose our lives in order to gain them.

When liberty is repudiated, the link between liberty and hope comes clearly into view. Tyranny expresses a resolve to leave nothing in the sphere of hope—a sphere without objective guarantees of the future—and to seek assurance in force. Tyrants are necessarily hopeless. This is the case as well with the masses on whose support every tyrant depends. Thus the Fascist and Nazi tyrannies that arose after World War I had their source in the despair caused by social and economic chaos. Security was sought in the will of the leader. Soviet tyranny, it must be granted, did not arise originally from despair. But neither, as I have already argued in my comments on Marxism, did it arise from true hope. Its origins lay in a godlike certainty concerning the historical future—a certainty founded on pride and on resignation to a universe without God. Lenin and Trostsky, like Mussolini and Hitler, were men without hope.

Liberty is fruitless, however, unless it brings change. Hence living with hope entails not only liberty but also openness to change, that is, to life in history. To inquire further into the politics of hope, then, we must consider how true hope involves us in historical change—both toward changes which merely happen and also toward changes we deliberately effect.

Liberty and Change

Deliberate social change is an undertaking freighted with probabilities of disappointment. The reasons are familiar, if usually ignored: our finitude and consequent inability to foresee all the consequences of our actions; the blindness and recklessness inherent in our pride. As governors of history we are handicapped not only by the limitations belonging to our creaturehood but by the sinfulness which disposes us to ignore our limitations, thus colliding with them more violently than we otherwise might. Attempts to effect specific historical changes practically never succeed altogether and sometimes, especially when they are very ambitious, fail catastrophically. All of this is illustrated profusely in the history of revolution and reform during the past two hundred years and should instill in reformers a realism which until now has been evident mainly among conservatives.

Social change nevertheless is incumbent on us. To resist all change is to fail in elemental responsibility toward those who suffer unfairly and remediably under the existing order. Efforts to move toward greater justice and harmony, even though of uncertain outcome, are commands of love. Unyielding defense of the status quo is morally tolerable only where no one suffers unjustly, and that, of course, is no-where. Compassion and absolute conservatism are incompatible.

Moreover, to resist all change is to fail in hope. How could it be said that there is hope in the mind of anyone who wants to keep an established society exactly as it is? Not by claiming that such a person may harbor a hope that is purely eschatologi-cal, for, as I have argued earlier, separating eternal hope from temporal hope is like uprooting a living plant. It will die. While hope is properly directed toward the end of history, it must be lived within history. Otherwise, it will become a mere idea, ab-stracted from life. Far from undermining social change, an eschatological faith evokes a spirit of reform. Such a spirit is essential to its own vitality. If the meaning of history lies in its eschatological momentum—its movement toward the end—then denial of the movement is denial of the end. A refusal to take part in history and in the changes it entails, turns eschatology into a set of dead words rather than a living faith.

This is to say that social change is a matter of situational obedience. It has not ordinarily been viewed in this way during the past century or two. It has been viewed rather as a goal arising from our own goodness and power—from purely human compassion and purely human mastery over historical developments; and it sometimes has been regarded, as in Marxism, as demanded by the full un-foldment of human productive forces. Historical change, in this humanist vision, is rooted in human will and power. It is therefore effected in a spirit of exaltation, rather than obedience. Much of the turmoil of our times derives from this fact. We have been ready victims of our finitude and pride.

Insofar as we face our finitude and overcome our pride, however, political re-sponsibility becomes less exhilarating and more irksome. Given a realistic hope, we are not allowed the simple and comfortable posture either of radicals of the kind who assume that extensive and salutary change is easily within our powers, or of conservatives who see the established order as beyond the possibility or the need of improvement. Efforts at social change must be made, but with the sobriety characteristic of an ethic of obedience rather than the elated self-confidence typically displayed by twentieth-century reformers and revolutionaries. True hope dissolves the ideological ardor of the left and the right alike. In doing this, it places us within the undisguised realities of history. This is why political responsibility is irksome. It can neither be evaded by the sentimental gilding of the established order practiced by conservatives nor approached with the doctrinaire self-assurance typical of radicals.

Summarily, true hope calls for a fusion of lucidity and compassion. We must try to view lucidly the circumstances that encircle us and condition all we do; and we must look compassionately on our fellow human beings. Banal as this principle may sound, practicing it is difficult; lucidity tends to banish compassion and compassion lucidity. The persistence everywhere of parties of right and left, of preservation and change, testifies to the stubborn human inclination to accord primacy to one obligation over the other. This inclination is attributable to deficiencies of hope. On the right, hopelessness takes the form of inflexible adherence to existing laws and institutions. On the left it is manifest as casual confidence that merely human powers suffice for effecting all needed reforms; everything being within the scope of human understanding and control, hope is not needed. Thus, for example, neither the typically-reactionary Russian émigrés of the 1920s and 1930s, nor the Bolsheviks from whom they fled, were truly hopeful. True hope, animated by the idea of destiny, enables us to pay our debts both to what is and to what ought to be.

When we think of change, at least in the twentieth century, we are apt to think primarily of government. This is not entirely wrong, since government has a necessary role in social reform. It is partially wrong, nevertheless, for it reflects the assumption that change must be under human control—rationally planned and methodically executed. In this way it obscures our relationship with passing occurrences, a relationship we can summarily characterize by saying that human beings are immanent in history. Even when armed with all of the organized intelligence and power of government, they are partially immersed in the stream of events. Only God is wholly transcendent. In affirming action too unqualifiedly, and in too thoroughly banishing qualms concerning its consequences, the idea that government makes us masters of social change weakens hope. There is hope only where there is trust in forces not entirely human. Hope therefore depends on a willingness to wait—a willingness not ordinarily found among those who resort instinctively to government whenever a common problem is encountered. It is vital to a balanced understanding of social change, therefore, to see at the outset that beneficent change comes not only from government but also from something at the opposite pole from government, that is, liberty.

Liberty emerges as a primary standard as soon as we begin to think about social change realistically. This happens, first of all, because realism tells us not only that all present societies are imperfect, since change is needed, but that societies will always be imperfect. Liberty, therefore, is indispensable. It guarantees a sphere of life protected against the surrounding society in its enduring imperfection. People who count unreservedly on the success of attempts to transform society are not likely to cherish liberty. Why worry about being protected against a social order that is perfect or being rapidly perfected? When such an order intervenes in my personal life it can only be to my own advantage. However, if society is resistant to reform, and if this is due to human qualities that are not ephemeral, but as enduring as finitude and moral fallibility, then liberty becomes a permanent need.

Moreover, liberty promotes change. That, too, is a reason why the ideal of liberty shines out once we begin thinking about change realistically. The kind of change promoted by liberty of course is limited. Institutionalized liberty entails the subjection of power to set procedures and permanent restraints. In this way, liberty does slow the accomplishment, and restrict the scope, of social change. It does this, however, only so far as change depends on government. Radicals who think that liberals, because they value liberty above all else, are in reality conservatives, could not be more mistaken. Liberty is not conservative. Rather, it places at the foundations of society an abundant source of change and a powerful motive toward change. Let us examine both the source and the motive.

The source is the human energy and imagination released by liberty and leading people to do things productive of change. Thucydides believed that one of the decisive advantages Athens had over Sparta, in the Peloponnesian War, was the liberty which aroused in Athenians a more intense vitality than the highly-disciplined Spartans could achieve. The typical leftist assumption that liberty must often be suspended for serious changes to be achieved is dubious at best. Liberty does not inhibit change as such; it inhibits only the kind of centrally-organized change which so many reformers have allowed themselves to equate with change itself. Thus capitalism, although supposedly the idol of conservatives, invariably is an agent of social transformation. It is often forgotten that Karl Marx, while condemning capitalism in some respects, greatly admired it in other respects. He saw it as unleashing human enterprise and calling forth momentous historical developments.

Modern reformers have often assumed, of course, that changes arising from liberty will never be fundamental because they will never displace large property owners from their privileged and dominant positions. The history of capitalism in the twentieth century partially confirms this assumption. But it also, through the development of "consumers' capitalism," partially disproves it. Even Marx thought that capitalism would tend gradually to empower the masses, and this it has done, even though wealthy property owners have induced the masses to acquiesce in their power and privileges. Indeed, the tastes and preferences of ordinary people are far more carefully and continuously consulted under capitalist regimes than under any communist regime that has ever existed.

When we speak of enterprise, however, we should not think just of business enterprise, although that is neither an insignificant nor invariably noxious source of social change. Enterprise can also be artistic and literary, educational and ecclesiastical. Liberty normally multiplies organized agents of change. One of the most important non-governmental sources of change may be the Church. Granted, the most outspoken reformers have often been religious skeptics and disdainful of the Church. Yet significant social changes have often been motivated by conscience—for example, the modifications in the raw capitalism of the early industrial revolution—and if there is one institution that more than any other enlivens and directs conscience it is the Church. In the American Civil Rights Movement, the Church was the leading agency. No doubt the upshot of change that is diverse in its origins, and spontaneous in its upsurge, is unpredictable and may be harmful. The way capitalist advertising and entertainment have undermined respect for both moral and cultural standards shows how profound and questionable changes coming from liberty can be. But changes coming from government can also be profound and questionable. Centralized planning and action, to put the point moderately, do not safeguard us from perverse and incalculable human initiatives.

It is not only by removing restraints, however, that liberty gives rise to change. The very principle of liberty contains a motive toward change. The motive is provided by the sweeping nature of the principle. Actual liberty is never more than a fragmentary realization of ideal liberty. It is never available equally to everyone, regardless of race, wealth, and social standing; it is never as complete as it ought to be, but always pertains to certain specified actions, like speech and worship, while neglecting other important actions, like work; it is never protected against all possible agents of infringement, such as private employers or family members; and it is never supported by all the conditions, like literacy and leisure, which are necessary for it to be fruitful. In short, the cry of liberty demands far more than any actual society can provide. Indeed, it conceals an anarchistic impulse; liberty would be perfect only if all organized power and all social restraints were done away with. Logically, therefore, the quest for liberty cannot end in conservative satisfaction with an established pattern of liberties. It always highlights the flaws and inadequacies in every such pattern and in this way prompts historical movement.

In other words, the idea of liberty implies ceaseless liberation. It instigates the identification of groups, such as racial or religious minorities, lacking the liberties enjoyed by the majority; it evokes efforts to render liberty more significant through such means as improving education and health care; and it produces checks on hitherto unchecked powers. It is a well-known fact that the demand for liberty is usually voiced by rising groups, like the bourgoisie which created modern liberalism, and that when such groups are satisfied, the demand in its original form dies down. But liberty is not easily contained. If some groups gain it, why not others? If the bourgoisie is set free, why not the workers too? Attempts in our own time to open up to women, to blacks, to the physically-handicapped, opportunities long considered normal by many others is illustrative of the natural dynamics of liberty.

The imperative of liberation stems, of course, from the same idea that underlies liberty itself: that a human being is a creature of peculiar dignity and ought to be permitted, therefore, to be an independent center of life. Human dignity entails responsibility—for shaping both one's own life and the life of one's people—and liberty, so to speak, is an allowance of responsibility. Since elites, however distinguished they may be with respect to intelligence, education, experience, and other desirable attributes, do not possess a larger share of dignity than others, every person has a claim to liberty; and in the absence of exceptional conditions, such as serious criminality or severe mental disability, every person has a claim to the same liberties others enjoy. The notion that every human being is sacred is one of the most potent moral ideas ever conceived, and it is partly its connection with liberty that makes it so. It causes every circumstance and power that limits liberty to be forcefully brought into question.

In other words, the project of liberation is strongly egalitarian. Hope, in its communality, is intolerant of exceptions, such as those pertaining to race, religion, gender. The goal is dialogue inclusive of all persons and all insights. Admittedly, it is difficult, even dangerous, to make the rule of equality precise and inflexible. Although this rule arises from the imperative of liberation, the rule and the imperative can come into conflict. The equality required by liberty may create conditions that threaten liberty. This was dramatically demonstrated by Alexis de Tocqueville in his analysis of American democracy. For example, equality militates in favor of uniformity; and by depriving individuals of the security provided by rank and traditional station it tends to make them slaves of public opinion. Moreover, the creation of equality often requires force; an unqualified commitment to equality would unquestionably lead to despotism. Nevertheless, since hope is for boundless communication, it must always be uneasy in the presence of drastic inequalities—of wealth, of social standing, of political power. And such uneasiness is largely independent of ideology. Sensible conservatives and sensible progressives alike will be conscious of that intrinsic dignity of personality which renders definitive and inalterable inferiority of status unfitting for any person or group.

The egalitarianism implicit in liberation becomes particularly sharp and insistent in the face not merely of inequality but of oppression and exploitation. An outcast race, a religious group that is permanently poor and powerless, an economic class systematically deprived of opportunities possessed by other classes: all of these offend authentic hope. The Bible is unequivocal in this matter, both in the

Old Testament and the New. God has a particular concern with the disinherited and downtrodden, and anyone indifferent to their fate is in rebellion against God. Not that God necessarily despises the rich; but the claim of liberation theologians that there is some sort of divine preference for the poor is not a manifest misreading of Scripture. Granted, care is needed among Christians to keep the question of moral commands separate from that of practical possibilities. The Christian view of human nature and history indicate that oppression and exploitation will never, within history, be wholly eradicated; here liberation theology was often seriously in error. But this does not imply that such conditions are ever morally acceptable and merely to be taken for granted. Christian hope anticipates a community at the end of time from which people are not excluded even by death or sin, much less by race, gender, or sincere belief. And if such hope is intransigent because it looks beyond history, to a time when human weakness and perversity have been subordinated to divine might and righteousness, it is also tenacious within history, believing that fidelity to ultimate things implies obligations toward penultimate things.

Still, there is a certain modesty implicit in the pursuit of liberty. This must be not merely conceded but insisted upon, for it is one of the strengths of the liberal persuasion. It can be useful to distinguish between liberation and social transformation. Liberation is a relatively sober ideal, in spite of the fact that it often figures in inflamed radical rhetoric. It means multiplying the areas of life in which the individual is protected against a society too flawed to be admitted into the most vital areas of personal existence. Social transformation, on the other hand, means altering society comprehensively and swiftly in order to achieve communal perfection. Liberation and social transformation are thus not only different but are mutually antagonistic. Liberty will always place obstacles in the way of social transformation by establishing substantive and procedural limits on centralized action, whereas social transformation—were it possible—would render such limits gratuitous. In comparison with social transformation, liberation is a relatively conservative standard. Within any of the Western constitutional democracies, a party pursuing liberation must seek to conserve existing institutions, since these provide for at least minimal liberties. And such a party will never aim at the social perfection which would render liberty pointless.

Although relatively conservative, however, the idea of liberation is also manifestly reformist. Widening liberty, in the sense of increasing both its amplitude and the numbers of those possessing it, is a task that is never finished. To be sure, we know that there are limits on liberation. But we can only encounter particular limits and cannot define them comprehensively prior to experimental efforts at liberation. We must assume that society as a framework of liberties is indefinitely—albeit not infinitely—perfectible. Every situation in which human beings are burdened by restrictions not dictated by stern necessity speaks to us with the voice of destiny: like the ancient Hebrews in Egypt, burdened people must be freed.

It does, of course, make a difference how liberty is used. It would be senseless to assume that liberty negligently used—in the exclusive service, say, of entertainment, recreation, and physical gratification—would make the same contribution to social progress as liberty used conscientiously. The spirit of liberty, as we have seen, is one of obedience to the necessities of human destiny. Liberty is an invitation to historical responsibility. Thus a truly liberal person is not simply permissive but is mindful of major social problems, thoughtful about solutions, and at the very least careful to live without making them worse. The liberal spirit involves a consciousness of destiny and the cultivation of hope.

One way Christianity makes for responsible liberty is by widening love beyond the private sphere. It is often thought that love for relatives, friends, and fellow-workers—those seen face-to-face—is particularly wholesome. This is partly true, but too simple. One can love people near at hand while being indifferent to all others and thus historically irresponsible. Christianity, of course, casts doubt on the value of such love. Neighborly love, as we have seen, is for concrete persons and not for abstract humanity; yet every person in the world is a potential neighbor. Love for husband or wife, or son or daughter, is right only if those loved are perceived as being the human race incarnate. Christianity calls for private love to be in this way continually universalized. In doing this it provides a foundation for historically responsible liberty. It places the private life implied by liberty in a global context and thus gives it historical significance.

It is a somber fact of our times that the most serious reformers have often been enemies of liberty. While one reason for this has been their anticipation of social perfection, another reason has been their mistrust of free peoples, that is, their want of hope. Ironically, they trusted human beings organized as a centralized governing elite—which one might think would warrant the profoundest mistrust—but mistrusted them as a populace possessed of extensive liberties. This irony is starkly exemplified in Lenin and his numerous avowed and unavowed followers around the world. It is exemplified also in the assumption, widespread even in the Western constitutional democracies, that in the non-industrial world liberty must be held in abeyance for an indefinite period of time while authoritarian governments effect industrialization and bring an end to longstanding injustices. But where reliance on organized human action is so heavy, there cannot be much hope. Trust is placed in human powers rather than divine governance, and in worldly progress rather than destiny.

Here we may see more clearly the connection between hope and the idea of change through liberty. While opposing change altogether is a sign of hopelessness, so is insistence that all change come about under centralized human direction.

True hope instills a willingness to walk in the darkness created by liberation, the darkness inherent in living into the future without the plans and centralized direction which provide the comforting illusion that we know precisely where we are going.

Let us remember "the universe of hope," as I called it in Chapter Two. Hope is based on the faith that the course of human events makes sense, that it leads toward truth and communion, even though it does this often in ways that are not fully comprehensible to us. Everything that happens enters into an all-encompassing destiny. To have faith in God and Christ, or like Dostoevsky's Porfiry to have faith simply in the ultimate direction of life itself, is to rely on destiny. The insistence that all change be under human command signifies an unwillingness to do this. Human initiative alone can be relied upon: this is the premise underlying the hopelessness of modern radicalism.

If the connection between liberty and change is denied by some, however, it is affirmed too unqualifiedly by others. The latter say that liberty is the only source of beneficent change. Illustrative is the nearly limitless faith some place in free markets, along with the axiomatic certainty that almost anything a government does will be harmful. Politics, according to this view, has no significant part in human destiny. This surely is false.

Government and Change

The need for governmental involvement in social change—and thus in history and in the enactment of human destiny—is partly a matter of mere common sense. It would scarcely need even to be spoken of were it not for doctrinaire opponents of government who insist that the natural harmony of society, typically envisioned as an economic order made both efficient and just by free markets, renders governmental intervention practically always needless, if not actually harmful. There is supposedly little that government must or can do. Common sense, however, speaks in somewhat different accents. It tells us that even though a government cannot act like a team of engineers, dismantling and rebuilding society as if it were a worn-out bridge, it is not entirely without competence and use. There must be a public agency to oversee social change, initiating changes that are needed but do not occur spontaneously, and checking changes that occur but are harmful, and government must be that agency. It tells us also that there are numerous imperative public tasks, such as national defense, crime control, environmental protection, and aid to the poor, that private agencies cannot ordinarily accomplish effectively, and that government must therefore take in hand.

One such task deserves to be particularly marked. I have argued in preceding pages that governments are responsible above all for liberty, and that liberation is egalitarian. One may infer that one task devolving on every government is that of moderating inequalities, and that this task becomes particularly exigent in cases of manifest oppression or exploitation. Governments should befriend the friendless. Granted, this will not happen as often as it should. A hundred years ago political analysts fearful of socialism assumed that once the poor were enfranchised they would vote to distribute wealth equally and would in that way impoverish the rich. Now we know that the rich usually have ample means for defending themselves, and that governments are apt to befriend mainly those already well-endowed with friends. The egalitarian obligation nonetheless remains. And within limits the obligation can be met.

There is a question, of course, as to how much even a well-intentioned government can do to remedy a condition like poverty. An age naive enough to believe that elected governments would normally, in the grip of egalitarian passion, wipe out wealth was also naive enough to believe that certain relatively simple governmental measures might eradicate poverty. In the twentieth century we have become more realistic. We are more sharply conscious not only of the tenacity of wealth but also of the intractability of poverty. We realize that poverty is probably ineradicable. But, to speak in the simple words of common sense, the poor can be helped; and the same is true of other disadvantaged groups, like American blacks. A government indifferent to the plight of such groups is not merely irresponsible. It is despairing, in the sense of having no part in the hope which envisions a community that is humanly all-comprehensive.

A major issue here for industrial nations is capitalism. How far can we trust in the invisible hand of the market? The issue has been sharpened in the latter part of the twentieth century by the growing realization, not only that the socialist alternative provides a dubious goal, given the normal ineptitude of governments, but that capitalism is remarkably efficient and fair—fair at least to the extent of making for widespread prosperity. At the same time, however, it has become apparent that uncurbed capitalism, even while bestowing the pleasures of propriety on large numbers of people, creates drastic inequalities of wealth and may actively exploit oppressed minorities, such as foreign agricultural workers. The result, many times, is a situation in which no governmental policy can be altogether constructive. Complete governmental inaction allows for the erosion of community under the impact of severe economic injustices; yet bold actions in behalf of the poor may greatly lessen economic efficiency, thus reducing the material well-being of everyone. Such dilemmas have no solution. Yet they need not be utterly paralyzing. Capitalism is productive of great riches, and governments moved by authentic hope can see that these in some degree serve the cause of inclusive community. A broad answer to the question of how far capitalism can be trusted is: not so far as idolatry. The doctrine of laissez faire makes an idol of the free market. Still, by severing the ancient and sinister dependence of community on slavery, capitalism can serve the ends of hope. Within a social setting shaped by a politics of hope, it will do this.

A less familiar, but not less important, reason for governmental involvement in social change has to do not as much with material results as with moral and political consciousness. It is mainly through government that social change can be realized as a common responsibility and a common experience. We cannot see very far ahead in history, nor is the course of historical events under our control. But to forget that through our life in history we are working out human destiny, and that this is in some degree our common responsibility, even when it is not under the aegis of government, is to lose full awareness of our humanity. It is to sink into the non-historical life of the natural world. And it is necessarily to lose genuine hope. While liberty may provide the matrix of deep social changes, it turns people toward private concerns and in that way encourages them to forget that they live in history. Of course governments, too, may encourage historical forgetfulness; both in interpreting the past and in foreshadowing the future they are often unintentionally misleading, if not purposely dishonest. But governments always speak out of a collective situation, and probably not even schools, churches, or newspapers can more forcefully direct the minds of a people to the historical context of their lives. It might be said, accordingly, that in judging a government, the question of whether it accomplishes efficiently all of its practical tasks is no more important than the question of whether it helps people realize that they are participants in a temporal order of public events. Government should be the face and voice of historical responsibility.

Connected in these two ways with historical change—directing change in-sofar as human beings can do this at all, and enabling a populace to realize its involvement in change—government (and this is to say politics) has a significant role in the life of hope. True, since the time of the French Revolution this role has been grossly exaggerated. Government was often expected to bring every hope to fruition; politics was a redemptive activity. But our awakening to the falsity of such a view should not be allowed to blind us to the fact that we still need government in order to live as creatures with a destiny and not merely a nature. Life without government would not merely be bad in the ways Thomas Hobbes thought it would be—"solitary, poor, nasty, brutish, and short." It would be void of historical hope. The main question now before us, then, is what government must do to fulfill its role as the main medium of historical hope. In answering this question, three principles must be discussed.

1. *Temporal continuity.* A government should by all means avoid doing or saying anything to instill the idea that history is under sure human control, for if that were so we would promptly bring history to an end, relieving ourselves of its

uncertainties and tragedies and entering into some form of pleasant finality. The very idea of historical continuity would quickly become anachronistic. As it is, what government should do can be simply put: it should help us gain an enduring awareness that the common life we are carrying on, while not unaffected by our wisdom and our foolishness, comes out of the past and leads into the future. We are ineluctably temporal. We are immersed in history and cannot rise above it. Some things are forever behind us; nothing we now possess can be held on to permanently; and the future is not under our command. This fundamental condition, the source of so much anguish and confusion, is humanly irremediable. Governments should manifest a clear knowledge that this is so. They might do this merely by reminding us now and then that there is a past which has shaped us and can guide us even though it is behind us, and that there is a future which we can affect but cannot control, comprehend, or avoid. Thus the generation of leaders that enabled Americans to gain independence from Great Britain and establish a uniquely effective political system recalled in their public writings, such as the Federalist papers, that the experiences of ancient peoples shed some light on their pathway. And while they never pretended to know where the American venture would lead, the very care with which they tried to design a system suitable for all historical seasons, showed how steadily and intensely they regarded the distant future. Sensing that they represented one of the great turning points in history, they kept alive in themselves and in the American people a consciousness of historical continuity.

Awareness that our common lives on earth are structured by time, that they are defined by the past and ceaselessly reshaped by the future, is disrupted by despair and by exalted expectations alike. Both moods envision history as ending, either in an abyss or in paradise. Governments therefore should help people think of history as a scene of hope, where achievements of true significance are possible even though the whole sum of such achievements will never bring a perfect society. Living in history entails unending trials and dilemmas; fleeing from history is therefore a constant temptation. Resisting this temptation—countering the despair and exultancy in which peoples seek a refuge outside the course of collective affairs—is the first business of government. If that business is left unaccomplished, nothing else can go well.

A familiar example of how government can play this role is provided by the Roosevelt Administration at the time of the Great Depression. The President, partly through his ebullient personality, partly through actions swiftly undertaken after his inauguration, and partly through exhortation, was able to give a confused and discouraged people confidence that a happier future lay before it. Not that New Deal measures all were sound; they never did bring economic prosperity. Those measures did, however, along with the public words that accompanied them, help to overcome despair and instill hope, and in that sense they succeeded. They did this, moreover, without arousing anticipations of an impossible future. The New Deal placed itself within—not above—the nation's evolving political and economic institutions, and pursued policies which were candidly experimental. The goal was not to create a new world but to enliven American democracy and capitalism by placing them within a meaningful and hopeful historical setting. The depth of Roosevelt's roots in hope was shown by the way he called forth hope a second time, imbuing that hope with a spirit of resolution and self-sacrifice, when America was confronted by the totalitarian challenge from Europe and Asia. A lesser leader, intimidated by the Axis powers, might have joined in with the many discouraged voices arguing that America in the late 1930s had no world-wide historical responsibilities.

2. *Present necessities.* Political leaders guided by true hope, that is, hope shaped by a spirit of obedience, will not build imaginary cities or paint pictures of an ideal society. They will be politically modest. They will realize that in our finitude and moral errancy we cannot proceed immediately to the ultimate end ordained by our destinies. Their leadership will consist partly in trying to instill modesty of this sort in their societies. They will also realize, however, and seek to instill, an awareness that we are not in utter darkness. We can understand something of the historical circumstances which constitute the immediate form of our destiny. Hence, appraising practical possibilities with care, and prayerfully searching out moral necessities, we can see what here and now must be done. We can meet the demands of situational obedience.

It does not follow that we should act only in ways that circumstances make easy. In the eighteenth century, it would have been far easier for America to evolve into Commonwealth status rather than waging war with Great Britain; in 1861, inaugurating the Civil War was a far harder choice for the northern states than it would have been to acquiesce in southern secession. Washington and Lincoln discerned a national destiny which called for onerous and dangerous decisions. Sometimes it is not leaders who see the need for such decisions, but dissidents and martyrs. When that happens, then, given the force of destiny, the course of history may be better represented by doomed and isolated individuals than by the reigning powers. John the Baptist rather than King Herod, Alexandr Solzhenitsyn rather than the KGB, incarnated the fundamental movement of events in their times. The question history puts before us is not what we can readily do but what is required of us, and a private individual who correctly answers that question possesses lordship of a kind lacking in a dictator who subordinates every national resource to the realization of his will. Such an individual exemplifies, however, not the normal manner in which a destiny unfolds, but the difficulties and dangers a destiny may impose. A life of obedient hope is not framed by habits of weakness and acquiescence. Nations cannot practice the hope inherent in responding faithfully to the necessities of history unless they have, most of the time, governments moved, as well as strengthened and emboldened, by such hope.

In political, as in personal, life we must walk in darkness. Owing to our finitude, and the pride which deepens the blindness imposed by our finitude, we cannot see very far into the future. Acknowledgment of the darkness, and willingness to walk in the darkness, may be the primary requirements of political wisdom. We find these requirements hateful and humiliating. We desire profoundly to know with our own minds, and control with our own wills, all that lies ahead of us. This is our worldliness. As defined in earlier pages, the world is a humanly-defined realm, composed exclusively of comprehensible and controllable realities, in which we can achieve the mastery our pride desires. If the key to worldliness is mustrust of every agency but the self, the capacity for acting only in response to present necessities is a mark of the transcendental trust which arises when events are understood as governed by God's unforeseeable commands and as having the form not of a humanly-organized totality, a world, but of providential history. A weak and indecisive leader, plainly, is not the same as a leader with the strength to cast off all worlds and defer to the deepest impulses of destiny.

3. *Historical waiting.* Leaders and peoples will never perceive the necessities of history (which are the commands of God) unless they become practiced in waiting. Not always is it immediately clear what we should do. Hence the need sometimes to be still and attentive—attentive to the unfoldment of circumstances and to the emergence of the light in which we can see them truly. In private life, hesitation and attentiveness are little more than common sense, even if not always exercised; in public life, however, they are apt to be scorned, construed as weakness and incompetence. This is a matter often of playing up to an impatient populace. But a government watching for the necessities of an historical situation to come to light is, whether consciously or not, attentive to human destiny. In Christian terms, it is waiting for God. As wrong and dangerous as it is when governments claim divine authority, it still may be said that wise political leadership is a medium of divine leadership, and this it can be only if it possesses, and can instill in others, the capacity to wait and to pay historical attention.

Both the Old and New Testaments contain repeated warnings against willfulness and haste. After telling Israel that its strength will be found "in quietness and in trust," the prophet Isaiah notes that Israelites insist on "speeding on horses" and predicts that they will be left isolated, "like a flagstaff on the top of a mountain." (Isaiah 30:15–17 RSV) The demand for immediate action, "speeding on horses," arises from secular hope, with its confidence in human powers, whereas willingness to wait—"quietness and trust"—characterizes eschatological hope. People imbued with secular hope are apt to feel exasperated and suspicious if asked to wait before embarking on a course of political action. Waiting, in their eyes, delays the rectification of the world's injustices and is therefore morally compromising. And what is there to wait for? Secular attitudes in this matter cannot be casually dismissed if (contrary to typical secular views) humans are sinful. Waiting too nicely serves the interests of the privileged to be morally safe. It is probably a bad sign when waiting is found to be comfortable. Nonetheless, it is difficult to see how the duty of waiting can, for all of its moral perils, be morally evaded.

In the years since the French Revolution, the human race has written a long record of reckless and unwise actions. Even if prudence were our only standard, and religious considerations were entirely absent from our minds, we might make a strong argument for hesitation and caution. The argument can be much stronger if there is a power and meaning in history—Porfiry's "life," the Christian's will of God—which is wiser than human rulers. In that case our political designs should conform with the designs of history as construed by practical judgment and moral conscience. These, however, are faculties that ordinarily need time in order to work effectively. Hence governments must often pause, and leaders must be capable not only of rallying people for action but also of teaching them to be, on occasion, hesitant and watchful.

A politics informed with the spirit of situational obedience would be capable of waiting attentively not only for insights into the necessities which mark the way into the future but also for insights into the past. One of the most dangerous legacies of secular hope lies in the pleasure we take in breaking with the past, or at least in talking about that impossible feat. We are oblivious of the fact that a good future reflects a meaning which pervades the past, and that such a future, far from being a radical departure from the past, will always be united with it in the form of a single story, a destiny. Thus forgetting the past, even if it be a past we abhor, is not a suitable way of preparing to enter into a destined future. In other words, hope cannot be grasped through amnesia. Hence, a responsible government will not talk about shaking off the past but rather about the historical directions—the roads into the future—which the past puts before us. In America, it was not only the Founders who reflected on the political experience of earlier ages; Lincoln associated himself with Jeffersonian democracy and the Declaration of Independence. In the Soviet Union, the journey out of the long nightmare of Communism began when the government started recounting, and allowing private citizens to recount, honest Russian history. Political leaders at their best would be narrators of history, and as such they would instill interest in the events which have brought us into our present situation. They would teach us to abide patiently the gradual unfoldment of the human story.

A model of misgovernment, in this respect, is the methodical falsification of the past carried on by the totalitarian dictatorships of our time. It must be granted that modern despots have recognized certain vital truths—for example, that present politics presupposes an image of past politics, accurate or not, and that hope cannot survive when dissociated from memory. Liberal leaders are not always so sagacious. These despots, however, accept only a past which they have refashioned to harmonize with their own designs for the future. They do what no liberal leader can do for long; they deny and invent historical facts. There is, of course, no entirely objective history. Still, outside the boundaries of totalitarian states, the actual past does constrain human interpretation. One of the most important benefits of liberty is that historical interpretations are subject to public criticism. In this way the past is given its own voice. In contrast with the false hopes that necessarily arise where the false narratives of totalitarian leaders hold sway, true hope becomes possible where liberty allows for true narratives.

In sum, governments guiding nations in history should strive to maintain temporal continuity, attention to present necessities, and a capacity for historical waiting. These principles might be summarized as ways of recognizing our confinement to history. We are transcendental to the extent of being able to rise above instinct and immediate desire, and even above some of the narrative strands making up the historical process in which we are involved; but we cannot rise above history altogether. Hence we are responsible *within* history but not *for* history as a totality. The principle of temporal continuity calls on us to recognize that, confined to history, we must carry with us, on our journey toward eternity, all three segments of time—past, present, and future; the principle of immediate necessities holds that historical time brings to those who are watchful the authority and providence of transcendence, or God; and the principle of historical waiting applies to politics the wisdom of Isaiah—that God is not at human beck and call and that only those who can for a time bear darkness will be granted the light of divine leadership.

These principles all are known to traditional Christian wisdom and for Christians derive their authority primarily from this source. But such wisdom concerns the general nature of life and history—the Logos—and is not possessed exclusively by believers. Thus the idea that prevailing circumstances impose requirements on us, that these requirements draw their force from both moral and practical considerations, and that they are unlikely to be understood by people ignorant of the past which imposes them on us, can make sense to people of varying religious and irreligious orientations. Even the idea that the whole course of earthly affairs is pervaded by a sovereign, and in some sense sacred, design is entertained far beyond the bounds of the Christian Church. Numerous non-Christians in our time (for example, Franz Kafka, Karl Jaspers, and Albert Camus) have been sensitive to the mystery which Christians believe is fully revealed in Christ and is the sovereign power and meaning in history. All of this suggests that political leaders need not invoke the name of God, or even necessarily believe in God, in order to shape a nation's sense of historical responsibility in the spirit of true hope.

I have already referred to a dramatic exemplar of true hope, Abraham Lincoln. It is worthy of note that Lincoln exemplifies all three of the principles we have discussed. First, it was fundamental to Lincoln's presidency that he accepted his confinement to an historical situation—a situation excruciating to him and his countrymen but one that had to be lived through in order to be surmounted. Lincoln never pretended, either to relieve the minds of Americans at large or to relieve his own mind, that the situation of the nation was not perilous. Further, in framing Northern policy Lincoln disclaimed explicitly any knowledge of God's designs or of the ultimate outcome of the War. He professed that he tried only to do what had to be done at each historical moment and that he sought, in this way, to conform with the will of God. And finally, he lived almost constantly in a state of semi-darkness, waiting for events to light the way ahead. The grandeur of Lincoln's personality derives in large measure from his acting always, not as a sovereign of history, but as a servant—of history and of the transcendence he believed to be implicit in history.

Hope based on a concern for destiny, whether consciously Christian or not, would provide a political standpoint beyond the old, and now stultifying, polarity of radicalism and conservatism. This polarity is no doubt rooted in human nature. As I have suggested, it reflects the inherent one-sidedness of finite beings. Some are inclined toward idealism and others toward realism; some naturally love action and change, others quietness and stability. Also, as everyone knows, such biases are strongly affected by personal circumstances. Possessing or lacking wealth, power, and social status will for many decide their political orientation. In sum, by virtue of temperament and situation humans are almost inevitably divided between left and right. But the antithesis grew theoretically sharper and emotionally more bitter in the age of the French Revolution. Swift and comprehensive change *versus* slow and piecemeal change became a highly-charged issue. One can see this happening in Edmund Burke's response to the revolution in France. This suggests that only when the spirit of situational obedience is lost, and human historical sovereignty is thought attainable, does the division between radicals and conservatives begin to seem elemental and inescapable. It also suggests that error is intrinsic to the very division between left and right and probably affects both sides of the division.

The aspiration to control history is manifest among reformers and radicals of all sorts, and reaches its extreme among revolutionaries. Yet conservatives of the kind typified by Burke may also seek, in their own way, to control history. In spite of possessing a superior sense of the mystery and tragedy of human events, their dispute with radicals and revolutionaries may come down to the question not of whether but of how history can be managed. This happens when conservatism is equated simply with caution and prudence. The upshot is that neither side represents the principle that history is not humanly comprehensible or humanly governable. Yet that surely is the truth.

History is not a kind of material which, whether with imagination and bold-ness, or with infinite patience, we can shape as we will. It is rather a manifestation of the elemental mystery of being. It calls upon us to pay attention and respond to emergent conditions. If we could understand history to be not merely the super-ficial play of circumstance but "deep history," the fundamental direction of affairs, then we would strive not only to shape, but also to be shaped by, history. We cannot do this, however, if we are blinded by illusions of historical sovereignty. Then we will merely fall into vain quarrels, motivated by the failures necessarily attending all our efforts, about whether to move quickly or slowly, boldly or cautiously.

Leaders capable of discerning and responding to the destiny underlying daily events will be wiser than radicals or conservatives as such can be. Washington, al-though he led a revolution, cannot adequately be characterized as a revolutionary; and Lincoln cannot be described as a conservative even though his great work was the conservation of the American Union. The point is not to move swiftly or slowly but to move according to the necessities of the times. The very idea that there are such necessities requires us to abandon pretensions to historical sovereignty. God is not radical or conservative (contrary to frequent assertions by radical and conserva-tive Christians) and human beings fall under the constraints of such a dichotomy only when, by claiming godlike historical powers, they rebel against God.

The word naming the attitude which enables us to stand amid events with the quietness and trust invoked by the prophet Isaiah, of course, is "hope." To think of hope is to think of a readiness for change which is not, in the usual sense of the word, radical because it relies on a source of change beyond human control. It is to think also of a posture of political humility which is not conservative because, as the Bible shows in diverse ways, the transcendent power and authority manifest in history is not, in the way of human beings, conservative (in leading the Israelites out of Egypt, for example, God brought about what is for many the model revo-lution). People capable of true hope will not be deeply divided by questions about the rate of historical change. That issue will be left in the hands of the God whose leadership they will watch for in the historical circumstances of their lives. They may differ about what God requires of them but differences in that matter will be rooted in reality and not in illusions of human sovereignty.

The objection may be raised that I am prescribing a hidden conservatism. It may be said that a politics of hope will enthrone timidity and doubt, and that wait-ing for the leadership of God is a formula for inaction. I grant that authentic hope, as I understand it, would rarely inspire or allow revolutionary enterprises such as Lenin's and that it might sanction periods of inaction, although the prevailing spirit would be watchful rather than complacent. Are such limits intolerable? If so, one might reasonably ask whether we are in a state of rebellion against the very fact of our finitude (a rebellion disguised, perhaps, by professions of compassion for the poor and oppressed). Are such limits even tinged with conservatism? That is doubtful, for Christianity not only inculcates a humility that is antithetical to the revolutionary ideal of sudden, sweeping social transformation; it inculcates a critical attitude toward everything merely human and not divine, including the ancient traditions and long-established institutions typically revered by conservatives. As Christians see things, sin is ingenious and ever-present. Hence the pride and selfishness of reigning classes enter powerfully into the shaping of long-standing institutions and customs.

Christianity does not require respect for the conceits and prejudices embodied in a traditional order any more than it does for the arrogance and inhumanity of a revolutionary government. An example is near at hand. By the middle of the twentieth century the subjection of the black race in America was fixed in laws, customs, and institutions that had endured for over three centuries. The assault on these came primarily from Christian churches, especially black churches in the South, and was led by a Christian minister, the Reverend Martin Luther King, Jr. It is noteworthy, too, that while King was manifestly not a conservative, neither was he, in the usual sense of the word, a revolutionary. That he had hope, however, can be said of him unequivocally.

An allied objection to the politics of hope, as herein defined, is that it diverts us with fantasies of a heavenly utopia. Anticipation of a paradisiacal finality that interrupts, and in some sense contradicts, the course of history, it is charged, undermines political responsibility. As we have already seen, however, eschatological hope does not posit a meaningless series of events suddenly and senselessly terminated by the onset of the kingdom of heaven—a view that would indeed undermine political responsibility. Rather it assumes that history is meaningful precisely because it has an end (as Nicolas Berdyaev asserted, there can be no meaning in endless history) and is making for that end. History is a process through which the very evils that constitute history, and underlie the radical imperfection of every earthly order, are eradicated. These evils, however, have their source in sin, and sin does not gradually disappear in the course of an uninterrupted progression from earth to heaven. History and the paradisiacal finalities toward which history is leading cannot comfortably merge. The depth and tenacity of sin imply a final crisis. History must be inconclusive. It is not meaningless, however. It leads toward, even though not directly into, its transcendental end—a view strongly suggesting that only those who play a responsible part in the temporal process will have a part in the transcendental end.

Hope of an eschatological sort is a better basis for reform than hope that is purely worldly. On the one hand, it is immune to revolutionary impatience. If there were nothing beyond the world, worldly injustice could seem intolerable, as it did to the unbelieving Ivan in *The Brothers Karamazov*. It then becomes a source of unrestrained violence. In Ivan, Dostoevsky prophetically depicted the Bolshevik mind. The historical consequences of revolutionary impatience have been disclosed to the world not only in the tyrannical character but in the final collapse of the Communist regimes. We can see now that it is not in all ways a bad thing for historical injustices to be bearable.

On the other hand, eschatological hope is immune to historical discouragement. Reformers who count on success are bound sooner or later to be disappointed. They are likely then to fall into apathy or into fanaticism—either to abandon history or else resort to extreme measures in order to master it. A reformer moved by hope that looks beyond history is more likely to be steadfast than a reformer whose hope is confined to history. The fact that considerations rendering worldly injustice tolerable may be turned to their own interests by people who profit from injustice displays the dangers that lie, not in eschatology, but in human nature. Sin is ingenious, and alert to every opportunity. Safety is found, not in concepts, however true they may be, but only in the spirit that lives through them. Where eschatological concepts are reflective of an eschatological spirit, the will to reform can be both strong and patient.

Having discussed social change in relation to both liberty and government, there is no way of avoiding the age-old question of the best society. To what end *within history* should change be directed? This is not to ask what kind of earthly society fulfills hope. Since there is no such society, that question has no answer. Still, it is obvious that some earthly societies are unusually bad, and if that is so, then some are relatively good, and the best earthly society can in a general way be described. To do this is clearly necessary for understanding the political meaning of hope.

Society and Transcendence

The question of the best earthly society, if asked in full awareness that hope is eschatological and not earthly, leads immediately to the principle of social plurality. On earth, there can be no ideal society or social group. There must consequently be diverse societies and groups, with no one of them being allowed to stand as the sole and supreme end of historical striving. The principle has various familiar implications. Every nation should comprise diverse associations, with citizens free to join and separate themselves from such associations as they please. Also, as I have argued, there should be diverse nations, with commensurate rights of travel and emigration. Earlier discussions in this essay, however, suggest that one form of social plurality is preeminent. If we ask which among all human institutions are of greatest significance, we see that the primary expression of the principle that no society and no group is a fitting home for man must be the duality of Church and state.

This duality has been examined and discussed so voluminously that little needs to be said about it in principle. Neither Church nor state deserves unshared and uncontested authority. The two should be in some manner distinct and separate, even though complete separation is a manifest impossibility. Earthly society in its most comprehensive secular form, as well as in its most sacred form, is persistently deficient. Even the Church is only a foreshadowing of the paradisiacal end. If the eschatological premise is denied, the dualistic principle falls. Thus political perfectionists, from Plato to Marx, all have opposed the division of sovereignty. The whole of society, whether spiritual, as with Plato, or worldly, as with Marx, must be under a single sword. But given a realization of human sinfulness and hence of the inescapable imperfection of all earthly societies and groups, the idea of divided sovereignty is apt to arise spontaneously. Thus the so-called doctrine of the two swords (holding that even the Church must share authority in some way with the state), can be traced back to the close of the fifth century, to Pope Gelasius I, and perhaps even to Jesus' distinction between the things owed to Caesar and the things owed to God.

Needless to say, diverse motives have been at work in the history of political and social ideas. I am concerned, however, not with history but with the structural logic of social pluralism and, in particular, of Church and state. Here the eschatological issue is primary. Denying, as Christians have, that any final harmony can be found in history has meant that even the noblest of earthly societies could be affirmed only with stringent qualifications. Human beings cannot be at home either in the Church or in the state. To make this principle clear, and give it practical effect, the two institutions must share, and check one another, in the governance of lives. Denying all earthly homes, the doctrine of the two swords invites individuals to seek meaning, not in any social order, but in an order that is realized only through history and with the end of history. In other words, it turns our attention toward true, or eschatological, hope.

For such hope actually to arise, however, society must have a spiritual character. God, or transcendence in some form toward which hope can fittingly be directed, must, so to speak, have standing in people's minds. And for that to be the case, the Church must be independent and powerful. Other spiritual institutions, such as those encouraging and transmitting literary insight, may bring transcendental perspectives into a society. From the Christian point of view, however, the Church is prior in importance to culture and consequently, in the final analysis, a society's capacity for hope will depend on the status of the Church. Without the Church, situated over all the rest of society in people's esteem, society will be apt to degenerate into an affair of power and monetary profit, culture to fall prey to nihilism, and true hope to evaporate.

The mere presence of churches clearly provides no assurance that such will not occur. Late twentieth-century America is evidence of this. The Church can fail not only by being overbearing and intolerant, as liberals typically fear it will be wherever it is powerful, but also by being insipid—by merely mirroring fashionable opinions, for example, or by being unable convincingly to take issue with those opinions. Still, unless the Church is near the center of common loyalties and succeeds in being, in some measure, an earthly analogue of the kingdom of God, a society is almost bound to become a mere world, a place where humans devote themselves exclusively to worldly lusts and ambitions, and the aims of true hope are forgotten.

Moreover, the Church is essential to the very existence of the liberty which we have seen to be a prime requirement of the life of hope and the immediate goal of the state. This is because it marks off a sphere of life in which the state is not to interfere, and it assumes responsibility for defending that sphere. We tend to forget this because where there is one church alone, as in the Middle Ages, there may be little liberty. Nonetheless, the rise of the Christian Church was one of the decisive events laying the foundations for modern liberty. Not only did it establish the principle that the most personal and important matters are not under direct governance by the state; it brought about an institutional dualism (continued today in such forms as public and private, executive and legislative, and political and judicial) which is necessary for that principle to be operative. This is true even today, when the Church exists mainly as churches, with these often lacking in vitality and spirit. Only the churches can convincingly maintain that in defending personal, extra-governmental areas of life something is at stake which is not merely enjoyed or preferred but has eternal import. In short, only the churches can assert, without hyperbole, that liberty is sacred. Were the churches to disappear, the ideal of constitutional government—that is, government under the stable, publicly-known limits that make liberty secure—would be fatally weakened.

Spiritual life of course is not confined to ecclesiastical institutions, even though Christians believe that truth in its fullness is about (or, more precisely, is) God, and that the Church comprises man's principal truth-seeking activities. God's footprints are all around us; everywhere are beauties and harmonies reflective of the divine. Hence art and literature, science and philosophy, music and architecture, are spiritual activities and, entirely apart from the Church, constitute a spiritual realm, the realm of what is often called "culture." And this realm has its own institutions, independent of both state and Church, such as publishers, universities, and art museums. In view of the power with which great works of art and thought testify to the reality of transcendence, it is scarcely amiss to think of culture as a kind of secular church. As such, it has a vital role in sustaining liberty and enabling it to serve the life of hope.

To retain its full transcendental significance, however, culture is no less dependent than is liberty in all of its forms on the Church in the proper sense of the term. Secular culture is incomplete, and apt to be gravely distorted, unless the eternal values which give it significance are explicitly voiced and represented. Athens is fulfilled in Jerusalem. This is particularly true of those who merely enjoy, but do not create, the great works of literature and art. Without the transcendental seriousness of the Church, their lives are liable to become merely aesthetic—that is, devoted to higher pleasures—rather than authentically spiritual. But it is true even of the creators of culture, the writers, artists, and philosophers who create the major works of human culture. Some of the most eminent of them, it is true, have been unbelievers. Yet even the unbelievers have often depended on Christian themes; witness some of the great requiems, such as those by Verdi and Berlioz. And the works of all human creators need interpretations of the kind that can come, directly or indirectly, only from the Church. Can we fully understand the primeval splendor of a landscape by Cézanne, for example, without some reference to the God who created the heavens and the earth?

Such is the spiritual primacy of the Church. Primacy, however, does not imply power. It might be nearer the truth to say, in the matter of spiritual agencies, that primacy implies weakness. Hence the paradoxical truth is that the Church must be strong, but being strong in its own distinctive way, it must also be weak.

The weakness of the Church is inherent in the dependence of faith on liberty. Christians must resist the temptation to try to shape society according to distinctively Christian forms and standards. They must rather accept, however regretfully, the irreligious and pluralistic world which is almost bound to arise where science, technology, and industry are highly developed. They must resign themselves to a worldly world. The reason is simple. Anything else would be a denial of liberty, and that in turn would be a denial of the possibility of uncoerced—which is to say, authentic—faith. Christians presumably wish to address those who are free to accept the Christian message; but to leave people free to do that requires leaving them free also to close their ears and minds to the Christian message. Liberty is therefore inseparable from the possibility of widespread agnosticism and atheism. And under the incitements to worldliness which inevitably flow out of advanced industrialism, this possibility is almost certain to become a reality.

The secular sphere of existence, under organized governance, is of course what we mean by the state. Here again we see the imperative duality of Church and state. Christian acquiescence in secularism implies acquiescence in the independence of the state. This does not mean that the state can go its own way, without Christian pressure or resistance. As we discovered in earlier discussions, Christians are obliged by the command of love to assume a measure of political responsibility.

They are inescapably involved in politics. And since they are inescapably involved in the Church as well, the idea of a "wall" between Church and state is a fantasy—usually of the secular mind. What then is the meaning of the main current formula for the weakness of the Church, that is, separation of Church and state? Its only possible meaning is that Christians, while involved in state activities, must maintain a certain detachment, a detachment that is trying and difficult precisely because it cannot be pure and absolute.

This detachment has diverse aspects and these cannot be reduced to a single rule. But an example, suggesting what Christian detachment means, concerns the deployment of Christian symbols in the public world. It is doubtful that Christians who have foresworn trying to impose Christian faith on non-Christians can properly ask non-Christians to support expressions of Christian faith, such as nativity scenes on public property and prayers in public schools, with public funds. The issue, framed in Christian terms, is trust in the Holy Spirit. If Christians commit their cause to free assent this is because, more deeply, they commit it to God, the sovereign of history. Some of the most bitterly-argued issues in this connection are in truth rather trivial. The contested practices are neither powerful incitements to faith nor serious infringments on liberty. But the anxiety shown by some Christians to maintain such practices suggests an absence not only of trust in God but of hope as well. A Church sustained by hope should have the strength to stand, like an island in a stream, allowing secular history to flow unimpeded around it. It should be able to let God's destiny have its way, and human freedom its part, in the attainment of truth.

Another aspect of Christian detachment concerns the role of the clergy. Members of the clergy should not ordinarily pursue political, which is to say partisan and ideological, causes in public. This is partly because they are not necessarily well-acquainted with public issues and cannot be expected to be by virtue of their positions. In short, they may well be wrong. Moreover, their authority, although greater than that of most private citizens, is limited. To use it for political ends may be to squander it. What is important in the society at large is that they be heard with respect when they speak on spiritual and moral matters. That is more likely to happen if they have not spoken on politics in ways that arouse antagonism and doubt. Of course spiritual and moral matters merge with political matters. Speaking on the former without speaking on the latter requires considerable wisdom and discrimination. It is not impossible, however. The art of guiding the Church in history is partly that of giving life to spiritual and moral considerations, most of them having political implications, without publicly supporting particular political programs and personalities.

The spirit of Christian political detachment is indicated by another rule: that the most serious Christians should not generally aim at high office. The main reasons for thinking that high office does not further the fulfillment of a Christian's historical responsibilities lie in the Crucifixion. Jesus' destiny tells us several things about participation in history—that suffering may be more consequential than action; that weakness at times is power; and that obscurity and humiliation can serve spiritual ends more effectively than do fame and public glory. Such statements are paradoxical but not, I think, incomprehensible in the light of the Cross. Paul often employed similar paradoxes, as in characterizing himself and his fellow Christians as "unknown, and yet well-known; as dying, and, behold, we live; . . . as having nothing, and yet possessing everything." (II Corinthians 6:9–10) It would be difficult to derive unambiguous norms of political conduct from these paradoxes. They point, however, toward a dangerous anomaly in the life of a Christian, or anyone else striving to sustain a spiritual stance, who holds and cherishes a position which bestows fame, wealth, and power. That is the side of Pilate and Herod, not of Christ. The paradoxes of Christian power also indicate that the suffering and solitude often incurred by Christians do not necessarily entail inefficacy. Jesus changed the course of history in agony and isolation; as he approached the Crucifixion even his disciples, as the Gospels tell us, "forsook him and fled." While there can be no wall between state and Church, there is unquestionably deep tension between political power and true hope.

Such observations must be qualified, however, by the proviso that situations may arise in which detachment is inappropriate. Christians now look back in shame on the political detachment of the Christian clergy in Germany during the time in which the Nazis were coming to power. We are perhaps justified in borrowing for political theory a concept which Karl Jaspers used in analyzing personal life broadly—that of the "boundary situation." In politics, we might characterize a boundary situation as one in which normal rules of political engagement no longer apply. And we might say that a situation of this sort exists whenever the very order which makes possible the Christian fusion of detachment and involvement has come into peril. Thus a boundary situation exists when liberal democracy is threatened by totalitarianism. In these circumstances, the kind of fusion of the spiritual and political exemplified in the life of Dietrich Bonhoeffer may be not only appropriate but inescapable.

Where there is stable liberty, however—liberty not only to carry on a life in private but also to participate in public affairs—a degree of political detachment may be expressive of hope. The urgency with which Christians sometimes seek to advance their principles through political programs suggests an attitude akin to despair, a fear that the purposes of God will be unaccomplished unless a particular political group entirely succeeds. When Jesus at the time of his arrest told a resistant follower to put up his sword and let destiny take its course, he suggested, surely, that his followers in the public realm, although spiritually self-assured, should be politically unobtrusive. Carried by the main current of human destiny, they need not be insistent on directing the daily unfoldment of historical affairs. They should be willing to sheathe their swords.

It may seem that this is a formula not just for detachment but for extinction. This brings us to the question of how the Church can be, not only weak, but also in its own way strong. The answer lies in the fact that however weak the Church may be, it retains the power of speech, and this is the power of the Word. The ideal society from a Christian standpoint is one in which this power can be used to the fullest, that is, a dialogic society.

In the light of earlier discussions of dialogue, the nature of such a society needs little explanation. It would be a society in which a human being as such is respected, reasoned speech is taken seriously, and people are therefore inclined to speak and to listen to one another. A dialogic society in the fullest sense would be both universal and democratic. Its ruling standard would be all-inclusive discourse. No tyranny can be dialogical. Neither can a society so absorbed in commerce that most speech aims at advertising or entertainment; given its commercial preoccupations, present-day America is dialogical only to a degree. Nor can a society be dialogical if governed by an exclusive elite; the principle of dialogue is implicitly egalitarian. A fully dialogic society would be without ideological or religious chasms, and without the unbridgeable divisions created by class barriers or by undiscussable principles. And it would be a society in which Christians, however weak in the political order, could be strong in the public realm, for they could speak and be heard. Christians could then live in the world, neither as potential sources of religious oppression nor as an inaudible, self-absorbed minority. They would be not only public representatives of the Word but also participants in that universally human kingdom, the kingdom of words.

The idea of public dialogue assumes that even though Christians cannot properly ask their secular-minded fellow-citizens to acquiesce in public support of religious symbols, there is nevertheless something of importance they can quite properly ask of them. This is attention. They can ask that people listen to them— not as a peculiar favor but merely as they do (or *should* do) to any other group that speaks seriously and coherently. Receiving the gift of attention (which Simone Weil speaks of as a uniquely rare and pure form of human generosity), would be far more significant for Christians than being allowed to prescribe prayers for public schools or display nativity scenes in public places at Christmastime. And it is a gift they can rightfully seek since they claim, not necessarily assent, but only consideration. They ask simply to be heard with the courtesy and concern for truth that constitute the principles, if not always the practice, of public discourse in every liberal democracy.

Christians have a singular role to play in the realm of public dialogue. Christians alone can speak to the world about Christ, the Logos. In doing this, at the very least they broaden the range of discourse and voice claims of concern (whether recognized or not) to every person. They help to make the world a place where Christ's question, "Who do you say that I am?" is not casually ignored. Granted, a serious person in a free public realm may reply that Christ was a mere man; indeed many are likely to do so. Nonetheless, in a world where Christ's question is recurrently remembered and pondered would be a world in which truth lingers and is sought. A world where Christ's question is not even asked is in danger of falling into frivolity and into despair.

Christ is the preeminent symbol of earthly hope. No like figure is found in any other religion. But the hope made possible by Christ is not wholly welcome to the world, for Christ is a savior, and a savior is needed only where evil in the soul has substantial power and where things of substantial worth are imperiled. Christ makes us acutely conscious of human failure and the human plight. Unsurprisingly, he has often been scorned and banished. In the public realm, his name is not apt to be gladly heard. Yet if we close our eyes to the conditions revealed by Christ, we worsen our situation. We inhabit it blindly. And we are necessarily deprived of realistic hope. Christians in the public realm, provoking people to consider the identity of Christ, can prompt them to examine the circumstances of their lives and open themselves, in this way, to a recovery of hope.

Having sketched the earthly order sought by hope—disunited institutionally, united dialogically—we must turn, in concluding this chapter, to the individual person. The very idea of hope implies what we might call the unassimilated individual. Hope is for community. But you can only hope for community if you do not dwell in community. So hope must again be conceived of dialectically. As an orientation toward community, hope is sustained in a state of solitude. Solitude is implied also by the duality of Church and state. To belong to both institutions is to be unassimilated in either. This is not merely a theoretical consideration. Secular society will for many Christians be an alien scene, however firmly bound to it by their civic obligations they may feel. And even the Church, always more or less disfigured by moral and spiritual imperfections, will never be an entirely satisfactory haven. In short, if community is our destiny, individual separateness is our fate. This is the truth that lies in individualism in spite of our ontological oneness.

Someone might suppose that such individualism, while important perhaps in personal life, has little relevance to politics, where collective efforts are so conspicuous. So let us once again call to mind the concept of responsibility, which weighs so decisively on the side of individualism. Its individualizing implications for politics can be summarized quite simply: politics involves responsibility, and responsibility is in the final analysis unsharable. It sets each one apart in political, as in all other, relationships. You cannot allow any other person, or any group, to decide finally on your political beliefs and actions. You may look to others, both to individuals and to groups, for guidance and support; indeed, you must. But the very concept of personal responsibility implies that the fundamental issues of life, some of which are political issues, must be decided by each individual singly. It follows that individuals realize their nature as political animals not only in association but also in solitude and dissent. And the polity attains health not through social unity alone but also through individuals capable of thinking and standing alone.

This brings us to the concept of the prophetic stance. One who has and uses the capacity for standing alone assumes a posture of historical responsibility which, to signalize the presence of hope, we might call "prophetic."

The Prophetic Stance

The prophetic stance is the bearing amid historical events of one who is sustained and moved by true hope. The concept brings to a focus some of the main themes developed in the course of this essay. We can see this first of all by examining the two terms making up the concept.

The word "prophetic" is not meant to suggest knowledge of the future. As we have seen, such knowledge is largely beyond us, and hope normally requires that we "walk in darkness." The word is meant rather to denote an unconditional willingness to enter into the future—the future inscribed in one's destiny—in spite of the darkness obscuring it. The word "prophetic" is intended also to mark such willingness as pertaining to the historical, as well as personal, future. Hope is prophetic when it reflects fidelity to the God to whom the future belongs, hence also a concern, not with oneself alone, but with one's people and with all humanity.

The word "stance" suggests the posture of an individual rather than a group. This connotation is fundamental to the concept of the prophetic stance. The responsibility of standing among historical circumstances and events, attentive to the lives of the multitudes with whom one shares the earth, and alert to the demands of the prevailing situation, personal and historical, bears, like all responsibilities, singly on every individual. Discerning and meeting the obligations inherent in destiny is a task which cannot be left to others. In this way, the prophetic stance, even though it is a way of being related to history and the state, partakes of solitude.

It also, however, partakes of community; and here we see more fully how the concept of the prophetic stance recapitulates principal ideas set forth in earlier discussions. As we know, solitude and community are not contradictory, but rather are interdependent. Solitude is the communality individuals must strive to sustain under the conditions of fallen human existence—conditions which render all communities fragmentary and ephemeral. Communality is possible only by maintaining a degree of independence from all social groups, especially from those pretending to possess a communal perfection which in the nature of things no earthly group can possibly possess. The enemies of community are not those who stand somewhat apart in order to hear and respond to the voices of their fellow human beings. They are rather fanatical partisans for whom a particular group—a party, a nation, a class, a race—is seen as actually or potentially a flawless community. Even though such partisans obliterate their private lives and become wholly immersed in collective life, they do not attain community. Rather, they render community inaccessible for, along with their private lives, they obliterate the communal self and the solitude which are essential to the existence of earthly community even in the fragmentary and ephemeral forms which are possible.

The dialectical character of the prophetic stance is manifest. It is an eschatological disposition, the bearing of one who lives in history with hope that anticipates the end of history. It is a resolute orientation toward a fullness of community which implies the end of history, maintained in resistance to the anticommunal pressures of the societies that structure life within history. This tension is critical to the effort to stand prophetically, which is to say eschatologically, within history.

In other words, the locus of the prophetic stance is the spiritual space between community and society. Each one of us has to try to stand in this space and to meet the contradictory demands which doing this entails. This is simply because it is impossible to be truly communal, and politically responsible, merely by standing apart from society. One must go out to meet human beings where they are, and they are always in society. This is a harsh and difficult task. Moreover, it is largely unrecognized in contemporary social and political theory, since the very distinction between community and society is largely unrecognized. Hence, to grasp the concept of the prophetic stance we must examine more carefully than we have hitherto the nature of society, and in particular we must perceive the qualities which make it at once alien and inescapable.

If community is the end which we hope to reach, society is a necessity to which we are forced to submit and which, in the perversity of our spirits, we freely perpetuate and reinforce. The necessity is both practical and spiritual. The practical necessity of society arises, as we have seen, from the dependence of community on outward order. Such order is needed, to begin with, to realize a degree of economic efficiency and military security. Without these, life of any kind, communal or not, is impossible. And they render a stable and controllable organization of human beings absolutely essential, for purposes both of work and of military action. There can of course be communality of some kinds in economic and military organizations, such as cooperative activities and discussion forums not dictated by the function of the organization, but such communality is incidental to their central purpose and, from a practical standpoint, is largely dispensable. What is not dispensable is an order in which there is rigorous functionality and efficient hierarchical control. These characteristics, rooted in ineluctible physical demands, more or less pervade every society. This partly explains why figures like Socrates and Jesus, devoted to communication of the most searching and uncompromising kind—communication inconsiderate of practical necessities—are likely to fall afoul of society.

Society is necessary also for suppressing internal violence. Society provides the basic order without which community is impossible. Not any order will do, as we have already seen; the order needed for community is one allowing for extensive liberty. A familiar phrase for characterizing the kind of order that favors community is "the open society." The phrase is appealing yet it is harmful if it causes us to forget the necessity, along with openness, of the system of customary and enforced constraints that constitute society. Liberty without order cannot eventuate in community. The primal disorientation traditionally called "original sin" makes the need for order particularly pressing. Fallen man is naturally disorderly, that is, spontaneously in conflict with the conditions of community. This is one of the most compelling reasons why there must be centralized force, or government. Government is the ultimate guarantor of order among creatures who live in a state of more or less permanent rebellion against order.

In sum, social order is a practical necessity because there can be no community unless there is life, and there can be no life unless basic physical needs are met and physical safety secured. But social order is a spiritual necessity, too. This is because community rests on common respect for values such as truth and beauty, and such respect is not spontaneous. The values at the center of community must be given concrete form, as in works of art and literature; they must be given durability through tradition; and they must be inculcated through cultural and educational institutions of various kinds. If these functions were unfulfilled, community, as a sharing of values, would be impossible. Even the most creative individuals necessarily draw their values from society, however extensively they may refine and creatively alter them. This generalization applies even to the most exalted figures, such as Socrates and Jesus—one thoroughly Greek, the other profoundly Jewish. Community comes into being when social values are internally realized, creatively developed, and possessed in common. True, a society never provides more than crude and compromised versions of the best values it represents, nor is a society ever perfectly unified and coherent; there always are conflicts among the values it teaches. Men and women in their communality, those of extraordinary and ordinary gifts alike, must develop a capacity for criticizing and refashioning the values they have inherited. There must, however, be values in the outward order for them to inherit. People capable of community can be born and live only in a social setting.

Fully to understand the distinction of society and community, however, it must be added that society is a product not only of necessity but also of sin. In our fallenness we far prefer society to community. Society, as an objective, functional order, more or less subject to rational comprehension and deliberate control, can be an instrument of pride. Community cannot. Community, as communication, depends on the humility necessary for inquiring with others into the truth. Society, in contrast, is a structure in which almost all stations, except those occupied by the most impoverished and outcast, lend themselves in some measure to the proud enterprise of directing, or at least looking down proudly and disdainfully upon, other lives. Hence the functional distinctions required by economic and military necessity are reinforced by purely gratuitous distinctions, such as those of race. Society would be far more porous, so to speak, more open to intrusions of communality, were it not continually strengthened and hardened, and its necessities exaggerated, by the expansive self of fallen man.

Society may serve not only pride but another form of sin as well—that of despair. We have already noticed that there are two perverse impulses in fallen man. Pride is manifest in the imperial self, in the domination of other selves and realities. Despair, or diversion, is manifest in the abandoned self, in the self that is lost in routine, habit, and conformity. Critics of mass society, like Tocqueville and the great Spanish philosopher, José Ortega y Gasset, have dramatized the peculiarly modern temptation to think and behave as does everyone else, hence thoughtlessly and irresponsibly. Tyrannies, as well as mass democracies, illustrate how society can further self-abandonment. The tyrant, so to speak, monopolizes pride; all others (leaving aside the nationalism and racism which allow the rank and file small tastes of pride) abandon themselves to the will of the tyrant. Hence the possibility of analyzing Nazi Germany as an "escape from freedom." What must be emphasized, however, is that society in every form does in some degree what mass democracies and tyrannies do in extreme degree, that is, provide patterns of activity and belief which enable people more or less to forget that they are individuals.

Society is the world, the sphere of reality shaped by outward necessity and by our iniquitous diversion from truth, community, and God. In the degree to which we think and act purely as social beings, blind to all that transcends society, we are lacking in wisdom, we are foolish; since society is the sphere of the impersonal, with all relations determined by functional necessity and power, in our societal roles we are lacking in love, we are unrighteous; in society, even though our hearts are lifted up by pride, we are shrunken in being and ensnared in our mortality. Society, then, is the setting in which the dialectic of our destiny—crucifixion and resurrection—is necessarily enacted. As mere social creatures we must perish, in order to rise into the communality in which we find our authentic being.

The duality of community and society reverberates throughout human life and history. The task of standing between community and society, that is, of maintaining the prophetic stance and living with a hope that is both personal and historical, brings into every responsible person's life a multitude of tensions, all reflective of the dialectic of our destiny.

One of these tensions, that between Church and state, was our principal concern earlier in this chapter. To be sure, standing between community and society is not precisely the same as standing between Church and state, for these are both social institutions and must therefore be classed under the category of society. Since the Church is the major representative of community within society, however, bearing the tensions between community and society is bound to involve one in the tensions between Church and state. This is to reiterate an Augustinian theme. In Augustine's mind the Church was far from the same thing as the City of God; but within history it was a symbol and an agent of the heavenly city. The state, in like manner, was not for Augustine simply the city of man—the hypothetical gathering of those devoted to man rather than God and composed thus of the damned—for it included the saved as well as the damned. But on earth, the state foreshadowed the city of the damned; it provided a foretaste of Hell. At the end of time, the two cities would be disentangled from one another and established in eternal separateness. In history, however, they were mixed together, with every human being, although a member of only one of the two cities (that is, either saved or damned) a participant in both of the institutions representing them—Church and state. This is the human situation. To take cognizance of and meet the responsibilities inherent in this situation is what I mean by the prophetic stance.

A parallel duality, defining another of the tensions intrinsic to the prophetic stance and the life of hope, is that between the public and private realms. The public realm is the secular counterpart of the Church. It is where all persons ought to be united in the knowledge of all truth. The ideal is not irrelevant even though it cannot be perfectly realized. Wherever there is a public realm deserving the name, it is represented by places—parliaments, courts, universities, art museums, libraries—where the truth is told as fully as possible to all persons.

On the other hand, the private realm cannot be contrasted with the public realm as a place where community can legitimately be forgotten. Since community is the ultimate human end, it cannot legitimately be forgotten anywhere. The private realm, therefore, must be characterized as a place where community is sought, not by welcoming everyone indiscriminately, but by excluding some, or even by excluding everyone in order to attain the solitude that is a readying for community. Thus a home is properly a setting either for communication among family members and friends or for solitary communality. But it could not be such a setting were it open to the general public. The main premise of the private realm is that community of some kinds is more apt to flourish where people in great numbers, or having motives other than communication, or being in some other way unlikely interlocutors, are not present. Communality, then, does not mean taking the private realm less seriously than the public realm. Rather it means embracing the duality of the two realms and incorporating the tension between them into one's own personal destiny.

A different sort of duality expressive of the tension between community and society is that between open and closed societies. An open society, as we have seen, provides an environment in which communality has wide room for expression. A closed society tries to preclude, through ideological uniformity and propaganda, and to suppress, through terror, the communal acts which call community into being. It is a fact of great significance in history that societies tend toward one extreme or the other. Thus the totalitarian states of the twentieth century have been almost completely closed; they have been, so to speak, pure societies, with community almost entirely excluded. Liberal societies have been relatively communal. They have not, admittedly, been pure communities, but they have allowed for the coming and going of diverse and fragmentary communities. In history, though, there are no pure types. Every society is in some degree both closed and open—in some aspects society and nothing more and in other aspects potentially communal. Thus liberal societies are often in certain ways notoriously anticommunal, as is illustrated in America by many qualities of the capitalist system and by most of popular culture. On the other hand, not even the harshest tyranny can despoil people of every liberty; occasional words of truth were uttered, although in secrecy and fear, even in Nazi Germany and Stalinist Russia. In short, the duality of society and community prevails both among and within societies. And the duality is lived, in prophetic hope, both in deciding where to live (as did multitudes of emigrants from Nazi Germany), and in deciding where to stand within one's own society (modestly exemplified by those rare Americans who refuse to own a television set).

Such dualities are obviously rooted in human nature. Two inclinations mark out the moral structure of humans in our fallen state: to assert the imperial self, claiming ascendancy over all else, or to abandon the free self, along with all the burdens of thought and decision which freedom entails. There are two loves, as Augustine held, one for the infinite above all, the other for the finite to the exclusion of the infinite. Most of us gladly set our communality aside for many hours every day and acquiesce in the social necessities which largely depersonalize our human relationships. The worker on the assembly-line and the bureaucrat are symbols of this aspect of human nature and life. But the communal self is never wholly suppressed and not only comes forth in various areas of public and private life but breaks into the grids and hierarchies of society; even factory labor can allow for communal relationships, as in various forms of worker cooperation. Given this duality, maintaining the prophetic stance is a matter of resisting one's own anticommunal impulses and holding fast to the requirements of community—a complex and difficult task in view of the fact that the pressures of society are not only buttressed by imperious necessities but also quickened by our own iniquitous impulses.

Living in the moral and spiritual space between community and society involves a dialectical movement between social engagement and withdrawal. As noted, the very search for community necessitates, paradoxically, involvement in society; one must search out human beings where they are, in society. Not everyone is willing to do this, as exemplified, apparently, by as great a figure as Kierkegaard. Even though Kierkegaard wrote an eloquent book on love, he often writes as though communication is a necessarily futile endeavor, and his own life was marked by the isolation seemingly sought through the broken engagement with Regina Olsen. Social involvement is required wherever there are social relations susceptible of being internalized and rendered communal by human listening and speaking. On the other hand, as also noted, there are many times and places, even in the best and most open societies, in which community requires withdrawal. Indeed, withdrawal is one of the major uses of liberty, and modern totalitarianism aims at making withdrawal impossible. But, just as some are unwilling to be involved in society, some are unwilling to withdraw from society. And a refusal ever to disentangle oneself from society is no less fatal to communality than a refusal ever to seek the human companionship which is found only within society.

In all of this it can be clearly seen why no contradiction exists between the political character of the prophetic stance and its dependence on single, and in some measure solitary, individuals. Genuine political responsibility exists only in someone who is ready to stand alone against the world. It is not the case that politics belongs mainly in the public realm, even though in a civilized society much communication dealing with a people's destiny will occur in places such as legislative chambers and courtrooms. Politics also belongs in private conversations; and it belongs in the inner conversations which one person may carry on alone. It is impossible to imagine a great leader who is altogether a public figure and is uninterested in private and inner conversations. Wise politics depends on the ability of people to live dialectically—to dwell sometimes in the public realm and sometimes in the private realm and yet to unify their lives through a communicative and inquiring consciousness of man's communal destiny.

Through the kind of political thought and attention that animates prophetic hope, one tries to be an inhabitant of history, cognizant of surrounding circumstances—embodied always in one's neighbors—and of the transcendental commands they encode. When I think of the human race and ask, "Where are we and what must we do?" I am asking political and prophetic questions, for I am striving to know our common circumstances and our common responsibilities. To do this is a matter of love. If I could love all human beings in full lucidity I would be aware of my own personal destiny as identical with the destiny of the human race, traveling on the road from creation to the consummation of the kingdom of God. I would realize that my true and complete life-story is an incarnation of the true and complete history of the world. And I would realize that the unfolding of my own personal being, in its microhistorical character, can be responsibly carried out only as an act of participation in the history of the world. Such participation is achieved, within the severe limits imposed by our sinfulness and mortality, by inhabiting one's personal situation as an historical—that is, political—situation and by doing and suffering all that prevailing circumstances require. In a word, participation is achieved through situational obedience, with one's situation understood in its full historical scope. Standing in readiness for such obedience is the prophetic stance.

Although political, the prophetic stance is also spiritual. This follows from the fact that the ultimate object of hope is God. As we have seen, the unity of the political and the spiritual, which Christianity has normally regarded as illegitimate when given institutional form, is not only legitimate for individuals but obligatory. A whole human being is necessarily both political and spiritual. Only one whose life is bent steadily on God can achieve the political maturity required by the prophetic stance. And only one who is bound to the human race at large by a sense of political responsibility can achieve spiritual maturity.

The prophetic stance, although situationally obedient, can be legally disobedient and socially dissident. All political determinations of destiny should, especially if they prescribe individual actions, such as payment of taxes or participation in military ventures, be affirmed or denied within the precincts of private judgment. Such is implied by the very concept of personal responsibility. In many circumstances, one will depart spontaneously from common patterns of thought and activity, and one may feel obliged at some time to break the law. In all situations there remains the necessity of recognizing that public opinion is one of the most fallible of authorities; that custom and tradition have accumulated not only the wisdom, but also the prejudices, of passing generations; and that governments are vastly inferior in their righteousness to the most righteous individuals.

It is perhaps not excessive to suggest that the health of a polity depends on how many of its members are able to inhabit history with hope, that is, to maintain the prophetic stance and to abide the spiritual and political inconclusiveness inherent in the duality of community and society, and in such subordinate dualities as Church and state, and public and private. Society is at its best when fragmented and unconcluded, at its worst when unified and finished. The progress of history depends at last on individuals able to discern authentic values and to stand for them, in their own lives and in the common life, even when everyone around them seems lost in hedonistic or fanatical despair.

—————◦ epilogue ◦—————

HOPE AND CIVILIZATION

Underlying and explaining the widespread distress and confusion of modern life there may be one massive occurrence—the decay and collapse of Western civilization. No one, of course, can be sure. But what signs, among those one would expect to see if civilization were in fact disintegrating, are lacking? Cities and families are falling to pieces; personal safety is at hazard not only on the streets at night, but in national parks and in rest stops on major highways. The best-educated people, such as university professors and journalists, by and large deny that right and wrong, good and bad, are anything but opinions variable with time and place; most people, in most nations, spend their leisure hours immersed in the shallow, mass produced entertainment provided on television. In the largest and most powerful of Western nations, the United States, government is largely under the control of wealthy private interests; and public bodies are forced into fiscal irresponsibility by voters who demand a high level of government services with a low level of taxation. Over a million-and-a-half unborn children are put to death by their mothers every year; and among children who are born, many arm themselves with loaded guns before leaving for school in the morning.

Does modern despondency—that is, the weakness of hope—have anything to do with this situation? Obviously circumstances so troubling might contribute to our despondency. The question I am asking, however, is whether the reverse might be true. Does our despondency somehow contribute to our troubled circumstances? Does it have anything to do with the decline of Western civilization, if such is occurring? The answer almost certainly is Yes. As we saw at the outset of this essay, despondency deprives us of the determination and energy needed for taking part in public life. And to be convinced that the values that structure society

are disappearing will inevitably lessen our allegiance to those values. If all of this
is true, however, then the recovery of hope would be apt to stem whatever decline
is occurring. Learning to hope, raising our public morale and heightening our political energies, might give buoyancy to a sinking civilization. Let us think more
carefully about these hypotheses.

1

It is scarcely an exaggeration to say that hope is a vision of values, although
these are values yet to be realized; to be hopeful is to have one's mind centered on
things of worth. It is essential to realize, however, that these are religious propositions. There is only one pure and absolute value, and that is God; all other values
are such only because they derive from this one supreme value. So, at least, Christians believe. Clearly, people often cherish values which they do not associate with
God, but that tells us little about the intrinsic nature of values. The question is
whether there are genuine values which can be fully understood and not associated
with God or with some conception of an eternal, providential being. It is doubtful that there are. The exhilaration of perceiving an authentic value, as in witness-
ing a valorous deed, or looking upon the countenance of one who is loved, or contemplating a scene of natural grandeur, derives from the feeling of being in contact
with something indefeasible and eternal. Thus in the writings of Saint Augustine
truth is often spoken of as the greatest of all values. The reason for this lies in Augustine's sense that truth is a realization of something immutable and eternal; it
is a perception of God. A value which slips through our fingers even as it is apprehended either is not a value at all or else it is misapprehended. Illustrative are
physical pleasures. Some of these, like food and drink in moderation, are genuine
values. It is arguable, however, that their value is clear only when they are seen in
relation with eternity—when, for example, food is seen as bread given by God and
drink as wine intended by God, in the Psalmist's words, "to gladden the heart of
man." (Psalm 104:15 RSV)

Since hope is for and in God, being possessed by hope leads naturally to the
belief that values are disclosures of the eternal foundations of life and govern the
unfoldment of life. Values are seen as sources of destiny. Their role in forming conduct is thus greatly enhanced by hope. The idea that conquering modern despondency and recovering hope might help lift the morale of a declining civilization is
thus made plausible. All of this might be better understood by reflecting briefly on
three values, all fundamental in Western political and social life, and on the way
they are given meaning and vitality by hope. These are the sanctity of every human
being, often spoken of as "the dignity of the individual"; the value of truth, which
ennobles enterprises such as science and philosophy, and which renders lying a

grave evil even when it is unavoidable; and, finally, the value of community, symbolized in Christian discourse as the kingdom of heaven.

The Individual. If we rely altogether on empirical evidence, the idea that every
individual possesses infinite worth is a palpable absurdity. Even the greatest human
beings are ambiguous in value, as seen in the fact that they can always be carica-
tured and shown in this way to be, from one perspective, ludicrous. They may be of
commanding wisdom, but are necessarily far from omniscient and thus can blun-
der seriously. They are perhaps uniquely courageous and steadfast, yet can be seen
from some perspectives as merely stubborn. If they have uncommon sympathy
with those who are downtrodden and destitute, they may nevertheless be insensitive to those whose experiences are of another kind. Perhaps possessed of great
dignity and rectitude, they may sometimes be haughty and cold. If we think of
people who are not great but are only average—and think of them objectively and
dispassionately—their limitations will be conspicuous. They may be perceptive but
emotionally unstable, strong-willed but self-centered, intelligent but pitiless, conscientious but indecisive. Finally, there are many human beings—particularly in
prisons and mental institutions—who, *judged empirically*, are worth little or nothing; they fulfill no social functions, cannot be called either wise or good, or even
sensible or decent, and are often physically repellent. Facts such as these were obvious enough in ancient times and were affirmed even by great spiritual figures
such as Plato. The reason they are not obvious today is that Christianity has intervened. Now, tradition attributes infinite worth to every individual, and we are often
unable and unwilling to face the stark disclosures of empirical observation.

Hope, however, offers another vantage point. It enables us to see individuals
against the horizon of eternal life. Seen from this vantage point, it is apparent that
they have value of an entirely different kind, and entirely different order of magni-
tude, than was visible when viewed from a worldly vantage point. We judge them
spiritually, not empirically; we perceive them in the light of hope. Now we see that
a human being is somehow meant for eternity. Regardless of the qualities visible to
worldly observation, every person is exalted by virtue of a divine ordination to
everlasting life. Even those who repudiate and fail this destiny are not mere animals; they are recipients of the terrible dignity of being damned. Of course even
the elect, seen objectively, are finite and iniquitous. They are transfigured, however,
by grace, and from the perspective of the faith in which grace is accepted, and the
verdicts of the observable world are transcended, they exhibit the resplendence of
citizens of the City of God.

At this point we can see clearly why it is that love, as noted earlier, is implicit
in hope. Someone in whom we perceive transcendental glory is someone whom we
love. Such glory, however, is never an outward, manifest quality like height, color
of hair, or facial features. It is a momentary disclosure, in a human visage, of some-

thing beyond time and space. Love is a sacramental experience and, like every such experience, a momentary perception of the eternal future affirmed by true hope. In seeing a human being as one exalted by destiny, we see with the eyes of the love intrinsic to hope.

Truth. In like fashion, hope provides a perspective that reveals the value of truth. If we assume that the world is all-inclusive, that everything real is in the nature of an observable object in space and time, then there is no more reason to attribute intrinsic worth to the truth than to every human being. If there is no God, there is no reason even to assume, as Bertrand Russell drily noted, that the ultimate truth is very interesting; and it may be, as Friedrich Nietzsche asserted, that a view of the primal senselessness that reigns over all things—since God does not reign over them—would be so horrifying as to be unbearable by most people. For an atheist, the only tenable epistemological position is some form of pragmatism: the value of the various truths must be regarded as proportional to their practical utility, and the idea of a single Truth, worthy of loyalty and attention regardless of whether it helps us or hinders us in the conduct of our lives, is necessarily discarded. If, however, life is destiny; if the natural universe was created as a theatre for the unfolding of that destiny; if all events and all of history reflect God's guiding hand; if, in other words, all things are construed in terms of hope, then apprehension that ultimate truth may be either not very interesting, or too awful to be steadily looked upon, evaporates, and the idea of treating truth merely pragmatically becomes unthinkable. Now it is reasonable to regard truth with reverence, as did Plato and Aristotle, and Augustine and Aquinas, for all of whom truth was a mirror of transcendence. As in the case of human persons, the vantage point of eternal life—of hope—enables us to see in truth a value which is imperceptible within the confines of the world.

If every earthly value is a glimpse of God, then truth, as one of these values, must partake of the splendor and delight intrinsic to every vision of God. It must be beautiful. Within the confines of the world, of course, there are ugly truths, truths that disgust us, like those concerning Nazi extermination camps. But Christian faith implies that such truths will be transfigured at the end of time and lose their unsightliness. Even the most loathesome things will come finally to serve the meaning with which God in his sovereign mercy fills the created universe and all that takes place within it. An atheist, it may be said, is someone who believes this cannot happen—that some evils are everlastingly impervious to transfiguration. Auschwitz can never be beautiful. Yet as demonstrated in a great deal of Christian art, the Crucifixion is readily seen as beautiful, and the Crucifixion was for those who witnessed it an exceedingly ugly event. Its transfiguration has been accomplished in various ways—by prayer and meditation, by theological reflection, and by artistic perception, as seen in the great painters of the Middle Ages and the Renaissance. What the great painters have done with the Crucifixion provides a hint of what God will do at the end of the ages with all that is revolting and horrifying in the human record.

Moreover, as difficult as it may be for us to understand how every truth without exception can finally become beautiful, the idea that truth must invariably be sought and recognized, and that deceiving others under anything but the most stringent necessity is wrong, is affirmed by the voice of conscience in almost everyone. Even when it is not apparent that the truth will benefit us, we do not feel we can rightly ignore or obscure it. William James spoke of truth as merely "the cash value" of an idea. But however engaging a writer James may have been, many will sense that wholeheartedly and steadily adhering to such a view of truth would be a kind of metaphysical betrayal. The history of theology, philosophy, and science provides abundant evidence of the enduring human conviction that truth, whether useful or burdensome, whether beautiful or repellent, has no price-tag. Thus the perspective of Christian hope accords with a conviction we find within us, even in our fallen state.

Hope enables us to make sense of this conviction. It does this by placing truth in the context of destiny. If we could not anticipate the ultimate transfiguration of reality, then the idea that truth must be sought and safeguarded in all circumstances would be quixotic. Some things, we would have to think, are best forgotten or never known. As it is, hope and conscience join in telling us that all things are worth knowing and that not only our dignity and self-respect, but even our salvation, depend on our revering the truth even as we revere God. In hope we hold to the faith that all truth concerns the destiny ordained and disclosed in Christ. This destiny does not concern just humans but the physical and animal world as well. Mountains and sky and light, and fish and birds and "beasts of the earth," will participate in the final act of history, when God's sovereignty will be made fully manifest. Even the most trivial truths have their own dignity.

It is misleading, however, to discuss the value of the individual and of truth apart from one another. These are not wholly separate values attaching to wholly separate realities. This becomes apparent when we think of destiny as the basis of value, for destiny is both the essence of an individual and the object of truth. And it becomes apparent when we reflect that an individual is granted respect by being told the truth and, conversely, that we desire to tell the truth to, and even to search for it with, individuals whom we respect. It is therefore not surprising that the individual and the truth fuse in a third value.

Community. As we have already seen, community must be sharply distinguished from society. Community is the unity of humans in their essential being and is therefore unity of a kind which in no way represses or falsifies those participating in it. On the other hand, since society by its very nature defines and organizes its members on the basis of social functions, it is necessarily an agent of the repression and falsification that obstruct and impair community. When the distinctive nature of community is forgotten, and mere cohesive groups are thought of as communities, the road toward idolatry of races, parties, and nations is opened.

The act constituting community, as we know, is that of communication, and that act, in essence, is a sharing of the truth. There are two ways in which truth can be shared: as something sought or as something already known. In practice, these are not separable, for we cannot inquire into the truth without in some measure already knowing it; and never do we know the truth in a way that stills our desire to know it better or in a way that enables us to file it away in our minds without ever reexamining it. We bring community into being, then, when we engage with others in inquiry and in contemplation—or, more precisely, in contemplative inquiry and inquiring contemplation.

It can be seen, from this standpoint, how it is that community fuses respect for individuals and for truth. It is only when I speak seriously with someone—that is, when I speak the truth—that I show to the utmost my respect for the person with whom I speak. To clothe, feed, and shelter someone is, in some circumstances, absolutely necessary. Yet I do that, sometimes, for animals. Only with human beings, and only with human beings whom I respect, do I undertake to share the truth. And the most compelling reason for clothing, feeding, and sheltering people is to enable them to listen and to speak. Lying provokes outrage because it demeans those lied to; even withholding the truth, without misrepresenting it, is often felt to be implicitly disdainful of those from whom the truth is withheld. On the other hand, if we show our respect for others by speaking with them of the truth, we show our respect for truth in the same way—by centering our common life not on entertainment or recreation, or even on economic and political activities, but on trying to understand the truth of things. By sharing the truth with my friends, I dignify not only my friends but the truth as well.

The value of community is closely connected with the value of democracy. If democracy is the highest political ideal, this is not because the common people are the best rulers; sometimes they are very bad rulers, and it would be hard to show that on the whole they are better rulers than kings, landed aristocracies, or commercial oligarchies. The superiority of democracy lies in the fact that in principle it demands, and in practice tends to call forth, universal communication. For the people to govern, they must be given comprehensive information on public matters and must be interested onlookers, if not participants, in public debates. Much depends, in a democracy, on whether the system is regarded as mere majority rule or as the political basis of universal communication. As the former, democracy becomes nothing more than another power system. Government, wealth, and other kinds of superior status are gained by appealing to the vanity, prejudice, prurience, and other iniquitous inclinations of the people; truth is lost in a wasteland of flattery, misinformation, pornography, and innuendo. Such phenomena are manifestations of what is often called "mass society." If, however, democracy is treated as the political basis of universal communication, then it commands respect commensurate with the respect given the individual, truth, and community. It assumes a place among the great human values.

The way in which hope tends to awaken us to the value of community is suggested by the preceding discussion. If community is the realization simultaneously of the value of the human individual and of the truth, and if these values are clearly seen only within the eternal horizons affirmed by hope, then the search for community has logical grounds only in hope. As we saw at the outset of this essay, hope is for community, the kingdom of God. Where there is hope, there is communal awareness and concern. Despondency, on the other hand, can be expected to manifest itself in self-seeking which is devoid alike of respect for persons and love of wisdom. Impulses toward community are almost certain to be swamped by ethnic, nationalist, and ideological passions. There will be too few on the historical scene who, like the early Christian founders of the Church, are possessed of true hope and thus are fully cognizant of the transcendental nature, origins, and authority of community.

Hope does not merely enable us to argue the value of community, however. It enables us to *see* community. Grounded in the mysterious idea of the kingdom of God, hope makes us mindful of the fact that a true community is not merely a kind of social grouping. Without hope, however, community is apt to be forgotten, as has happened almost everywhere today. Only society is seen. Then the yearning for authentic unity, which is a yearning for community, is misconstrued. It becomes a drive toward social solidarity and in that way is debased. Tightly-knit nations, ethnic clusters, and parties—mere units of society, but easily seen—are mistaken for communities. Communal insight is obstructed by nationalism, ethnic loyalties, and hankerings for dictatorial simplification and discipline. Such obfuscation readily occurs, since community is not so conspicuous a fact that no one can fail to see it. Rather, it is fragmentary, ephemeral, and, in the sense of being inaccessible to objective observation, one might even say, invisible. Faith in the imminence of the kingdom of God—which, of course, is what we mean by hope—makes us aware that something often inconspicuous and evanescent, such as a sympathetic glance or a sudden shared insight, is in actuality a portent of the end of the ages and a sign of the meaning of all history. Such faith makes us sensitive to community and thus capable of taking responsibility for community in history.

The values illuminated by hope—values such as the individual, truth, and community—do not altogether banish the darkness which inheres in our fallenness. They provide no blueprint for reconstituting a failing civilization. They do, however, help us to find our way in history. They illuminate the existing situation and throw into relief the necessities of the moment. They enable us to realize, for example, that we must cherish such communal activities as serious conversation, not only in personal situations but in parliaments and press conferences and other public places. And they remind us that taking responsibility for community means trying to see that all people have access to the material goods, the education, and the leisure which are required for an interest in truth to become effective, and, moreover, that the air is not so filled with the noise of entertainment and advertising that serious speech is inaudible. In relation to the historical situations we inhabit, hope is like a full moon rising over a darkened landscape; it enables us to make out numerous features of the surrounding terrain and to find our way across it. If God is limitless, indefeasible value, then we can fittingly regard the values which hope enables us to perceive as lights by which God gives us guidance in the darkness of history.

True hope is notably realistic. The values we have examined are, in their Christian context, free of sentimental illusions. Thus respect for human beings does not depend on the false notion that they are good. They are respected as recipients of divine mercy and therefore, in spite of the evil they do, reflect in our eyes the glory of a forgiving and redeeming God. In other words, they are respected not for their present goodness, which is not very great, but for their destined goodness— a goodness visible only to the eyes of faith. Truth, too, is seen realistically. Christian reverence for truth is without romantic distortions of historical actualities; this is manifest in the fact that the center of Christian truth is symbolized by the Cross. Like an ordinary, fallen individual, the Cross is distinctly inglorious to worldly eyes. To eyes enlightened by faith in the Resurrection, however, it is paradoxically glorious. Finally, true hope is realistic in not setting community before us as a simple historical possibility, to be created by prudent or audacious governments. It is rather an indefinable and incalculable breath that passes among us now and again. Hope tells us that it will not be a visible and enduring reality while we inhabit history. In sum, true hope is realism of a kind which spurns both illusions and despair.

It is not, however, a realism which confines us to the things we can see and hear and touch. True hope draws into the forefront of our minds not only the values on which civilization depends but also the invisible foundations on which those values rest. In this way, too, it strengthens civilization.

2

The most serious intellectual error of recent centuries has arguably been that of equating the real and the visible. Causal factors have been various: declining religious faith, rising industrial productivity, increasing wealth, growing delight in the world of the senses; also, the development of science (which for all of its abstractions depends finally on empirical confirmation), and the rise of technology, bringing not merely visible but spectacular reslts. Whatever the reasons, it gradually has come to be assumed that what cannot be seen by any normal and reasonably careful observer is not real. To most people in the modern world such an assumption is apt to seem innocuous. Yet it replicates the sin which the ancient Hebrews thought worse than any other, that is, refusal to recognize the invisible God. The idolatry condemned in the First Commandment was, at least in large part, a will to worship only visible gods. A visible god is necessarily a being in the world—observable, calculable, and controllable—in short, not God. It is a god we ourselves have enthroned. Implicit in the worship of visible gods, then, is the human pride for which the supreme god is man, the creator of gods. The act which Camus found particularly disquieting in modern revolutionaries was what he called metaphysical rebellion.[1] Such a rebellion is concealed in the modern repudiation of the invisible. To raise the visible above the invisible is to raise man over God and over all the company of heaven.

Metaphysical rebellion necessarily undermines all major values. These values are comprehensible only as visible manifestations of invisible being—the glory of God, reflected in the dignity of a human personality; the harmonies of divine creation, bestowing sanctity on all truth; and the numinous splendor of the encompassing mystery of being, hallowing every true communal relationship. But if only the visible is real, then some human beings have no value at all and none have infinite value; truth may sometimes be useful but certainly is not sacred; and community is nothing but social solidarity. Likewise, every effort to state absolute moral norms must be regarded with skepticism, if not with indignation, as being implicitly intolerant. Beauty is construed simply as a source of sensual gratification and not in any way a disclosure of the harmonies of creation. In a universe made up exclusively of things we can see, the soul is a figment of imagination and God a grandiose illusion.

In such a universe, values of a very different sort are affirmed, although it is questionable whether these should be called values rather than personal preferences. Physical pleasure naturally comes to occupy the center of life, for it has great appeal, is readily available, and can be profitably sold. Continuous physical pleasure is impossible, however, so diversions of various kinds, such as entertainment and physical recreation, also become important. In addition, money, social status, and power take on great significance, for all of them enhance the pride which there

---

1 See Camus, *op. cit.*, pp. 29–76.

is no longer any reason to condemn, as well as providing ready access to pleasure and diversion.

Such a transformation of values is unavoidably destructive of civilization. This is partly because it produces deep dissatisfaction. As a creature of infinite imagination, a human being cannot help being alienated and finally enraged in a universe where there are only visible and therefore finite values. Some will try to convince themselves that finite values in great quantities are effectively infinite and thus will seek unalloyed satisfaction by building great personal fortunes or living amid expensive luxuries. Others will resign themselves to the quiet despair of small physical pleasures and trivial diversions. A few will break out of the imprisoning world by means of philosophy, art, and religion. But the populace at large will become an inglorious and distracted multitude that can be more or less marshalled and organized through corporate organizations, capitalist markets, democratic elections, and bureaucracy. Peace may therefore prevail for awhile. But underneath there will be only despair and rage; these will be inescapable in a universe which mocks and ignores the orientation toward transcendence which defines uncorrupted, and even in some degree corrupted, human nature.

In liberal nations, the old constitutional forms will, like the republican institutions of imperial Rome, be hollowed out and perverted, if indeed they remain in existence. Visions of the public good or the moral law will no longer have the force to guide and limit governments. Those seeking official favor in their search for wealth will come together in avid and single-minded pressure groups. Where moral conviction remains, it will become shrill and extreme in order to define and defend itself against prevailing amorality. Among public servants the upshot will be paralysis and hypocrisy. Authorities charged with defining the public good will at best merely negotiate compromises among competing interests and will at worst promote the interests solely of the powerful and wealthy.

The loss of invisible values will have no slighter an impact in the realm of scholarship and intellect. The effort to render all studies, even the most humanistic, quantitative and empirical will become widspread; professors and students in the universities will for the most part adopt relativistic attitudes toward moral questions; fashions such as deconstruction, denying that literary works have meaning, and denying accordingly that religious and moral treatises deal with realities external to themselves, will spread; and having lost awareness of the true values that render culture significant, intellectuals will become preoccupied with cultural diversity. In their efforts to master all available data—the visible facts—scholars will become narrowly specialized, while philosophical breadth and imagination will largely disappear.

In short, we will suffer spiritual uprootedness. The roots of all real values are invisible. Belief that only the visible is real will divide us from the only realities which, able as we are to look beyond every visible value, we really care about. Confined to a visible universe, we will be unable to maintain anything deserving the name of civilization.

At this point, however, we must be wary of a major misstep. That would consist in assuming that saving civilization is our ultimate aim. Such an assumption would obscure the major themes of this essay. True hope would be lost from sight.

3

A civilization is always more or less degraded by the pride, avarice, and irresponsibility of its human members. It is always an inadequate embodiment of the eternal values which entitle it to the name "civilization." This is why Augustine, living during the death throes of the Roman Empire (the imperial city itself having been sacked twenty years before Augustine's death), was relatively unconcerned with the fate of classical civilization. He was fully conscious of the difference between a civilization in history and the heavenly city destined to come with the end of history. It is partly because of the radical defectiveness of every civilization that it is difficult to tell today whether Western civilization is coming to an end. Are the egregious evils so apparent all around us signs of decay or are they merely manifestations of the human iniquity which will always deface even the greatest human achievements? We cannot surely know. What we can know, however, is that a civilization is an order built, maintained, and inhabited by a fallen race. With all of its splendors, it is something very different from the City of God.

Saying these things is a way of reminding ourselves that authentic hope is eschatological. It looks beyond history toward eternal life. It is uncompromising allegiance to values which are necessarily compromised when they are incorporated in the institutions and practices of sinful human beings. Jesus' proclamation of the imminence of the kingdom of God—the one, definitive manifesto of human hope—was a deeply subversive, although not in the usual sense of the word revolutionary, act. It affirmed the imperfection and inconclusiveness of every human order. On the other hand, when humans commit themselves unreservedly to the preservation of a civilization (which happens, or comes close to happening, in Burkean conservatism), they commit an idolatrous act. They treat as divine a mere human artifact. This might all be simply expressed in the proposition that there cannot be (if words be given their due weight) a Christian civilization. A civilization is such a vast and august thing as to invite idolatry. One of the great merits of eschatology is that, without temporizing for a moment with the illusions and arrogance of revolutionaries, it reduces civilization to its proper relativity.

The commonplace that no civilization can last forever contains an essential truth: time is the enemy of civilization. And in the last analysis we humans are on the side of time, not of civilization. Time must finally be allowed to have its way with civilization. *Hope is willingness to entrust our lives to time.*

This is the main idea I have tried in a variety of ways to set forth and defend in the foregoing pages. Sin is evasion of time. In giving way to nostalgia, for example, we flee from time into the past. Evading time is accomplished mainly, however, by constructing worlds—orders of life in which everything has its assigned place, and all events are foreknown if not willed. There are personal worlds, occupied perhaps by only a single individual; and there is also "the world," the surrounding order of society, treated as objectively knowable, humanly controllable, and morally final. A world is always a kind of fortress against time. Sin, as I have tried to show, is in essence worldliness, whether in proud mastery of a world, in distracted aban-donment of oneself to someone else's world, or, as is almost always the case, a subtle mixture of these. To entrust your life to time, however, is to acknowledge the impermanence and imperfection of all worlds. It is to dwell within the situation in which time has placed you, suffering and doing what you must, in the faith that by submitting to the demands of time you are submitting to the demands of God, the Lord of time. "God intended man to have *all* good, but in his, God's, time," writes the theologian Hans Urs von Balthasar; "and therefore all disobedience, all sin, consists essentially in breaking out of time. . . . Hence the importance of pa-tience in the New Testament, which becomes the basic consitutent of Christianity, more central even than humility: the power to wait, to persevere, to hold out, to endure to the end."[2]

Affirming time in this fashion is not contrary to eschatology. We trust in time, not because we take time to be good in itself, but because we believe that time will carry us into eternity. Time will have an end and without an end would be mean-ingless. In other words, the structure of time is eschatological. Time is essentially a preparation for eternal life. By meeting the requirements of time, as these are in-corporated into our personal and historical situations, we are made fit for life in the presence of God. This is what we mean when we speak of justification and sancti-fication.

The basis of this faith is the life, death, and resurrection of Christ. The signifi-cance of time, and its eschatological structure, are revealed in this event. In Christ God entered into time. God entered also into the suffering and death inherent in time. Human beings are thus warned against trying to reach eternity by ascending above time. Only by living faithfully within time, and by submitting to the suffer-ing and death to which Christ submitted, is God encountered. Time thus is given great worth. Yet its worth is only relative, for it lies in its being a pathway beyond

---

2 Hans Urs von Balthasar, *A Theology of History* (San Francisco: Ignatius Press, 1963), pp. 36–37.

time and into eternity. The Cross must therefore be understood not only as man's appointment to time but also as a judgment on man's normal and fallen life in time—that is, a judgment on human civilization.

We see here, as we have seen recurrently in this essay, that eschatology provides a balanced outlook. It tells us that we can rightfully hope for goods we experience in time, yet that these goods have real value only as foreshadowings of eternity. It tells us that history is meaningful but inconclusive. In politics, eschatology denies the validity of either Burkean conservatism or revolutionary radicalism, but it also suggests a way of inhabiting time that embodies the fragmentary truth that each contains.

Eschatology offers a balanced view also of civilization. It is obvious that civilization, like time, has great worth. It is a gift that time bestows, even though it eventually takes it back. The alternative to civilization is outward disorder and inward confusion. Barbarism, although sometimes obscured by romantic sentimentality, means the eclipse of values. No realistic person can be indifferent to the fall of a civilization. Nevertheless, the worth of a civilization—again like time—is relative. If the kingdom of heaven is at hand, then the fall of a civilization is a serious matter but not an ultimate concern. Worse things can happen. To live responsibly in time, then, is to defend the good order and authentic values that a worthwhile civilization represents; it is also to accept the fact that time erodes civilizations and finally brings them all to destruction. This describes the poise Augustine achieved and it sets a standard—one particularly pertinent in troubled times—for all of us.

INDEX

222

Christianity, 1, 3, 7, 9; as source of anti-semitism, 8; as religion of hope, 9, 10

Church: and concept of truthfulness, 101–104; and doctrine, 104; and community, 167; as source of change, 178; and state 194–199, 205; and the prophetic stance, 208

Cicero, 3, 4

Civil War, American, 133

Communication: universal, 6; as sharing of truth, 214

Communism, communists, 137, 159–161; failure of, 16; delusions of, 87; and rejection of liberty, 169; and idolization of state, 169

Community, 96–97, 180, 213–216; and self, 73–74; Christian concept of, 98–99, 137; and state and society, 158–159; and the Church, 167; and liberty, 170; and destiny, 200; and the prophetic stance, 201–205; as distinct from society, 203–204; and the public and private realms, 205; and the prophetic stance, 206–208

Compassion and lucidity, 176

Conscience, civic, 13–14

Conservatism, 191–192

Courage, 146–147

Cross, 62, 111, 116, 124, 135, 139, 216, 221; and justification, 66–69, 71; and love, 113; and eternal life, 144; and death, 145

Crucifixion, 57, 63, 71, 78–79, 105, 112, 118, 212–213

Dante, 78

Despair, 138, 143

Destiny, 81, 82, 96, 123, 182; at the core of Christianity, 58–59; and common sense, 61; and history, 63–64; and justification by faith, 66; and trust, 83; and selfhood, 83; and hope, 86; and fidelity to god, 109; and love, 114; and prayer, 118–119; and the past, 124, 126–127; dialectic of, 137–138; and kingdom of God, 149; power of,

149–150; concept of, 153, 174; and human finitude and fallenness, 157–158; and the prophetic stance, 201, 208; and love, 207; as the basis of value, 213

Dialectic, dialectical, 63, 72, 88, 138, 148, 159, 202; and ecstatic suffering, 137

Dialogue, 99

Dialogic society, 199–200

Didion, Joan, 59

Dignity of the individual, 45

Dostoevsky, Fyodor, 5, 48–49, 58, 130, 131, 182, 188, 193; and concept of destiny, 61–62; the Grand Inquisitor, 106, 171; on prayer, 118; eschatological faith, 126–127

Egalitarianism, 179–180, 183

Eros: see love

Eschatology, eschatological, 40–42, 187–188, 192–193, 221; of light, 48; vision, 89; and history, 133; as defining hope, 148, 157, 219; and the prophetic stance, 202

Eternal life, 142–143

Evil, evils, 131; of the 20th century, 15–17, 20–21; transfigured, 76; conquest of 129; and the state, 169

Faith, 6, 9; see justification by

Fallenness, 87, 96, 100, 117

Finitude, 132, 175

Forgiveness, 126, 129–130

Freedom, 4, 17

Freud, Sigmund, 23

Freudian psychology, 127–128

Fromm, Erich, 172

Fukuyama, Francis, 17

Gelasius I, Pope, 194

Gibbon, Edward, 164

Gnosticism, 6, 59

God: as personal, 35; as jealous, 36; as compassionate, 37; and self-love, 39–40; in time, 40–41, 56–57, 62, 80, 220–221; and Hell, 50–52; as source of destiny, 57–59; and original sin, 65;

Life, eternal, 143–144
Lincoln, Abraham, 7, 133, 168–169, 190, 191
Locke, John, 84
Logos, 6, 139, 147, 161, 189; doctrine of, 2; Christ as, 7–8, 156; and non-Christian religions, 9; as Word of God, 35–37, 49, 88, 102–104
Love, 9, 43–47, 52, 71, 99–100; and kingdom of God, 112, 137–138; as *eros,* 113; as *agape,* 113; eschatological character of 114; neighborly, 155, 181; Christian, 181; as sacramental experience, 212
Lucidity and compassion, 176
Luke, 118, 148
Luther, Martin, 106

Machiavelli, Niccolo, 167
Manichean dualism, 59
Mann, Thomas, 51–52
Marcel, Gabriel, 133
Marx, Karl, 5, 20, 23, 79, 157, 177, 194
Marxist, Marxism, 1, 32, 45–46, 80
Mass society, 17–18, 97, 214–215
Mercy, divine, 112
Metaphysical rebellion, 216–219
Moses, 35, 118

Nation-state system, 164
Natural law, 4
Neibuhr, Reinhold, 3, 55
Newman, Cardinal, 89
New Testament, 8, 42, 56, 57–58, 78, 180, 187, 220
Nietzsche, Friedrich, 2–3, 5, 23, 48, 119–120, 212
Non-Christians, 1–3, 6

Obedience, 81, 95; and prayer, 118; and suffering, 138–139; and hope, 148, 158, 159; and waiting, 161; and liberty, 172–173; situational, 86–94, 123, 157–158, 186, 190; and remembrance, 128; and death, 145; and change, 175; and the past, 188; and the prophetic stance, 208

Objectivism, 3
Old Testament, 8, 35, 42, 50, 66, 129, 180, 187
Original sin: see sin
Ortega y Gasset, José, 204

Pascal, Blaise, 6
Paul the Apostle, 41, 64, 68, 69, 72, 84, 101, 107, 114, 198; and unbelievers, 2; and hope, 9; and the Law, 66; and hope as exaltation, 81–82; and detachment, 124; and penitence, 128; and ecstatic suffering, 72, 137–39; and sting of death, 144
Penitence, 128–129
Peter, 38, 82
Philosophy, 10; of history, 4; and faith, 119–123
Plato, 4, 76, 88, 122, 156, 166, 211; and the good, 33; and beauty, 48; and *eros,* 55–56; and death, 105
Plotinus, 3, 33, 55, 57
Poverty, 183
Power, 168
Pride, 31, 54, 87, 175
Private realm, 205
Progress, doctrine of, 19–26
Public realm, 7, 205
Punishment, 130

Reality, realities, 4, 5, 216
Redemption, 98, 112, 126, 148, 159
Reformation, 99
Remorse, 128
Responsibility, personal, 208
Resurrection, 63, 78, 105, 121, 216
Retribution, 66, 129
Revelation, 6, 9, 32–35, 37, 63
Revolution, 159, 221
Righteousness, 20, 67, 69, 136, 137
Roosevelt, Franklin D., 185–186
Russell, Bertrand, 212

Sacramentality, 104–107, Eucharist, 105
Sartre, Jean-Paul, 3, 4, 59, 173
Secular, secularism, 2–6; radical, 5, 32; agnostic, 5, 36; and doctrine of